THE LONG GALLERY, SUTTON PLACE, GUILDFORD, SURREY, ENGLAND

ENGLISH FURNITURE
FROM GOTHIC TO SHERATON

A concise account of the development of English furniture and woodwork from the Gothic of the fifteenth century to the Classic Revival of the early nineteenth with the minimum of descriptive text and the maximum of illustrations

BY

HERBERT CESCINSKY

WITH MORE THAN 900 ILLUSTRATIONS

DOVER PUBLICATIONS, INC.
NEW YORK

To those who love a home
which is more than a mere dwelling
who appreciate the work of bygone ages
when the craftsman lived for
the joy of his art

PUBLISHED IN CANADA BY GENERAL PUBLISHING COMPANY, LTD.,
30 LESMILL ROAD, DON MILLS, TORONTO, ONTARIO.

PUBLISHED IN THE UNITED KINGDOM
BY CONSTABLE AND COMPANY, LTD.,
10 ORANGE STREET, LONDON WC 2.

This Dover edition, first published in 1968, is an unabridged republication of the second edition, as published by Garden City Publishing Company, Inc., in 1937.

Standard Book Number: 486-21929-1
Library of Congress Catalog Card Number: 68-19173

MANUFACTURED IN THE UNITED STATES OF AMERICA

DOVER PUBLICATIONS, INC.
180 VARICK STREET
NEW YORK, N. Y. 10014

CONTENTS

PREFACE TO THE SECOND EDITION

When this book was written, its make-up was somewhat of a novelty to me, and something like an experiment. I had the idea that to place each chapter in lecture form, and to supplement the text with illustrations taking the place of lantern slides, might be a convenient way of presenting a subject, and also of imparting such knowledge of English furniture and woodwork as I happened to possess. Unlike the lecture, where the slides are thrown on the screen for a few moments only, the illustrations here remain for leisurely consultation, and can be examined over and over again, if necessary. One may add that the text is equivalent to having the lecturer also at command, to repeat what he has said before, and as often as one wishes. The only disadvantage that I can see is that the reader has not the lecturer before him in the flesh, but, speaking as one of the confraternity, I doubt if this be a drawback at all. I know that the lecturer can be questioned by his audience but judging by the letters I receive, so can an author. In addition, a writer who cannot put his case in better language, or marshal his facts in more orderly way than even the best lecture ever delivered, had better give up the game of authorship and take to something more manual, such as selling gasoline, for example.

I can remember in my boyhood days (long ages ago) hearing Professor Huxley—the grandfather of the present generation, Julian and Aldous—hold a Norwich audience of working men enthralled for an hour while he talked about a piece of chalk. He was a concise and fluent speaker, a born lecturer, but when his address was published later on (in Lay Sermons), I noticed it had been re-polished for publication.

ENGLISH FURNITURE FROM GOTHIC TO SHERATON was originally published at $25, yet the first edition sold outright. Other than in the second-hand market, no copies remain. Now the Garden City Publishing Company has re-issued the book, and if it be a "seller" again, I prefer to think that the make-up will be responsible for such sale. This is not false modesty; no one who has known me for long has ever accused me of such a vice; it is, I think, a literal statement of fact.

H. C.

PREFACE

IT MAY INTEREST a reader to know how, as well as why, this book came to be written. I may not claim that it is any more than a re-presentation of an old subject, one to which I have already devoted many pages in other books. I may claim, however, that in re-iteration there is often improvement in presentation, as books on applied arts, in particular, often educate authors more than readers. The latter can (and, I grieve to say, do) skip; the author must marshal his facts and his thoughts; and in the writing and proof correcting he learns his own lesson, again and again.

During the winters of 1927 and 1928 I delivered a course of lectures on the subject of English Furniture and Woodwork, at the Metropolitan Museum, extra-mural classes of New York University. I had the idea at the time (nearly every Professor has) that this course of thirteen lectures, covering a vast subject, was merely purveying information in tabloid form, something akin to a series on the Languages of Europe, devoting each lecture, of one hour, to a different language. Lecturing, even with lantern slides, must, from its nature, be evanescent in its effects on the audience, as I found, to my chagrin, at the examination which concluded each series. The same lecture, written down, and illustrated with photographs in place of slides, could be referred to again and again, in short, might have just that permanency which the lecture so conspicuously lacked. On the other hand, with the lecture, the audience has a view of the lecturer (I had almost written "the showman") and may ask questions afterwards, but I have rarely found that such questions have any material relation to the subject of the lecture itself.

My friend, Henry W. Frohne, an American architect, and for some years an editor of art journals, attended one of these lectures, which must have been something of an ordeal to one who saw, even more clearly than I did, the futility of the effort. He was far too keen-sighted to fall into the common error of confusing lecturing with instruction. It was at his suggestion that these lectures were afterwards expanded into this book. His, also, was the idea that a minimum of explanation and a wealth of illustration can often teach a lesson in this particular field, in which many words and few pictures often fail.

After such efforts as "English Furniture of the Eighteenth Century" (in three volumes), "Early English Furniture and Woodwork" (in two) and "The Old-World House" (also in two books) I formed the idea that, on the subjects of English Furniture and Woodwork, I had expressed all that I knew, but I must confess, on looking through these pages, that Henry W. Frohne has been a wise director, guiding me, in the way of compression here and expansion there, until, in this book, I have set down all I know on the subject and in the most concise way. The chapters are really in lecture form, and the illustrations are the slides. Both may be studied from the easy chair at home, picked up at odd moments and referred to at will, something like a talking-machine record, which may be played again and again.

When one passes the half-century mark in years, and has lived that life with the furniture and furnishings of the past, it is little wonder that, like the shoemaker, to whom there is nothing like leather, the antique has the greatest appeal. I do not refer here solely to furniture or woodwork; it is the numbers of other works of art, not only in their beauty, but in their variety, which make the successful home. The warfare of the Middle Ages has something of a counterpart in the business life of the present day, and the business man, on returning from the day's war, lays aside his bow, spear, shield and sword, doffs his armour, and endeavours to get away from the present. How can he do so better than by delving into the past? Again, with the things of bygone ages, pictures, oriental porcelain and pottery, enamels, silver, miniatures, fabrics or other works of art-craftsmanship, he has not only the interest of variety, the unwritten history of the past, which is often more eloquent than the written word, he is also living with the things which gladdened the hearts and delighted the eyes of generations long since mouldered to dust. There has been a gap in the everyday humdrum existence which has clarified the mind and enlarged the intellect. There is no greater pleasure, to my mind, than in the appreciation of fine things, necessarily made in an age when time was of little account, and when the craftsman gloried in his work. Modern conditions have killed all this; the refuge is only in the past. The Orient offers the only exception at the present day, and the Oriental is fast falling into the commercial stride of the Occidental. The thing made for the million, and produced in a hurry, cannot be fine. Perfection of workmanship is of little account compared with the fire of inspiration. In all art works, talent does what it can; genius what it must, as Frank Harris remarked. If I had to preach a crusade, in these days, it would be not against the Powers of Evil, but against Rubbish, in the production of which, it would seem, the Powers of Evil have a hand.

H. C.

February, 1929.

CHAPTER I

The Dawn of Construction in Wood

IN THE ATTEMPT to write the history of a nation's art-handicrafts, one is compelled to make an arbitrary beginning somewhere, as the age of utility, when mankind first began to adapt the raw materials of nature to his own needs, would carry us back into unknown ages. One is obliged to begin with the dawn of art, and art begins with decoration. This is a truism, but one which is too often ill-comprehended, mainly because one is apt to confuse decoration with ornament. While often allied, ornament is decoration, of course; decoration is not necessarily ornament. This difference must be clearly understood if confusion in terms is not to result. A piece may possess decorative form, in shape, proportion or otherwise, yet be destitute of ornament. It is, nevertheless, a work of art, and has every claim to be regarded as such; whereas, without form, proportion or ornament it can have no title to be so considered. On the other hand, any attempt at ornamentation, however crude and primitive, establishes such a title, even if other form and proportion be absent. Art, therefore, can arise in two ways, at least; it can be constructional, or it can precede construction, but primitive art, arising, as it does, in very lowly ways, can easily be overlooked. Take the dug-out boat of Robinson Crusoe and compare it with a modern yacht. The lines of the latter are deliberately studied, so as to make it a thing of beauty on the water, whereas, with the former, utility was the only consideration to the castaway. Had Crusoe devoted any of his time to ornament, the chiselling of a pattern round the rail of his vessel, one would have recognised and acknowledged the attempt at decoration, but had he spent the same amount of time in shaping the hull, in order to render it pleasing to the eye—that is, going beyond the confines of mere utility—many might have failed to recognise the boat as a work of art; which it would have been, in fact.

In the first dawn of art, in English furniture and woodwork, exterior or interior, construction and art are interchangeable terms, as art implies deliberate selection, and one must select before construction can be possible. One cannot take rough wood, and, in its crude state, make anything from it, without giving definite shape and form to each piece so that it will fit another. To do so one must have a selective eye; the constructed thing must be decorative before it can be assembled; it must take on a definite artistic quality, even if ornament be entirely absent.

Conversely, a thing may be ornamented without being constructed, and thus art (which includes ornament as well as decoration) may precede construction. Thus, the inscribed bones of the reindeer epoch are art works, by reason of the ornamentation, which indicates the guiding hand and observing eye of man, with capacity for selection and rejection. This everyone will admit, but what is so frequently unobserved is that construction devoid of ornament may still be artistic, no matter how crude the art may be.

The art of the stone-mason is much older than that of the woodworker, in England, and it is instructive to follow the development of the latter, where the methods of the former are copied faithfully, until, in the later years of the thirteenth century, the carpenter begins to awaken to the possibilities and properties of his material, and then, for the first time, he begins to construct instead of build or hew. The persistence of early type is also remarkable, and must always be looked for by the earnest enquirer. Thus the mason's miter, borrowed from the ages when English woodwork was in its infancy, is found as late as the seventeenth century, and constructive methods, or the lack of them, persist to much later periods than one would expect. Knowledge or trade tradition, which is the same thing, does not extend to the whole of a trade nor of a craft, and primitive construction is a dangerous guide in attempting to date a piece of woodwork.

One who starts out to a certain distant point and makes a minute error of one second of an arc in his direction at the starting point, will find that the divergence from the true line assumes serious proportions as he proceeds on his quest. In the same way, one who fails to apprehend the conditions of the Middle-Age craftsman at the outset, will equally fail to realise the significance of much which follows in the developmental history of English woodwork. The years up to the close of the fifteenth century were an age of pictures, or rather, of pictorial representation. The standard of living was exceedingly low, and this was true of both lower and upper classes. The church monopolised the enlightenment of the time. Reading being a rare accomplishment, books were practically unknown to the laity. Amusements were few, and not of a very elevating character. It was the age of stories and legends, either oral or commemorated in carvings, stained glass or mural paintings. The rood or chancel screen, unembellished with pictorial representations of the saints, was a rarity; even the walls of the early churches were decorated in the same manner. Taste was coarse, even in the holy places, and if one examine the carved ends of choir stalls, where later defacing by the minions of Cromwell has not destroyed them entirely, it will be found that the subjects are usually Rabelaisian, to say the least. Those in St. Michael's Parish Church (now Coventry Cathedral) will serve as examples.

The mediæval church was the meeting house of the people; their place of amusement. The chancel alone was sacred, and even to this day the nave remains the property of the parish, maintained by the common funds, whereas the chancel is in the charge of the church. Many accounts still exist in church records, of drunken bouts, known as "ales," which show the monetary contributions of the parish to these orgies. Apart from these, and certain outdoor sports such as archery contests at fairs, the lower classes had no amusements whatsoever during the Middle Ages. Hunting and hawking were not for them.

The standard of living being crude in the extreme, furniture was equally scanty, both in variety and amount. A rough trestle table, a few stools and a chest would be all, even in the yeoman's house. The bedstead was for the wealthy only; for the lowly, straw or rushes on the floor was enough, or all they could afford.

To understand the dawn of construction in English woodwork, it is necessary to bear in mind the early sub-divisions of the trade itself. Up to the middle of the thirteenth century such divisions had not arisen, the carpenter being the sole craftsman in wood. Right up to the end of the Dissolution of Monasteries, which may be said to extend from 1525 to 1550, he was still supreme. He was assisted by the woodcarver, and, in such great works as the choir stalls at Winchester (typical thirteenth-century work at its best) it is doubtful whether the credit for excellence is not due almost entirely to the carver. These great canopies are hewn from great baulks of English oak, united only at the divisions between the stalls. They are, in the highest degree, ornamental; in the lowest only are they constructive.

We are apt to judge of the age of this early woodwork by its technical perfection, oblivious of the fact that progress does not always conform to modern theories in this obliging manner. Thus, the pulpit of Chivelstone Church, in Devon, (a very progressive county in early woodwork) is hewn from the solid oak log, yet has ornament of linenfold panels, an unmistakable sign of the very late fifteenth century, if not of the early sixteenth. It *should* be thirteenth century, or earlier, only it *isn't*.

So much for theories based on construction principles. The fact is that while the carpenter had progressed in constructional knowledge, or in tradition (which is another name for the same thing) a distinct race of craftsmen had arisen, workers of lesser status, and utterly without trade traditions, the *huchiers* or "arkwrights." (The mediæval language of documents in England, up to the end of the fourteenth century, is a kind of bastardised Norman French, hence the term "*huchier*.") The "ark" was the place of safety and was used to designate the chest, the important piece of furniture made not only to hold silver, fabrics and other valuables, but also the vehicle of their transport from place to place. The man who fashioned anything from wood, metal or other material, was the "wright" (hence the modern word "wrought") and the name persists in the "shipwright" and the "wheelwright." The "arkwright" was the maker of chests, and he ranked far below the mediæval carpenter, the constructor of timber houses and of the woodwork in cathedrals and churches.

In the Middle Ages, all art sprang from the church, and the best craftsmen were nearly always churchmen, monks or lay brethren. It has been computed that, at the time when Henry VIII began to suppress the great monasteries, nearly one-third of the entire wealth of England was in clerical hands, and wealth, in those days, was tangible;§ (in more ways than one, as the church found to its cost) in land, buildings, gold, silver, jewels, vestments, fabrics, illuminated missals, tapestries and similar property, not in mere figures on paper, as at the present day. Not only did the church aggrandise nearly all the wealth; all education, in the sense of book-learning, and the entire range of the arts and crafts were in its hands. Art flourished only in the shadows of great monastery or mighty abbey. If we investigate the building of any of the wonderful English cathedrals of the period, if we seek for the creator of illuminated missal, of carved and decorated altar or predella, of chancel or parclose screen, it is always an abbot, monk or lay brother whom we find, that is, if we succeed at all. The art of the woodworker culminated in the fifteenth century; that of the worker in stained glass some two hundred years before, but from 1425 to 1520 is still the golden age of the English craftsman, when living was cheap, famines almost unknown, wages high, and leisure abundant.‡ It is in those years that innumerable rich, but small parish churches arose everywhere throughout England, where, in wonderful screens, stalls, pews and font covers, the leisure, piety, and artistic emulation of the craftsman had full sway. Nowhere do we find any records of this work being paid for in money; bills exist for gold, colours, timber, but of wages there is no trace; it was solely a labour of love, and it serves to indicate the amount of spare time which the artisan of the fifteenth century possessed. This period sees the English church at the zenith of its power; the next half-century witnesses its nadir.

In the investigation of early records, one is apt to be confused by names which have since acquired other significance. Thus, the master-carpenter (such as "Master" Hugh Herland, who built the great oak roof of Westminster Hall in 1395) was the mediæval equivalent of the later architect, and, in no sense a workman. William of Wykeham, Bishop of Winchester, Counsellor to King Edward III, Chancellor of England, builder of Windsor Castle and founder of New College at Oxford, was the master-carpenter of Winchester Cathedral as well as a great prelate.

§Tangible; from Fr. tango—to "touch" in vulgar parlance, to borrow or seize.
‡Plagues were of frequent occurrence, however.

We find another worker in wood, during the Middle Ages, who is difficult to localise, so elusive is he. This is the wandering craftsman, carpenter, carver or mason, usually of foreign birth, almost an outlaw, certainly a soldier of fortune, a brigand. Pietro Torrigiano, who superseded "Master" Pageny as the designer of the tomb of Henry VII in Westminster Abbey, at the invitation of burly Harry (and, incidentally, introduced the Renaissance into England), is an example of the type, truculent, lawless, yet a fine artist withal. He is in good company with Villon and Cellini.

The work of these men, whether in wood, stone or metal, is far above the average level of the time, and renders the task very difficult of dating without apparent anachronism. The laws regulating labour were severe, if not savage, during the fourteenth and fifteenth centuries. No artisan could leave his village or town without the consent of the abbot or lord of the manor. To wander afield without such sanction rendered him liable to arrest and hanging from the nearest tree, without trial, as a "rogue and masterless man." Those licensed to travel were known as "journeymen," a name which has persisted to the present day, but has entirely lost its earlier significance. It is curious that the old Cinque Port of Winchelsea, on the south coast of England, has never had this ancient statute formally repealed, with the result that the mayor still has this mediæval power to hang, without trial, any unemployed man he finds in the village. Needless to say, the "privilege" is not exercised, but such was the law against vagabondage even until the end of the sixteenth century.

It is difficult, in the case of the very early work, to segregate furniture from woodwork, as in churches; for example, the chair was a fixed thing, i. e. the abbot's throne or the monk's stall. Thus, the usual definition of "furniture" as something movable does not apply. The earliest piece of all was the chest, for the reasons already given. The table is rarer, for two reasons. In the first place, the table on legs or trestles was usually a huge thing, intended chiefly for the great hall or the guard room (there is one, at Cefyn Mably, which is over thirty feet long) and, very occasionally, we find a table specially made for the old game of shuffle-board, a pastime which has survived to the present day in country inns, under the name of "shove-ha'penny." A coin is placed at the extreme end, just overhanging the edge, and is projected up the table by a smart blow of the open hand. The winner is the one whose coin stops the nearest to a mark at the other end. One driven right off the table is "dead."

These old shuffle-board tables may have been general once, but they are extremely rare now. There is one at Astley Hall, Chorley, Lancashire, which is illustrated here. It has twenty legs, and the top is a herring-bone parqueterie of finely-figured oak. Two of the original counters are still preserved, in form similar to a modern four-ounce brass weight. The table must have been placed in position before the Long Gallery at Astley was completed, as it is impossible to remove it now without taking it apart or breaking down a side wall.

The mediæval chair is the rarest piece of all, if the word be used to define a secular piece as distinct from a clerical throne or stall. Even in the guildhalls of the time, the stool was the usual seat, and until nearly the close of the sixteenth century, a domestic chair was almost unknown. Even as late as this the chair was a seat of dignity reserved for the master or the mistress of the house, and for the stranger to have occupied it, uninvited, would have been a grave insult. It is not until after the Restoration of 1660 that the chair became the usual seat at the table, for meals.

Next in importance is the bedstead, but here we are without any very early examples. We know, from preserved records, that the bed of William of Wykeham was a gorgeous affair of silk, velvet, bullion and embroidery, but whether it was a piece of wooden furniture or a couch placed in a recess in the wall (which is more probable) and dressed with valances, back-cloths and curtains, we are unable to say. Beyond a few examples of late fifteenth-century bedposts which have survived (and of which the English nationality is questionable) we know of no bedsteads prior to the days of Elizabeth. From that date on, until the end of the eighteenth century, if not almost until the middle of the nineteenth, the bedstead was of the four-post kind, with tester and hangings. It is only within the last hundred years that the science of ventilation and draught-exclusion has reached such a stage of perfection as to render the open bedstead a practicable thing. In the English country districts, even in the late seventeenth century, the usual oak bedstead was in the form of a panelled box, open only on two sides, and roofed in the same way as the more aristocratic "four-poster." The trundle-bed of New England is a good example of the unhygienic carried into days within living memory.

It is necessary to bear in mind the earliest dates when certain pieces first appear, or we are likely to make the same error as the man who demanded a book illustrating Romanesque gas fixtures. Certain experts rely upon crudity as evidence of extreme age, and they fall into grievous errors, in consequence. They ignore the fact that after the Dissolution of Monasteries, when the culture of England in art and handicraft was driven forth to haunt forest and thicket as outlaws, a new race of inferior craftsmen arose, with none of the former fine traditions, with only dim memories of the early glories of the Gothic; and this new craftsman-class began in the old, unconstructional manner of the early thirteenth century, and this as late as the middle of the sixteenth. Thus, the Burwaston cupboard, in the Victoria and Albert Museum is, or was, described as mid-fifteenth century, although there is no evidence that the chest evolved into the standing cupboard until after 1500. There is no cultured Gothic example of a standing cupboard extant in England; no later developments from the Burwaston example are extant. One would expect such were it correctly dated. The whole question of Gothic furniture and woodwork in England is so tangled up with conflicting phases and sources of evolution that it will be necessary to straighten out this tangle before any progress can be made with our enquiry. Even if truth and accuracy were not desirable for their own sakes, the history of the development of a nation's domestic handicrafts is too important to allow ignorant guesswork to pass for knowledge. This is a definite branch of sociology, one which has been neglected as of little or no account, hitherto, but is now accepted as possessing far-reaching influences on the life of a people. How a nation lived in its homes is now recognised as having far greater importance than facts as to how many of the same people perished on this or that battlefield in quarrels in which they had little or no personal concern. We manifest great interest in the chair or throne of Tut Ankh Amen, although we, in England, have little in common with the domestic life of the ancient Egyptians; but we are not concerned in knowing how the generality of our people lived in the days of the Wars of the Roses, although we preserve the date and full account (generally apochryphal) of each battle and teach this "history" as something worth-while in our schools and colleges.

Another late arrival in the field of the English woodworker is the wainscot or wall panel. Panellings appear only at the very close of the fifteenth century, and even then they are exceptional. In the mediæval house of the great hall, the private apartments had either bare stone or plastered walls, or these were hung with arras or tapestry. In some instances—which may not have been as exceptional as we have thought, hitherto—patterns or rough pictured scenes were painted on the plastered walls (the "wattle-and-daub") but these, covered at a later date with whitewash, paint or woodwork, would disappear when the house was demolished and their presence hardly be suspected. Two examples are preserved in the Museum at Saffron Walden, in Essex, discovered almost by accident during the demolition of some old houses in the district. In churches, these wall-paintings must have been almost general. Those who are interested can be referred to "Mural Paintings in English Churches during the Middle Ages," by Frank Kendon.

The great hall, bisecting the entire house from ground to roof, was ill-adapted for panelling in wood, and the same is true of churches composed of nave, aisles and chancel, and with one or more chapels. Even in the latter, which partake of the character of private apartments, the walls were generally used for the insertion of memorial tablets, piscina and the like. The altar-end of the chancel was probably panelled at a very early period, but the Dissolution of Monasteries in 1525–50, the edicts against the use of altars under Edward VI and Elizabeth, and the deliberate vandalism under Cromwell, when destruction of church monuments was carried out on a systematic and wholesale scale (to say nothing of "restoration" in Victorian times) have left nothing of these panellings of the fifteenth century or earlier. The detached reredos fragment (it may have been a predella) in Norwich Cathedral is enough to show, in construction and the high standard of its fourteenth-century painting, something of the glories of the early churches in England.

With this general survey, we can proceed to trace the rise and development of wainscotings in England from the last years of the fifteenth century to those of the eighteenth, in text and illustration, with some, at least, of the false conceptions and premises cleared from our path.

EXAMPLE OF LATE FIFTEENTH OR SIXTEENTH CENTURY DEVONSHIRE PULPIT CUT IN THE THIRTEENTH CENTURY MANNER. THIS IS CUT OUT FROM THE SOLID TRUNK WITHOUT ANY CONSTRUCTION. ILLUSTRATION TO THE RIGHT IS A CLOSE-UP TO SHOW GREATER DETAIL

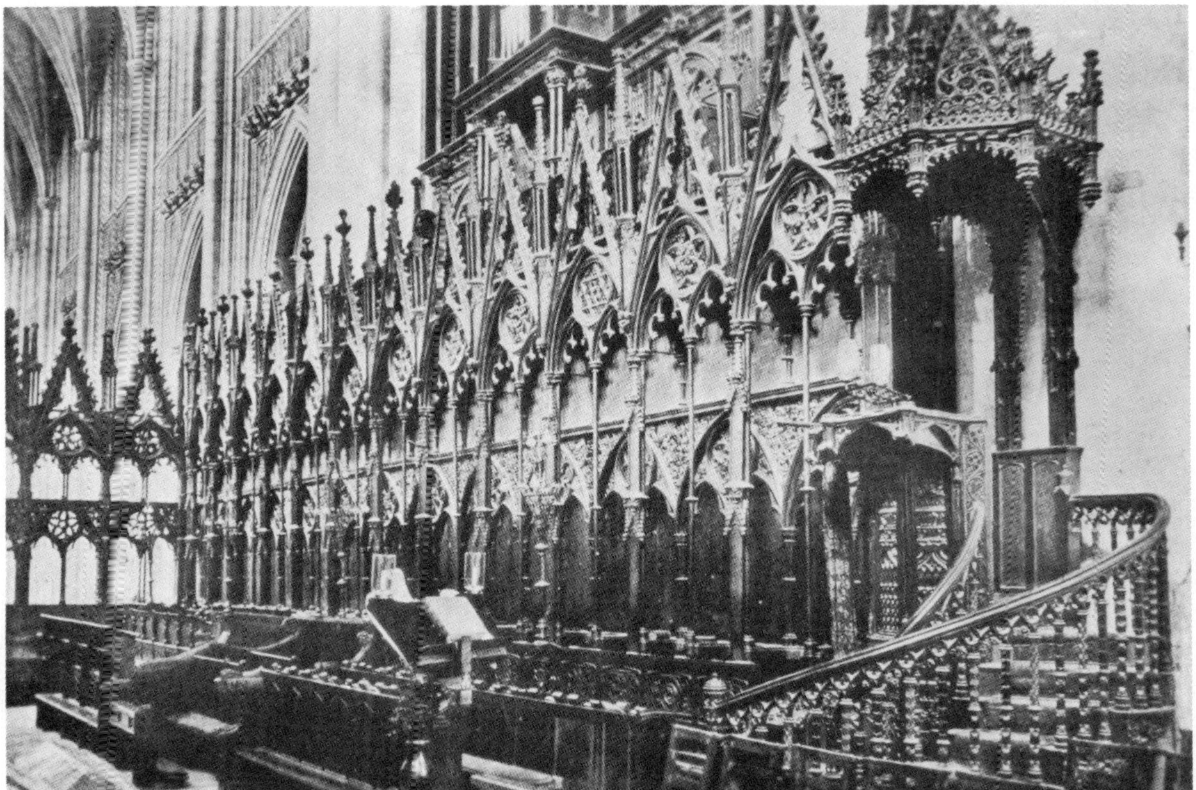

CHOIR STALL CANOPIES IN WINCHESTER CATHEDRAL, THIRTEENTH CENTURY.
THESE GREAT CANOPIES HAVE BEEN HEWN FROM SOLID OAK BAULKS

CARVED OAK CHEST FRONT, MID-FOURTEENTH CENTURY. THE WORK OF A FOREIGN WANDERING CRAFTSMAN, AND IN NO SENSE TYPICAL OF ITS TIME

FRONT OF AN OAK CHEST, LATE FOURTEENTH OR EARLY FIFTEENTH CENTURY. MADE IN ENGLAND BY A WANDERING ARTISAN, PROBABLY OF GERMAN ORIGIN

EARLY SIXTEENTH CENTURY OAK CARVING, INTENDED FOR THE FRONT OF A CHEST. THE WORK OF A FOREIGN ARTISAN IN ENGLAND, PROBABLY FRENCH. THIS ILLUSTRATES THE HIGH QUALITY OF MUCH OF THIS FOREIGN WORK

DETAIL OF SHUFFLE-BOARD AT ASTLEY HALL

THE PLAYING END OF THE GREAT SHUFFLE-BOARD TABLE AT ASTLEY HALL, CHORLEY, LANCASHIRE.
EARLY SEVENTEENTH CENTURY

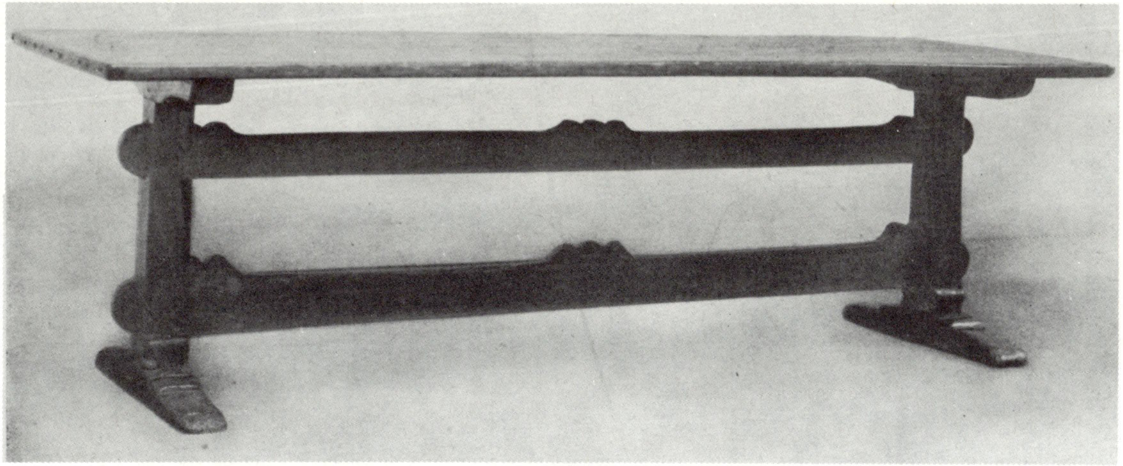

OAK TRESTLE TABLE FROM COWDRAY, SUSSEX. THE TYPE OF THE FIFTEENTH CENTURY

OAK TABLE AND BENCHES FROM BABLAKE SCHOOLS, COVENTRY. LATE FIFTEENTH CENTURY

TYPICAL OAK TUDOR CHAIR, DATED *1574*. CHAIRS WITH LEGS DO NOT APPEAR UNTIL THE CLOSE OF THE SIXTEENTH CENTURY

(LEFT) OAK TUDOR CHAIR OF THE PALATIAL KIND, LATE SIXTEENTH CENTURY.
(RIGHT) MID-SIXTEENTH CENTURY OAK CHAIR OF THE DOMESTIC OR YEOMAN TYPE

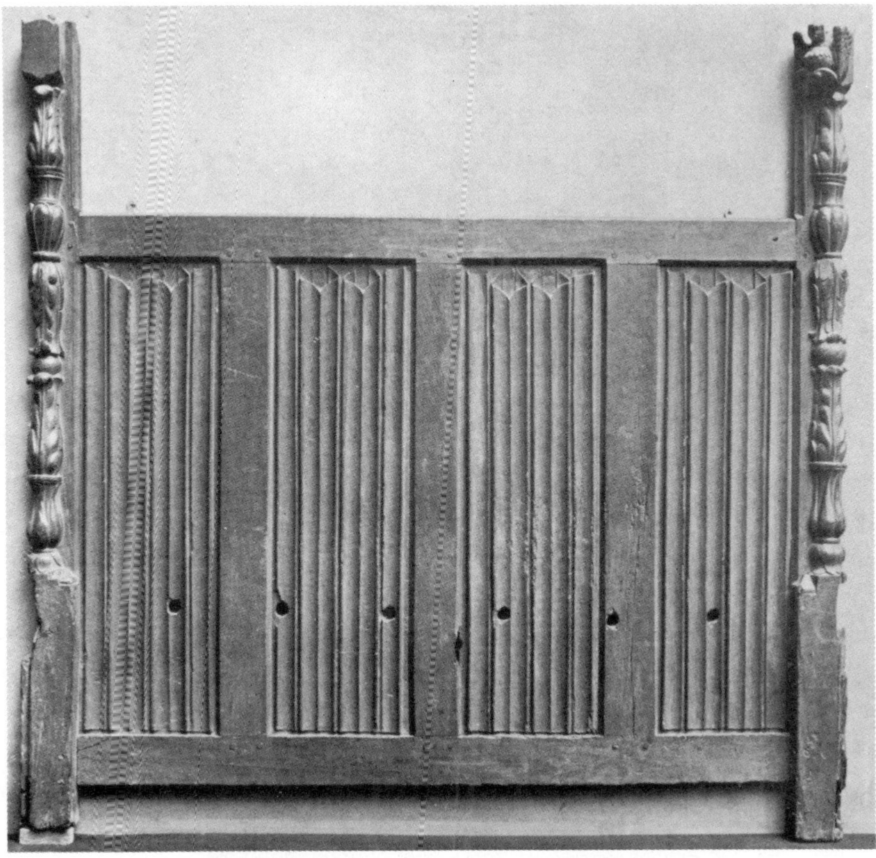

EARLY SIXTEENTH CENTURY OAK BEDSTEAD HEAD WITH THE ORIGINAL CORD HOLES IN THE LINENFOLD PANELS

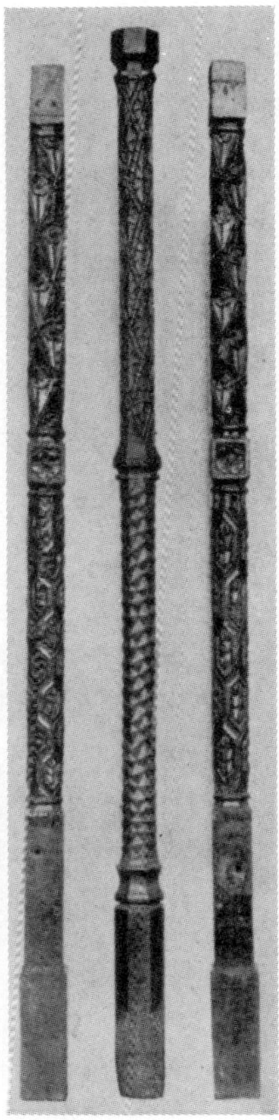

OAK BEDPOSTS OF THE LATE FIFTEENTH CENTURY

EARLY SEVENTEENTH CENTURY OAK BEDSTEAD OF THE YEOMAN TYPE

MID-SEVENTEENTH CENTURY OAK BEDSTEAD OF THE PALATIAL TYPE. FROM ASTLEY HALL

OAK CHEST. THE FLAT CARVED GOTHIC OF THE LATE FIFTEENTH CENTURY. THE WORK OF THE CARPENTER

OAK STOOL OF THE LATE GOTHIC PERIOD WITH RENAISSANCE DETAIL. EARLY SIXTEENTH CENTURY

OAK BOX CHAIR. LATE SIXTEENTH CENTURY. BEFORE THE DEVELOPMENT OF THE CHAIR ON LEGS. *c. 1590*

OAK CHAIR. TUDOR TYPE OF *c. 1520* WITH FINE CONSTRUCTION AND CARVED GOTHIC DETAIL. THE WORK OF THE CARPENTER

OAK HUTCH OR DOLE CUPBOARD CONSTRUCTED FROM SLABS OF TIMBER, CRUDELY PIERCED AND CARVED. THE WORK OF AN ARKWRIGHT IN THE "POST-DISSOLUTION" YEARS. *c. 1540*

OAK CUPBOARD, THE WORK OF AN ARKWRIGHT IN THE "POST-DISSOLUTION" YEARS. THE CORNICE AND BASE ARE MUCH LATER ADDITIONS

A COMPLETE OAK CHEST MADE FROM ENGLISH OAK BY A FOREIGN ARTISAN. EARLY SIXTEENTH CENTURY

LATE THIRTEENTH CENTURY OAK CHEST FROM GREAT BEDWYN CHURCH, WILTSHIRE. THE WORK OF A PRIMITIVE ARKWRIGHT

POST-DISSOLUTION "GOTHIC," OAK LIVERY CUPBOARD FROM BURWASTON, SHROPSHIRE. NOW IN THE VICTORIA AND ALBERT MUSEUM, LONDON. ERRONEOUSLY DATED "*c. 1500*," REALLY MID-SIXTEENTH CENTURY

OAK MUNIMENT CHEST IN ST. MICHAEL'S PARISH CHURCH, COVENTRY. THE WORK OF A CARPENTER IN THE LATE FIFTEENTH CENTURY

OAK "CHIP-CARVED" CHEST OF MID-SIXTEENTH CENTURY. POST-DISSOLUTION "GOTHIC"

DOLE CUPBOARD OR AMBRY OF MID-SIXTEENTH CENTURY. POST-DISSOLUTION "GOTHIC." THIS CUPBOARD IS SAID TO HAVE COME FROM IVYCHURCH, AN OLD HOUSE AT ALDERBURY NEAR SALISBURY

CHAPTER II

The Gothic

POSTERITY has created styles by a process of segregation, by ignoring those examples which lead up to the full development of a manner, and which also serve as "bridge-pieces" in its decline and connect the one with the next. The statement is literally true, therefore, that there never was a new style, in building, decoration or furniture; nothing but a gradual evolution, one fashion merging into another, almost imperceptibly. It is well to remember this, even when for the sake of clearness of comprehension it may be necessary to treat each style as though it were a separate entity.

It is impossible to understand the Gothic without visualising both its origin and its development, and also appreciating the cardinal principles of the style itself. Many theories have been adduced as to the former, none of which bear the stamp of probability. The possibility that the Gothic, (or the Pointed style, to give it a better name), may have arisen simultaneously in various countries has escaped notice, hitherto, in spite of the importance such a fact would acquire, could it be established.

The high regard in which the circle was held, and from very early times, as typifying eternity, especially in primitive religions, would engender some method of describing the circle with some degree of accuracy. The ancient Druidic rites were always held in a circle, either drawn on the ground, or built in trilithons as at Stonehenge and Avebury. To insert a central peg in the ground, attach a cord with a marking peg at the end, and by walking around the central pivot with the cord stretched to its full extent, thus to describe an accurate circle, would be an easy discovery. From the cord and peg to the hinged compass or divider would be the next transition. Now let us examine the potentialities of such an instrument. From circle to semi-circle, then to two half-circles, side by side, and so to intersecting circles, would be only progressive steps. We obtain, in this interlacing, the pointed arch of the Gothic, a new form for the stone-mason. Now a few words are perhaps in order, as to the value of this new form.

The trabeated or lintel architecture of the Greeks had been superseded by the arch of the Romans, but, even with the latter, any height to the keystone demanded a width of, approximately, twice that height. Mediæval cathedrals in England were built, nearly always, on restricted sites, on the top of a hill, as at Durham, or in a fen, as at Ely. They were constructed with regard to defensive possibilities as well as for worship, as sanctuary would avail little against the foreign invader. Majesty demanded height, which, with the arcuated style, a restricted site would interdict. The advantages of the pointed arch, produced possibly haphazard by the user of the compass, must have been strikingly apparent to the mediæval mason, one seeking for height without corresponding width. An arch which demanded no keystone, and which lost nothing of its strength by excessive height gained, in fact, by being thus constricted; this would be an epoch-making discovery, indeed, and thus the Gothic may have arisen, and in several countries, at approximately the same period. To say that the idea was brought back from the East by the crusaders is far-fetched, as there was no Gothic in England until long after the first crusade. The warriors of Europe were not of the type to assimilate the arts of the East; they were there on quite other business. The Seljuk architecture of Turkey and Asia Minor has been cited as the prototype of the European Gothic, but this is so undeveloped, in itself, that independent origin is to be suspected.

The Gothic style in England has been divided into periods and sub-divisions, by the same process of artificial segregation to which allusion has already been made. It may be convenient to mention this classification here, as it does mark the full development of each manner. From 1066 (William I) to 1154 (Stephen) we have the Norman with its Romanesque, circular-headed arch. From 1154 to 1189, we get the transition from the round to the pointed or lanceolated form. From 1189 (Richard I) to 1272 (Henry III) we have the so-called Early English, when geometrical tracery begins to appear. From 1272 (Edward I) to 1307 we find geometrical tracery absolutely without any free decorative forms. From 1307 (Edward II) to 1327 is the true Early English, or Geometrical Pointed style, with free forms appearing in tracery and in the decoration of mouldings. The period from 1327 to 1377 is that of the Decorated or Curvilinear, and from 1377 (Richard II) to 1399, of the transition from the Decorated to the Perpendicular, the latter persisting until about 1546, being then gradually submerged, during the last forty years of that time, by the Italian Classical style or Renaissance.

It is difficult to find examples of woodwork prior to the Decorated period (the great canopies of the choir stalls at Winchester are highly exceptional) and furniture, that is anything worthy of the name, comes even later. The principles underlying Gothic construction in stone building are greatly abrogated in the case of woodwork, and in furniture the style becomes mere decoration. The reasons for this are self-evident. The following explanation of the constructive principles of the Gothic apply, therefore, almost entirely to building, but it is impossible to apprehend the furniture and woodwork of the time without a proper appreciation of Gothic buildings, to which the style properly belongs.

Gothic ornament, right up to the middle of the fourteenth century, if not later, is not only constructional; it is actually constructive ornament, that is, where the details of construction are given ornamental forms. In this, the Gothic is unique; the same may be said of no other style, before or since. The sketches here will explain this point, one of great importance to the student who desires to appreciate the spirit of the style itself. Tracery in windows does more than split up the glazed surface into panels; it actually strengthens the window itself. In this sense it is ornamental construction. Being geometrical, not only does the tracery have a definite ornamental form, but, what is more significant, looking out to the light from a darkened church, each panel or pane has a similar decorative shape, the form carefully studied. If we reversed the design, making the panels opaque and the tracery transparent, the result would still be satisfactory, whether viewed from within or without. With the Renaissance it is the ornament which has the decorative value; with the early Gothic it is the silhouette of the ornamental construction, as well as its form, which possess equal importance.

The Gothic has already lost many of its early fine principles before woodwork appears at all. In any case, the constructive character of the ornament, which is an integral element of stone buildings, is absent in the woodwork, even in such examples as rood, chancel or parclose screens. Here tracery is merely decorative, the real construction of muntin, joist or bressummer being masked behind carvings or disguised by other ornamentation. What is worse, an appearance of false delicacy, of inadequacy, is often purposely given by piercing, tracery, crocketting, or pinnacled tabernacle work, as at Atherington. This, while very charming in its result, giving an effect of extraordinary richness to the whole composition, is far removed from the fine principles of the Early English or Decorated Gothic of the thirteenth and fourteenth centuries.

Although the Gothic, in woodwork, and especially in furniture, ceases to be a constructional style, some understanding of the various periods with their leading characteristics is necessary, if one is to comprehend the various phases of the style itself. In addition, an understanding of the Gothic is of the utmost value in appreciating the English furniture styles which follow, right up to the eighteenth century. With compass and T-square only, to copy the examples illustrated here will teach more than a volume of explanation. It is impossible fully to appreciate the Gothic without learning to draw it.

In spite of many divergencies from strict building canons, in timber houses, roofs, screens and furniture, there are certain details which are valuable indications of periods, and these, coupled with a knowledge of the progress of the woodworking trades at various stages, will prevent ignorant dating, as in the instance of the Burwaston standing cupboard illustrated in the previous chapter. One must apprehend the guiding principles of the style itself in order to be able to classify much of the early woodwork in England, and these points can be better explained by illustration and note than by empirical statements in the text. In the early Gothic, at least, nothing is designed or executed in haphazard or freehand fashion. Everything is confined within strict rules; every detail belongs to its style and its period, and this is true until almost the close of the fifteenth century, after which ornament becomes more free and sporadic. Of the post-dissolution Gothic woodwork and furniture there is little or nothing to be said. If it were not for the fact that these debased examples had been accepted as the work of the Gothic in its full glory, by persons who should have known better, one could afford to ignore them entirely. Both in style and in constructive knowledge, the post-dissolution woodworker had become utterly depraved; the flower of the craft had turned to the new manner, the Renaissance. The glory of the Gothic had departed, and the new style from Italy, France and the Low Countries had taken its place.

A few words in explanation of terms and the illustrations may be necessary. The word "tracery" is self-explanatory. The uprights of a window are known as muntins; the cross-rail, where such exists, is the transom. Where tracery is not constructed from moulded muntins, straight or shaped, but is cut out from the solid stone, it is known as plate tracery. The window from Charlton-on-Otmoor is an example of this. Cusps are formed at the junction of two half-circles; in some examples they are solid, in others they are pierced or open. Both styles are shown here, with their dates. Cusping is rare in the early thirteenth century, but cusps have been found in Norman work; so it is dangerous to dogmatise in this particular. In the Early English and the later Gothic, cusping is abundant. The interlacing of circles in a Norman window, producing the lancet-headed light, is shown at Sutton Courtney, Berkshire, which seems to suggest that the theory of the origin of the Gothic, ventured here, is not so wide of the fact. The great window from Raunds in Northamptonshire is a notable example of the strictly geometrical style without cusping. At the Chapter House at York we have geometrical tracery with cusps but utterly without free forms. These appear in the Rose Window of St. Mary's at Cheltenham, with the curvilinear ribs still, however, produced with the compass. Cusping, as may be observed, is here the paramount form of tracery ornamentation.

Examples in which the arch-head to windows is replaced by the square form (which is adopted later on in the Tudor Gothic for domestic buildings) are to be found, occasionally, even as early as the fourteenth century, as at Dorchester. The last phase of the Gothic is the Perpendicular, where, in windows, the lower mullions are carried right through to the upper tracery, as at Swinbrook in Oxfordshire. The examples chosen for illustration are, naturally, typical of their time and style, and they are useful in showing each manner in the most representative fashion. There are others in which the several styles overlap, which illustrate two manners at the same time, but, in view of the gradual evolution which took place, these are inevitable. The sketches here (which are from authentic sources) should be sufficient, however, to give some idea of development of the Gothic in its various phases, and this is indispensable for the proper understanding of English woodwork and furniture in Gothic times.

THE OAK SCREEN AT ATHERINGTON, WEST OR NAVE SIDE

SUTTON COURTNEY CHURCH, BERKSHIRE. INTERLACING CIRCLES, TRANSITIONAL NORMAN

CHARLTON-ON-OTMOOR CHURCH, OXFORDSHIRE. MID-THIRTEENTH CENTURY PLATE TRACERY

RAUNDS, NORTHAMPTONSHIRE. GEOMETRICAL TRACERY WITHOUT CUSPING. THIRTEENTH CENTURY

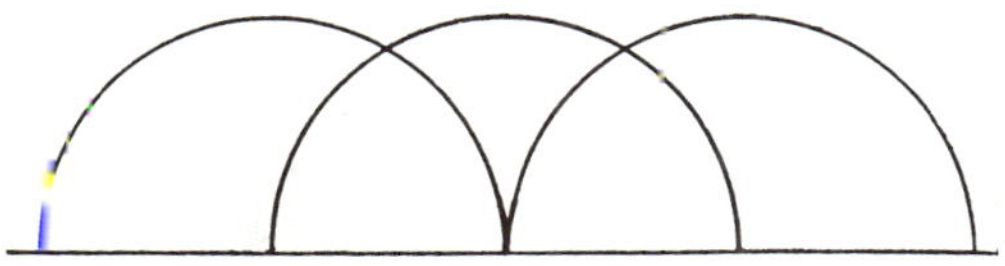

THE INTERLACING OF CIRCLES PRODUCING THE POINTED ARCH

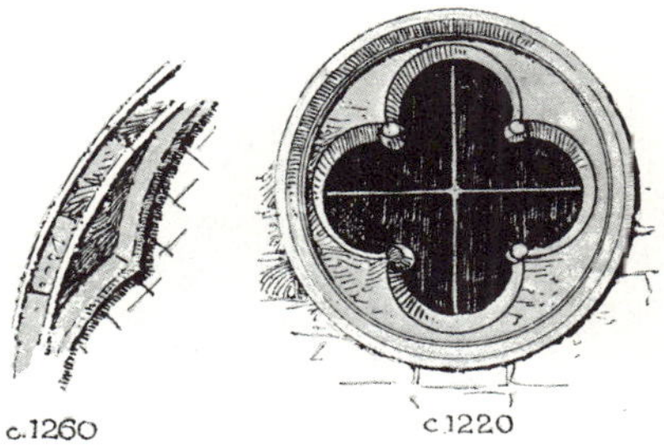

EXAMPLES OF CUSPING, SOLID AND PIERCED

CHAPTER HOUSE, YORK. GEOMETRICAL TRACERY WITH CUSPING, THIRTEENTH CENTURY

DORCHESTER CHURCH, OXFORDSHIRE. CUSPED TRACERY IN SQUARE-HEADED WINDOW OF THE FOURTEENTH CENTURY

SWINBROOK CHURCH, OXFORDSHIRE. PERPENDICULAR TRACERY OF LATE FIFTEENTH CENTURY

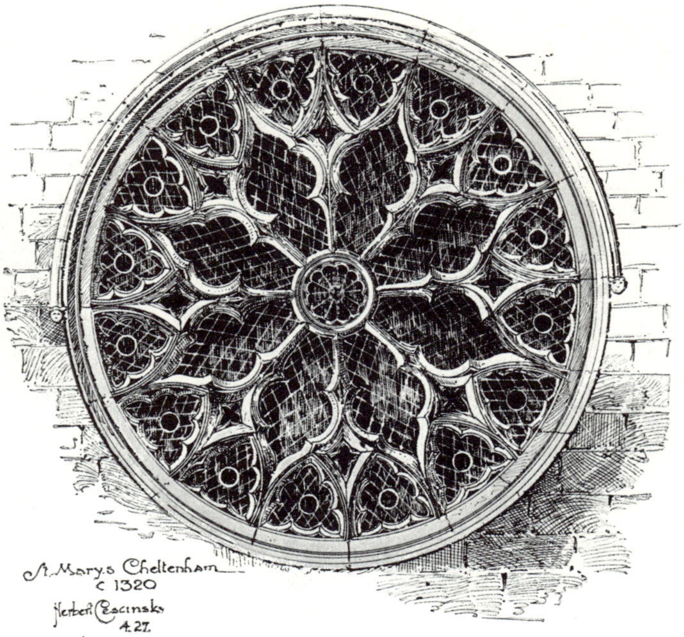

ST. MARY'S CHURCH, CHELTENHAM, GLOUCESTERSHIRE. ROSE WINDOW, FOURTEENTH CENTURY, THE ZENITH OF THE DECORATED GOTHIC WITH THE APPEARANCE OF FREE FORMS IN THE TRACERY

THE SIMILARITY IN GOTHIC SCREEN DETAIL IN THE FOURTEENTH CENTURY CHANCEL SCREEN ON APPLEDORE CHURCH, KENT, AND IN CULBONE CHURCH, SOMERSET, TWO HUNDRED MILES AWAY

CHAPTER III

The Half-Timber House

As far back as the fourteenth century, if not still earlier, a friendly rivalry appears to have existed between the stone-mason, the bricklayer and the carpenter, in the building of houses. Of the products of the three, the half-timber house is infinitely the most picturesque, and, at its decorative zenith, is peculiar to England. Houses of timber are to be found all over Europe, in Holland, Germany, Switzerland, Austria, Norway, Sweden, Denmark, in certain districts of France; and the American settlers on the eastern seaboard adopted the same method. The familiar "clap-boarded" house of New England is really the old English house of timber and plaster, boarded over at a later date (after shrinkage of wood and plaster had taken place) to withstand the rigors of the New England winter.

In all these countries, however, utility was always the first consideration. In England, during the fourteenth and fifteenth centuries at least, the decorative quality of the timber house absolutely dominates the utilitarian, yet, with Gothic throughness of principle, every ornamental detail is contrived to serve a useful purpose.

While the oak-and-plaster, or the oak-and-brick house seems to demand a setting of old, growing timber, yet we find the style used, to almost an equal extent, in cities and in streets, as in the celebrated Rows of Chester, and the old houses of Staples Inn, fronting Holborn Bars, in London. The latter, isolated as they are at the present day, were merely survivals from the Great Fire of 1666 which destroyed so many of these old London timber houses existing at the time of the Restoration. With narrow, tortuous streets, stories, each overhanging the one below, until, at the top, the buildings on either side of the street almost touched, the highways of Restoration London must have been more picturesque than sanitary. At this period, the water for household consumption was conveyed in pipes hollowed out from the trunks of trees (some of these were taken out and replaced by modern iron ones within the last thirty years) and of sanitation there was none; the central open gutter of the street was the "kennel," the channel for sewage and refuse. On rainy days, the water from roofs was discharged directly into the street. Sometimes also slops were thrown from windows; rain-water heads and leaders were almost unknown. Umbrellas were unheard of until more than one hundred years later, and the satins and velvets of the cavaliers must have suffered grievous harm when the wearers were caught in a storm in the open.

During the seventeenth century many of these old timber houses were masked by a facing of brick, with a parapet gutter and low-pitched roof, the gables being removed at the time. These pages are written in an old house, dating from 1660, in Kensington Square, which had been re-faced in the days of Queen Anne. Exteriorly, its original identity has been lost, but within, the old powdering closets (to give them a polite name) still remain as they were built. Kensington, now one of the fashionable quarters of London, was, at this time, a remote country village, separated from London by open fields which it was dangerous to cross, after nightfall, if one wished to avoid the attentions of footpads.

It is impossible to follow the development of the English house, from the fourteenth to the sixteenth centuries, without some knowledge of the important changes in house-planning which took place in that space of time. The great hall, which was general until about 1500, effectually bisected the house from ground to roof, and this was the living room for the family, retainers, visitors and guests. Even in small houses, of the lesser yeoman class, we find these roof-high halls; and if we substitute the less pretentious term of "general living room" for "great hall" it may be said, with literal truth, that such an apartment was to be found in every English country house, almost down to the cottage, until the close of the fifteenth century. Everywhere we find these roof-high living rooms—or the remains of them—complete even to the double-sided oak screen which formed the passage, borrowed from the great hall, leading from entrance door to the "buttery" or kitchen regions. As a rule, later conditions, change of habits or of domicile, have sub-divided these halls either laterally by partitions, or vertically by joists and ceilings. Thus, the original timbers of the roof are to be found only in attics, and here, hidden away, one encounters such details as crenelated, cambered tie-beams, ornamented braces, or even traceried spandrels, obviously never intended to be concealed in this fashion.

A representative example of a hall-screen in a yeoman's house of small size now only a farmhouse, used partly for the storage of hay and fodder, is still to be seen in the old Kentish village of Smarden. Others abound on the English countryside, but they are usually so altered as to be unrecognisable except by the antiquary.

Corridors and passages, other than the entry from main door to kitchens, were unknown in houses prior to the sixteenth century; one room opened directly into another. With the great hall, also, which effectually divided the house into two parts, more than one staircase was necessary and sometimes there were three or more. They were nearly always unimportant, often hidden away behind doors, and sometimes—very rarely in original examples—we find the central-newel, or "vyse" staircase, where the treads and risers are notched into a central vertical post, winding round from floor to floor, in the same way as a stone turret stair. The English staircase began to assume dignity and importance only after the great hall had disappeared from the house plan, replaced by the long gallery and the great parlour.

The Long Gallery is nearly always on the first floor (in America it is known as the second), rarely on ground level, and never, as far as I know, on the upper floors. There is a long gallery at Lyme Park, on the second (third) story, but as the entire house was re-built by Leoni in the early eighteenth century, this gallery must have been contrived at the time. The old panelling of the original 1613 long gallery has been re-used, but has been made out with portions copied in deal, stained to resemble the oak, to replace flanks used in the Great Drawing Room on the floor below. The pattern of this long-gallery wainscoting at Lyme is interesting, of arcaded, interlaced and inlaid pattern, in a design which is very rare. I know of only one other example and in the same district, at Tissington Hall, Derbyshire, but this is neither inlaid nor carved. Panellings will be described and illustrated at a later stage.

Ornamental plasterwork belongs to the timber-house period but is rarely used for ceilings. The usual devices were either heraldic, shields and coats-of-arms, or grotesque animals, distributed in unconnected fashion on walls. The symmetrical plaster ceiling belongs to the brick or stone house of the seventeenth century. There is little doubt that foreigners were responsible for the introduction into England of these modelled or cast-plaster ceilings. The foreign influence is very marked in some of the Lancashire examples, as at Speke and Astley Halls.

We have already seen the danger of attempting to square facts with theories; the half-timber house offers no exception to the rule. One would look for the house of wood in forest counties, for stone buildings in the neighbourhood of quarries, and for brick structures where clay is abundant, yet accurate investigation will show that no such easy solution of the problem presents itself. East Anglia possessed no forests (other than Epping which can hardly be said to be in the district at all, situated as it is, many miles from Suffolk and Norfolk) yet in these two counties we find the richest timber houses of the fifteenth century. It is true that wood houses are to be met with almost throughout the length and breadth of England, but rich examples are extremely localised, in Cheshire, Lancashire, Derbyshire, Devonshire, the eastern Welsh Counties and in Norfolk and Suffolk; and perhaps northern Essex may be included. In Kent, Surrey, Sussex, Hampshire, Middlesex, Buckinghamshire, Berkshire or Hertfordshire, timber houses are also found, but very rarely in any degree of elaboration. In Cornwall, the neighbouring county to Devonshire, they are practically non-existent.

Where rich woodwork is encountered in small parish churches, fine timber houses may be expected in the same localities, but not invariably, as the former is far more general than the latter. Industries appear to have become localised in certain districts at very early periods. Thus, Kent, Surrey and western Middlesex favoured brickwork, and there we find those beautiful two-inch bricks of fine cherry colour, laid with wide, flat mortar joints, and carved and twisted chimneys of the same material are plentiful —or were until the rage for demolition of the last forty years set in. The old portions of Hampton Court Palace exhibit many wonderful specimens of carved brick chimneys, but Hampton Court was built by a mighty prelate and added to by a king.

In the Midlands, stone is the more usual, and in Cornwall, as at Aberdeen, granite is the building material for the great houses, harsh and forbidding, equally to the workman and the beholder. Whether it was a demand for a particular style which brought carpenters, bricklayers and stone-masons into certain localities, or whether the predilection grew out of this localisation, it were rash to say with certainty. To presuppose such a thing as a public demand is always hazardous; the public usually takes what is offered to it.

England must have been in a disturbed state, convulsed with periodical civil wars, in the days when many of the finest of these timber houses were built. The moat, with which many are surrounded, must have been dug for defensive purposes, as stagnant water can hardly have contributed much to either the comfort or the convenience of the inmates, yet Great Tangley in Surrey, Ightham Mote in Kent, and Moreton Hall (the finest black-and-white house in England) are all moated and the last-named, although dating only as late as the middle of the sixteenth century, narrowly escaped siege by Cromwell's Ironsides.

I like to hear of a moated house, especially if it be known as the Grange. It seems to me, for no reason that I can define, that a moat must presuppose the existence of a ghost, and Ightham Mote should have several, if half the legends about the history of the house be true. There is a circular cover to the floor of the dark corridor leading from the dining room to the "With-drawing Chamber," and beneath is the moat. A guest well wined, and this cover removed, an "after you, please!" before "joining the ladies"—and the moat would tell no tales. That murderous *oubliette* requires a lot of explaining away, even in these days.

Many moated timber houses could be named here, if space permitted. Baddesley Clinton in Warwickshire dates back to the fourteenth century; Birtsmorton Court, in Worcestershire, is not much younger, but its great hall is now a farm kitchen and its fine banqueting room, 50 feet by 24 feet, is used for the making and storage of cheeses. *Sic transit gloria mundi.* Compton Wynyates is a jumble of stone, brick and oak timber, but a charming medley withal, and it has its moat. There is another fine timber house, that of Catesby, the gunpowder-plot conspirator, Ashby-St. Leger, eighty miles north from London, on the Holyhead Road, where the plotters assembled at six in the evening of the fatal day when Guy Fawkes was arrested, which should, in my judgment, have been moated; but perhaps it is sombre enough without that feature.

The English timber house plays up nobly, as it were, to its material, British oak, *Quercus robur* The first story being built, oak uprights filled in with herringboning of "brick nogging," on a base of brick or stone, the joists were placed across and allowed to overhang (thereby preventing the joist-ends from decaying) with the ends finished with brackets or carved with devices. The posts of the next floor being tenoned into a wall-plate placed at the outer extremity of the joists, and this repeated with each successive story, the room above was always as much larger than the one below by the amount of the joist-projection. Occasionally, a double-overhang at front and ends was attempted, which necessitated the diagonal "dragon-beam," into which the joists were tenoned at right angles to each other, so that they could project in each direction. To support the "dragon-beam," the corner-post was necessary, that picturesque adjunct to so many of these fine black-and-white houses of the fifteenth and sixteenth centuries. To complete the picture, the corbelled bay, or straight mullioned windows, perhaps an oriel of full house-height, glazing of diamond quarries with emblazoned panels inset, overhanging gables with pierced and carved barge-boards, roofs of red sand-faced tiles, and last, but by no means least, bold brick chimneys, chamfered, facetted or carved, not pigmy affairs, as if chimneys were things to be hidden, but noble erections worthy of the house, crowning it with glory, as it were, and with a fitting background of great oaks, beeches, chestnuts, limes or elms, and you have the English half-timber house at its best, a worthy monument to a people to whom the house, its beauty and its dignity, meant much; not something of the moment but for succeeding generations to love and treasure. How different is the house of the present day, which, in the words of the house agent, possesses, among other amenities, an easy access to every possible means of getting away from it; close to trolley cars, omnibuses and railway stations, and complete with a garage to hold a powerful automobile to make the flight rapid and effectual.

THE WEST FRONT, HAMPTON COURT, MIDDLESEX. THE OLD WOLSEY BUILDINGS, SHOWING THE CARVED BRICK CHIMNEYS OF THE SIXTEENTH CENTURY

ROBERT RAIKE'S HOUSE, GLOUCESTER. LATE FIFTEENTH CENTURY

OLD FIFTEENTH CENTURY TIMBER HOUSES AT BRENCHLEY IN KENT

OLD HOUSES, HIGH STREET, ROCHESTER, KENT. EARLY SIXTEENTH CENTURY

OLD HOUSES AT WORCESTER, ENGLAND. EARLY SIXTEENTH CENTURY. THE TIMBER WORK BECOMES MORE PERPENDICULAR IN DESIGN

OLD HOUSES AT STAPLES INN, HOLBORN BARS, LONDON. LATE SIXTEENTH CENTURY. ALMOST IN THE HEART OF THE CITY OF LONDON. STAPLES INN WAS FORMERLY ONE OF THE INNS OF CHANCERY

INTERIOR OF THE WOOL-HALL, LAVENHAM, SUFFOLK. A LATER BALCONY WAS ADDED FOR ACCESS FROM ONE SIDE OF THE HOUSE TO THE OTHER ACROSS THE HALL, ONE STAIRCASE BEING REMOVED. FIFTEENTH CENTURY

UNDER THE ROOF IN SPARROWE'S HOUSE ON THE BUTTERMARKET AT IPSWICH. CRENELLATED CAMBERED TIE-BEAMS AND MOULDED HAMMER-BRACES OF THE GREAT HALL (NOW CEILED). FIFTEENTH CENTURY

THE LONG GALLERY, HARDWICK HALL, DERBYSHIRE. A SEAT OF THE DUKE OF DEVONSHIRE

DRAGON-BEAM, WITH CARVED BRACKET-SPANDRELS, AND JOISTS TENONED IN TWO DIRECTIONS.
LONG MELFORD, SUFFOLK

PROJECTING CORBELLED BAY WINDOW, BRACKETED JOIST ENDS ABOVE, AND ENTRANCE DOOR ON RIGHT.
LAVENHAM, SUFFOLK

CORNER-POST, END OF DRAGON-BEAM, AND JOISTS PROJECTING BOTH WAYS IN A DOUBLE OVERHANG OF THE STOREY ABOVE. LAVENHAM, SUFFOLK, FIFTEENTH CENTURY

DETAIL OF GUILDHALL, LAVENHAM, SUFFOLK, SHOWING CORBELLED BAY WINDOWS AND ELABORATELY CARVED CORNER-POST WITH ORNAMENTED MOULDING ABOVE

(ABOVE AND AT EXTREME RIGHT) EARLY SIXTEENTH CENTURY CARVED CORNER-POSTS OF ARMORIAL TYPE

PORCH OF THE FIFTEENTH CENTURY GUILDHALL AT LAVENHAM, SUFFOLK

FROM AN OLD HOUSE (NOW DEMOLISHED) AT BURY ST. EDMUNDS, SUFFOLK

SIR PAUL PINDAR'S HOUSE, BISHOPSGATE WITHOUT, IN THE CITY OF LONDON.
BUILT *1600*. DEMOLISHED *1890*

FRAGMENTS OF A GREAT HALL SCREEN FROM DEVONSHIRE. THE GALLERY ABOVE, AND THE ARCHES OF THE TWO OPENINGS, BETWEEN THE FLANKS, ARE MISSING. EARLY SIXTEENTH CENTURY

PAYCOCKES, COGGLESHALL, ESSEX. BUILT IN THE LATE FIFTEENTH CENTURY BY THOMAS PAYCOCKE, A WEALTHY WEAVER OF COGGLESHALL

OLD HOUSES ON LADY STREET, LAVENHAM, SUFFOLK. ON THE RIGHT CAN BE SEEN THE ANCIENT SHOP WINDOWS (NOW CLOSED UP). FIFTEENTH CENTURY

CHAPTER IV

The Timber Roof of the Mediaeval Carpenter

ANY ACCOUNT of the mediaeval carpenter would be incomplete without some reference to the timber roofs of the Middle Ages, which are one of the outstanding features of the craft of the woodworker, from the earliest times of which we have any knowledge up to the period when the Great Hall is superseded by the Long Gallery, namely, the latter years of the sixteenth century. With the advent of the Long Gallery and the Great Parlour, the former open roofs of oak give way to the closed ceilings of plaster.

Between stone and timber construction there are certain cardinal points of difference which must be stated here in order to render easy of comprehension much of what follows. Stone construction, especially in the Gothic, is vertical; the lintel is almost unknown in England, from Norman times onward. Stone will bear great vertical stresses but is incapable of sustaining lateral strains, and lintels, therefore, must have thickness proportional to their span. It was because of this quality (or absence of one, perhaps) that the Roman arch (which is constructional and constructed) developed in the way that it did throughout the Roman Empire. On the other hand, a timber beam, especially if cambered, will take a great strain without sagging; rot, decay and worms are its only enemies. Wood, however, owing to its nature, demands construction of joints such as the mortise and tenon, halving, grooving, notching, fingering, rebating or dove-tailing. This jointing introduces another problem, one with which the mediæval carpenter had to contend on all occasions, namely, the weakening which is inevitable to joining two pieces of timber. With the mortise and tenon, for example, the tenon takes from the strength of the stile, the mortise from that of the rail. The same applies to furniture also, but here the considerations are not so serious, as a piece of furniture rarely receives any great strains. With the timber roof, on the other hand, stresses are present everywhere, and they have to be calculated and provided for, if the roof is to have permanent stability.

The whole problem of the mediæval timber roof was in the nature of an engineering proposition, demanding great knowledge and still greater care. One has to realise the many difficulties with which the carpenter of the Middle Ages was confronted before one can appreciate, to the full extent, the triumph of the achievement. How perfect was this knowledge in the fourteenth century may be gathered only from the rare examples of roof-construction of this period which remain. It is the later type only which is defective, such as at Eltham Palace and the Hall of the Middle Temple, where the former fine principles had been forgotten or where construction had become debased. It is the same with all domestic arts; the craftsman begins with imperfect knowledge and progresses until he reaches the zenith of his trade; then the decline sets in and the older, fine traditions are either forgotten or become depraved.

If it were possible to instance examples of the earliest timber roofs, we could trace their true evolutionary order, the development of the science of their construction, noting each advance in its turn. Unfortunately, the wood roof is so old in England that all the earliest examples have perished or long since disappeared. To make the problem more difficult, it is not as if the advance were cumulative, each improvement banishing the older, and more imperfect method forevermore. We find perfectly constructed roofs of the fourteenth century (as in Westminster Hall, at once the largest and the finest example in the world) with others, of far later date, which abound in structural errors, as at Eltham and elsewhere. The inventive skill which lifted the aisle posts of the timber barn and poised them high in the air, as hammer-posts supported on hammer-beams, is older than we know—probably of early thirteenth-century origin, yet the roof of York Guild Hall is constructed with posts to the floor, barn-fashion, although it is no earlier than the middle of the fifteenth century. High or low development of the craft of the mediæval carpenter, therefore, is no criterion of age; we are hundreds of years too late on the scene for this to be the fact. The pitched roof is a great advance on the flat or lean-to types, yet the latter are to be found dating only from the late fifteenth, if not from the early sixteenth, century.

With the flat roof the constructional problems are few in number. The walls must be adequate to withstand the weight, and the beams placed across them must be stout enough to avoid sagging. Transversely across these beams are the joists, then, at right angles, i. e., in the same direction as the tie-beams, are the rafters. Above these, in turn, close-boarding is nailed, and, last of all, is the final covering of lead or zinc. On a flat roof tiles or slates are useless, as water would percolate through their joints or overlaps; they may be used safely, therefore, only on a sloping roof.

The flat roof collects rain, snow or leaves, especially if any tendency to sagging develop, as it usually does, so the next development is the slightly pitched or cambered type. The pitch is effected either by cambering the beams themselves, or by firring them up with additional pieces of wood, known as firring-pieces. This roof, therefore, is known as the firred-beam type. From these roofs to the high-pitched or gabled kind is more than a matter of degree; new principles are involved and these demand some consideration here.

The first new factor with which the constructor of the gabled roof has to contend is the thrust, the tendency to flatten out and collapse, either by pushing the walls outwards, or the rafter ends off the wall-heads. The second is the liability to wind pressure from the sides, which may blow the entire roof off the building; and the third is the tendency to sag along the length of its apex, at the ridge. There are other minor problems which will be considered later, but before doing so, it may be desirable to define technical terms.

At the top of the pitched roof is the ridge-purlin, or ridge, the long beam into which the upper ends of the rafters are housed. In many of the older roofs of the domestic type this ridge-purlin is dispensed with, the rafter-ends being "fingered" together, hence the irregularity of skyline which many of these roofs present, owing to sagging of the ridge tiles. From the ridge, down the sides of the roof, are the rafters, and, where occasionally a thicker one is introduced, at intervals, for strength or for other purposes which will be explained later, this is known as a principal rafter, or principal. Both rafter and principal are notched, at their lower ends, into the wall-plate which rests on the top of the outer walls, along their length. One or more horizontal beams, fixed across the rafters between the ridge and the wall-plate, known as purlins, serve to stiffen the rafters and prevent sag in their length.

To obviate wind-strain on the slopes of the roof, which would have the tendency to push the entire roof off the walls, vertical posts are tenoned into the wall-plate and carried down the inside faces of the walls, supported on brackets or corbels; these are known as wall-posts. The cross-beams, which span the roof at various heights, are known as tie-beams when at wall-head level, and as collar-beams, or collars, when tenoned into the principals at a higher level. A vertical post, fixed between ridge and collar, or between collar and tie-beam, is a king-post; where two are placed between purlins and cross-beams, one on either side of the roof center, they are called queen-posts. A diagonal bracket supporting a beam at its wall-end is a brace; where it is curved it is known as an arch-brace.

A beam, projecting into the hall, at right angles to the wall-plate and tenoned into it, is a hammer-beam. It demands a brace underneath to support it, otherwise it would rest merely on its tenon. The vertical post above, tenoned at its foot-end into the hammer-beam and at its other into a principal, is a hammer-post. Its function is to prevent sagging of purlins or principals. Sometimes we find two tiers of hammer-beams, in which case the roof is known as a double hammer-beam. A false hammer-beam roof is one where the hammer-post, or an arch-rib, is set back from the outer extremity of the hammer-beam, the latter thus projecting into the hall without any useful function. A pendentive hammer-beam roof (a bad type and, curiously, always of late date) is one in which the hammer-post is carried down past the end of the hammer-beam, the latter being tenoned into it. The strength, therefore, depends, not on the solid lateral beam, but on the small tenon at its extremity, which bears the weight of the post and all that it carries. Middle Temple Hall and Eltham Palace are both of this pendentive type and, although of late date, have required periodical overhauling and restoration, in consequence of this defect in constructive principle.

In timber-roof construction, where strength and stability are both of the highest importance, and where every timber has to bear strains, the tenon is a joint to be employed only vertically; used horizontally it has the defects incidental to its form. Though sometimes unavoidable, it should always be reinforced by the use of brackets or braces. With furniture or panellings these strictures do not apply, for obvious reasons.

The hammer-beam roof is a logical necessity when the hall is too wide in span to allow of tie-beams from wall to wall, or where it is inadmissible to bring the hammer-posts to the floor, as in barn construction. The hammer-beam type is known as a compound roof; one with tie-beams, but without principals or purlins, is said to be single-framed; with both principals and purlins, it is double-framed.

Between secular and sacred roofs, those of dwelling houses or churches, there is no absolute line of demarcation; neither may they be divided into decorated and undecorated, although we may have the barn roof at the one end and Hampton Court Great Hall at the other, but between these are all stages of elaboration. Any classification, therefore, is subject to wide exceptions. Many secular buildings, such as St. Mary's Hall, Coventry, an old guild hall of the cloth-workers, have a semi-sacred character, and all artwork, until the close of the fifteenth century, was at least church-inspired if not actually from the hands of monks or lay brethren.

There can be no doubt about the secular character of the largest oak roof in the world, that of Westminster Hall. The old building, of William Rufus, in which, at Whitsuntide, in the year 1099, the Norman king held his first court, was considerably decayed in 1395 when Richard II decided on its restoration. The original roof, as far as we know, was of timber, in double-aisled form, with posts to the floor, in the manner of York Guild Hall. At that date no other construction would have been practicable with the available knowledge of the period. Even in 1395, only a king's master-carpenter, invested with almost royal powers, could have attempted the roof which exists at the present day. Master Hugh Herland, or John Godmeston, the clerk of the works, could impress any carpenters, or other labourers "where or whenever found, *Except In The Fee Of The Church*, with power to arrest and imprison contrarients," and to take stone, timber, tiles and other materials at the king's charges. It was from the royal forest of Pettelwode, in Sussex, (does the name survive as Petworth?) that the oak was obtained, but of this old forest no trace remains at the present day.

It is curious, and tragic, that this mighty roof, of fine Sussex oak, *Quercus pedunculata*, which might have defied the centuries for all time, nearly crashed to the ground, owing to the ravages of the wood-worm, *Xestobium tessellatum*, a tiny antagonist, barely one-quarter of an inch in length, yet, in countless millions, enough to eat away Herland's mighty trusses almost to powder. But for one apparently slight oversight, a failure to provide for adequate ventilation to the timbers, no such attack would, in all probability, ever have occurred, and H. M. Office of Works would have been spared some eleven years of responsible and difficult labour of restoration. To-day, the great roof is invisibly reinforced with steel, and secure, it is to be hoped, for centuries to come. Unique as it is, this triumph of English mediæval carpentry is little known, even to the Londoner, and seldom seen by the visitor, yet it nestles under the angle of the Houses of Parliament, so may hardly be dismissed as inaccessible. To those who may make a pilgrimage of inspection (perhaps in consequence of these notes!) one or two words of advice may not be out of place. When one stands on the stone floor and looks up into what is almost a forest of British oak, it should be remembered that each timber has its proper purpose, and takes its share of strain. Even the great spandrels, pierced and carved, serve to stiffen beams and braces, yet I have known persons, who should have been better informed, regard the whole work as mere decoration.

WESTMINSTER HALL (ELEVENTH CENTURY) HAS THE LARGEST TIMBER ROOF IN THE WORLD (BUILT IN *1395*). THE HALL IS *238* FT. LONG, *68* FT. WIDE, AND *90½* FT. FROM FLOOR TO RIDGE. EACH HAMMER-POST IS *21½* FT. IN HEIGHT, CUT FROM A BAULK *25* IN. BY *38½* IN., WEIGHING *3½* TONS

HAMMER-BEAM ROOF WITH HAMMERS CONCEALED BY A CARVED CORNICE, AND VAULTED TO WALL-POSTS IN THE MANNER OF THE STONE-MASON. A FINE DECORATIVE ROOF OF THE FIFTEENTH CENTURY

UNORNAMENTED BARN ROOF, FIFTEENTH CENTURY. BRACED TIE-BEAMS WITH KING-POSTS, COLLARS ABOVE; RAFTERS WITH THREE PURLINS, NO RIDGE. HAMMER-POSTS TO THE FLOOR (REINFORCED WITH STONE AT THE FEET) WITH HAMMER-BEAMS TENONED INTO THEM

TIMBER HOUSE OF FIFTEENTH CENTURY BEING RESTORED. NOTE ABSENCE OF RIDGE AND SAGGING OF THE PURLIN UNDER THE COLLAR-BEAMS; CAMBERED TIE-BEAM WITH MOULDED AND BRACED KING-POST ABOVE. PRINCIPAL AND COMMON RAFTERS WITH DOUBLE PURLINS ON LEFT

TYPICAL OPEN-ROOF CONSTRUCTION OF THE FIFTEENTH CENTURY. YEOMAN HOUSE TYPE. CAMBERED TIE-BEAMS, NOTCHED ON WALL-PLATES, ARCH BRACED TO WALL-POSTS; BRACED KING-POSTS, COLLARS ABOVE REINFORCED BY A PURLIN UNDERNEATH. NOTE THE PEGGING OF THE TIMBERS

DOUBLE HAMMER-BEAM ROOF. UPPER TIER FALSE, WITHOUT HAMMER-POSTS; LOWER TIER OF THE PENDENTIVE TYPE, COLLARS TENONED INTO PRINCIPALS; TWO PURLINS, RIDGE AND CARVED WALL-PLATE

ROOF WITH HAMMER-BEAMS AND HAMMER-POSTS, THE LATTER ALTERNATELY OF THE PENDENTIVE TYPE. PRINCIPAL AND COMMON RAFTERS, WALL-PLATE, PURLIN AND RIDGE, ALL CARVED. FIFTEENTH CENTURY

(A) TRUE HAMMER-BEAM, WITH HAMMER-POST TENONED INTO IT. ILLUSTRATING THE CONSTRUCTIONAL STRENGTH OF THE VERTICAL TENON

(B) THE PENDENTIVE HAMMER-BEAM, WHERE THE HAMMER-POST IS CARRIED DOWN PAST THE BEAM, THE LATTER BEING TENONED INTO IT. ILLUSTRATING THE WEAKNESS OF THE HORIZONTAL TENON

(C) THE PENDENTIVE HAMMER-BEAM IN THE EARLY CONSTRUCTIONAL MANNER, WHERE THE EFFECT OF THE PENDANT IS OBTAINED WITHOUT LOSS OF STRENGTH. BOTH HAMMER-POST AND PENDENTIVE ARE TENONED, VERTICALLY, INTO THE HAMMER-BEAM

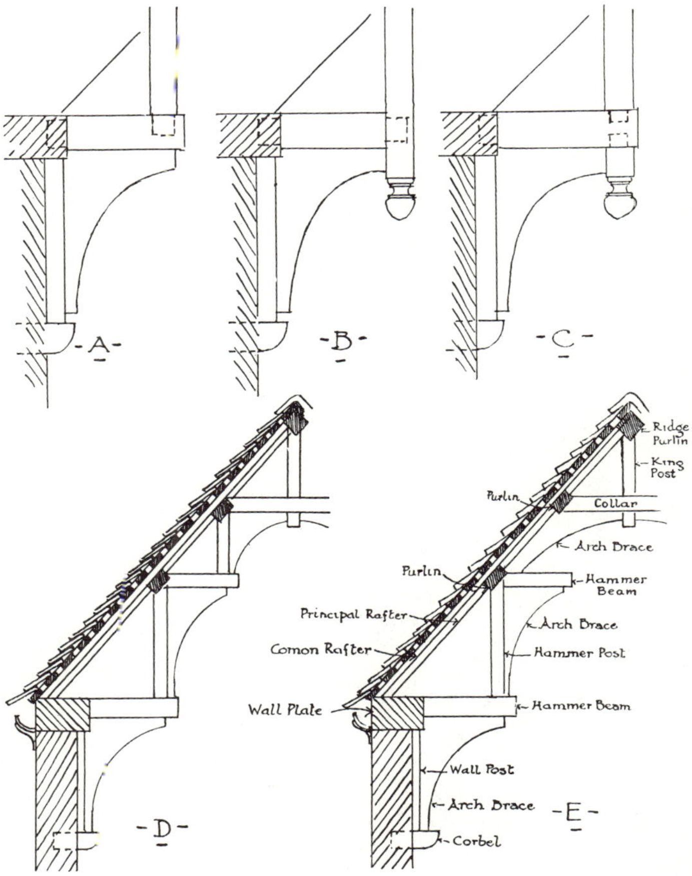

THE HAMMER-BEAM ROOF, WITH TECHNICAL TERMS INDICATED

(D) TRUE DOUBLE HAMMER-BEAM, WHERE THE HAMMER-POSTS ARE TENONED INTO THE OUTER EXTREMITY OF THE HAMMER-BEAMS

(E) DOUBLE HAMMER-BEAM ROOF WITH THE UPPER TIER OF HAMMERS FALSE, I. E., THE ARCH-BRACE UNDER THE COLLAR IS CARRIED TO THE BACK OF THE HAMMER-BEAM, WHICH IS CARRYING NO WEIGHT AND, IS, THEREFORE, MERELY DECORATIVE

NOTE HOW THE HAMMER-BEAM ROOF IS CONSTRUCTED IN A SERIES OF TRIANGLES, THEREBY GIVING THE MAXIMUM OF RESISTANCE TO SAGGING STRAIN IN EACH PART

SCISSOR-BRACED WAGON TYPE OF ROOF, WITHOUT COLLARS OR RIDGE. BRACKETED WALL-PLATES AND FIVE PURLINS. DEVONSHIRE TYPE OF THE FIFTEENTH CENTURY

LOW-PITCHED CAMBERED TIE-BEAM ROOF, THE BEAMS ARCH BRACED TO WALL-POSTS, WITH FIGURES OF SAINTS ON THE CORBELS

THE LIBRARY, DURHAM CATHEDRAL. LOW-PITCHED ROOF WITH KING- AND QUEEN-POSTS, TIE-BEAMS BRACED TO WALL-POSTS. SUPPORTED ON STONE CORBELS

INGENIOUSLY DESIGNED LOW-PITCHED ROOF OF CLERESTORY TYPE. CAMBERED COLLAR-BEAMS TENONED INTO THE GREAT HAMMER-POSTS, WHICH ARE CONNECTED BY SUBSIDIARY COLLARS. THE HAMMER-POSTS ARE OF THE TRUE TYPE, THE PENDENTIVES BEING JOINTED INTO THE HAMMER-BEAMS BELOW

HOUSE IN COURSE OF DEMOLITION SHOWING COUPLED PRINCIPAL RAFTERS WITHOUT RIDGE, (COMMON RAFTERS REMOVED) PURLINS, TIE-BEAMS, AND COLLARS

PITCHED ROOF WITH RIDGE, TWO PURLINS AND CARVED WALL-PLATE. COLLARS WITH KING-POSTS, ALTERNATELY ARCH-BRACED TO HAMMER-BEAMS AND WALL-POSTS. EARLY FIFTEENTH CENTURY

COLLARS AND SCISSOR-BRACED COMMON RAFTERS. WALL-POSTS AT EACH SEVENTH RAFTER. THE VERTICAL STRUTTING AT THE FOOT OF EACH RAFTER IS KNOWN AS "ASHLARING"

CHAPTER V

Panelling and Interior Woodwork: The Small Panel

THE USE OF WOOD, either as wainscoting or for panelling in the covering of walls, dates no earlier than from the close of the fifteenth century. The Great Hall, double-sided screen, which borrowed from the hall itself the passage leading from the entrance door to the buttery (this passage is always referred to as "The Skreens" in documents of the time) which is identical in construction with much of the later panelling, is considerably older than this, and shows that the knowledge of framing and panelling was very early in the history of English woodwork. Similarly, we have the same principle in rood and chancel screens and in the panelled flanks at the back of church altars. Of room wainscoting we have none prior to about 1480, if as early. Church woodwork and great hall screens were, undoubtedly, the work of the carpenter exclusively, but there are many reasons for supposing that secular room panelling was often made by the arkwright.

There are obvious causes for the inadaptability of panelling in churches and sacred edifices. The church plan is divided into nave, chancel, aisles and chapels, in which outer walls (available, as a rule, only in aisles and chapels) are broken up by windows, and the free wall spaces are utilised for memorial tablets, tombs, *piscinae* or subsidiary altars. The walls of the chancel are nearly always devoted to screenwork, stalls or choir seats, and, at a later date, to the pipe organ. Clerical houses usually affected a severe simplicity, except, as in the instance of William of Wykeham, a great prelate, where the walls would be adorned with arras or "painted cloths." In his will, dated 1403, he leaves to Robert Braybrooke, Bishop of London, his silk bed and the "whole suite of tapestries" in his Palace of Winchester.

With the laity, the Great Hall was also ill-adapted for panelling, owing to its height and fenestration, and it is only when domestic privacy was attained, when rooms had become smaller and of lesser height, when plaster ceilings had replaced open roofs of timber, that panelling or wainscoting began to replace walls that were bare or painted or hung with cloths or tapestries.

The term "wainscoting" is here used to indicate a close-boarded covering of a wall without either framing or panels, the mediaeval equivalent of the modern "match-boarding." It may be incorrect to use the word in this way, but to do so makes clear the distinction between it and panelling.

It has already been pointed out that we do not know how general may have been the use of plaster, painted with figure or floral subjects, before panelling became general. There are many reasons why the presence of plaster and paint would hardly be suspected, whereas with panelling, even if covered with canvas and reams of wall-paper, the woodwork, if present, is almost certain to be discovered when the wall is pulled down. It is only within recent years that the attention which has been directed to the possibility of these wall-paintings being present under later papers, panelling or whitewash, has led to the more careful demolition of old houses, with the result that a number of these painted walls have been discovered. One, from a house at Stodmarsh, in Kent, is illustrated here, and the subject, Diana and Actæon, is not one which would have been painted on the walls of a labourer's cottage. The date is probably as late as the early sixteenth century, to judge by the costume of Actæon. It cannot well be earlier.

Oak was the timber generally used for wall-paneling up to the end of the seventeenth century, but imported woods, such as walnut and Memel deal (the former is not an English timber before about 1650, as it was planted in England, for the first time, in 1565, by the Earl of Pembroke and Montgomery, at Wilton Park, near Salisbury) are known in comparatively early times. There is, or was, a room panelled with deal, with close framing and small panels, in the oak manner of the time, at Parnham Park, Beaminster, in Dorset, in the room known as the "King's Chamber," which dates either from the last years of the sixteenth century or very shortly thereafter. There are records also in which these deal rooms are mentioned, and they were evidently highly prized. At Rotherwas, in Herefordshire, there existed, until the last twenty years, another room from about 1640 panelled in walnut of foreign origin, either Dutch or German, but the actual work was unmistakably English. These, however, are so exceptionable that it may be stated, almost as a definite fact, that quartered oak was the usual wood for panelling until the last decade of the seventeenth century.

We have already seen the inaccuracy of assuming knowledge to be non-existent because it is not exhibited at any given period. For example, we find wall-boarding or wainscoting at an earlier date than panelling, and the latter indicates a higher stage of development than the former, yet we cannot assume that the woodworker of the time had to discover the art of framing and panelling, even if he, personally, was obviously unacquainted with the mortise and its tenon. We know that this knowledge was possessed by the woodworking trades as early as the middle of the fourteenth century. What we do not know is whether the carpenter, who represented the highest degree of skill and tradition of his time, made this early panelling and wainscoting or whether this type of work was left to the lesser craftsmen, the arkwright or *huchier*, or, to give the latter the name which begins to come into use in the first years of the sixteenth century, the "joyner," or joiner.

Panelling may be said to coincide with the last years of the fifteenth century, in its inception, and to bridge, therefore, the Gothic and the Renaissance. If we accept the earliest date of the Renaissance in England as 1509, the year when Henry VIII ascended the English throne as the second of the Tudor line (he begins at once to prepare for the tomb of his father in Westminster Abbey, displacing Master Pageny and appointing that Italian soldier of fortune, Pietro Torrigiano, thus rejecting the Gothic and accepting the new style) then there remain only some twenty years during which any Gothic panelling could have been made.

There are three patterns which may be said to belong to this Gothic period, the last two of which carry us into the Renaissance. The first is a purely Gothic wall-boarding, without tongue-and-groove joints, the boards merely nailed to the wall and the butt-joints masked with an applied tracery. This is exceedingly rare; only one example has been discovered up to the present date, but that does not prove how much or how little of this work may have been done at the time and replaced later by framed panelling or destroyed in subsequent demolitions. The one example which we have is painted in the same manner as the base of a fine chancel or rood screen, but there are reasons for supposing that much of the oak panelling and even the furniture of the fifteenth century, if not also much of that of the sixteenth, was originally painted, decorated or lacquered. I have seen examples in which the painted decoration appears to be original.

The second pattern is the curved-rib or "vine" panel of which many varieties are to be found, all possessing the same basic idea. The third is the linenfold. As it and the curved-rib may have evolved in the same way they may be here treated together. The curved-rib is rare in company with Renaissance details but the linenfold is much more common; it belongs, in fact, more to the Renaissance than to the Gothic.

Nearly all decorative motives begin by having some useful purpose, and both the curved-rib and the linenfold panels may have commenced in the same way. As everyone knows, to insert a panel into the groove of a frame necessitates chamfering the former, or actually making it thin enough to allow of insertion in the groove. With a framing, the stiles and rails of which are rarely as much as one inch in thickness, the groove cannot be much more than one-quarter of an inch, and a panel of this thinness might easily bulge or split. It is usual, therefore, to make the panel stouter, and to plane the borders down to the requisite thickness to permit of its insertion in the framing grooves. This chamfer, in the early work, is generally very broad, often enough for the two slopes to meet in the center in a ridge. A panel, chamfered in this way, with a central rib, will stand better than one of the full thickness, unchamfered. This would soon be discovered in the Middle Ages, when the greatest attention was paid to the proper cutting (quartering) and seasoning of timber. There are many examples of this central rib on the backs of panels, especially in church doors, which, from their exposed situation, would be prone to warp or split in time.

From the central ridge on the back, to the bringing of this feature to the front, making a decorative device of it, would be only a step, and the next stage would be the vertical moulding of the panel-front in the form that we know as linenfold. It is certain that this imitation of the folding of linen was not devised until much later, as there are many examples to prove this fact. The early vertical-moulded panels have the ribbing carried from top to bottom, with the result that the face of the panel must project over the framing mouldings, as at Yarnscombe. To get rid of this overhang the mouldings would have to be cut back, this cutting would be given a decorative form, and the linenfold would result. Where the folding of linen, or more properly, the creasing of parchment, is deliberately imitated, such examples are always late, after 1500 at least. In the great hall screen from Brightleigh in Devon (already illustrated in Chapter III and shown again in this chapter, in its "restored" state) which is late fifteenth-century work, there are early examples of linenfold panels which bear little resemblance to the actual folding of any material, possessing, if anything, rather a heraldic significance than one based on natural forms.

The central-rib, or "vine" panel may have evolved in much the same way, the rib being diverted to form another kind of device, but retaining its stiffening property at the same time. The old Gothic tradition of making ornament serve a useful purpose would not die out easily; it is only with the Renaissance that decoration becomes purely and intentionally an adjunct to construction.

Shortly after 1500 the full tide of the Renaissance sets in; either from Italy direct, as in the case of the tomb of Henry VII in Westminster Abbey; transmuted through France, as in the instance of Abbot Fuller's panels from Waltham Abbey; or at a much later date, from Holland and the Low Countries, of which variation of the style, the overmantel from Lime Street in the City of London may be cited as an example. With much of the early work, the traditional influence of certain of the English counties is marked. The carved woodwork of Devonshire has a richness, almost barbaric, found in no other district. There is, again, a strong foreign influence in much of the work from the Welsh bordering counties. The same is true, in another way, of some of the Lancashire work, each being unmistakable. These county characteristics are evidently the result of strong trade traditions of the time, as there are the same peculiarities in the panelling from Barnstaple and that from Exeter, although separated by the

OAK OVERMANTEL AND STONE CHIMNEYPIECE FROM A HOUSE IN LIME STREET, LONDON. DUTCH RENAISSANCE, EARLY SEVENTEENTH CENTURY

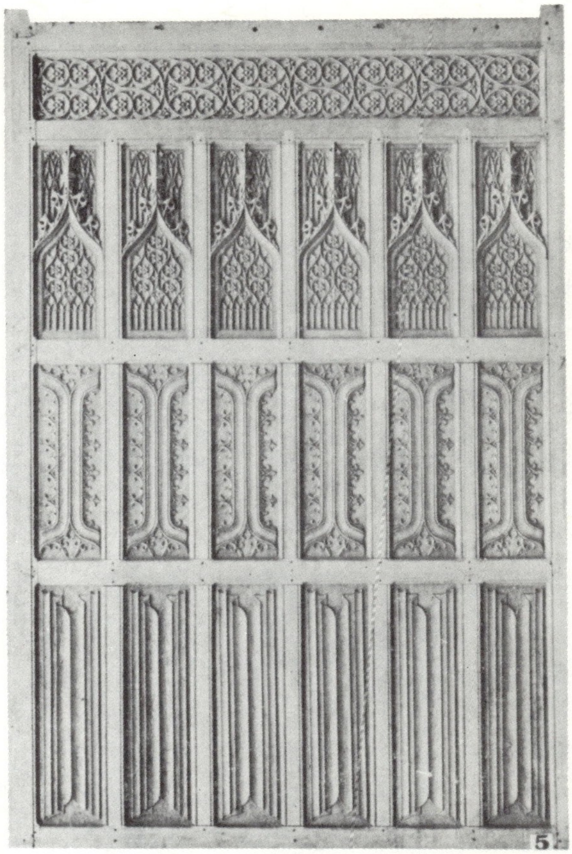

FRENCH FLAMBOYANT GOTHIC. OGIVAL TRACERY, THE CURVED-RIB AND THE LINENFOLD USED IN COMBINATION

OAK SCRATCH-MOULDED PANELLING WITHOUT MITRES. TENONS PEGGED AT JOINTS

PANELLING FROM WEST STOW CHURCH, SUFFOLK. EARLY OAK BOARDING, WITH APPLIED TRACERY TO HIDE THE JOINTS, DECORATED WITH POINTED ORNAMENT. FIFTEENTH CENTURY

FREE GOTHIC DETAIL WITH PLAIN PANELS. THE FRAMING "MASON-MITRED" AT THE CORNERS

CURVED-RIB OR "VINE" PANELLING, THE LAST PHASE OF THE TRUE GOTHIC

ARCADED AND INTERLACED PANELS AS AT TISSINGTON HALL AND LYME PARK. RAIL ABOVE ARCADING WITH CHOPPED-IN INLAY. EARLY SEVENTEENTH CENTURY

THE LINENFOLD, USED IN CONJUNCTION WITH FREE GOTHIC MOTIVES IN SMALL SQUARE PANELS

THE LINENFOLD USED IN CONJUNCTION WITH RENAISSANCE DETAILS IN UPPER TIER OF PANELS

INNER-FRAME, OR "STRAP" PANELLING FOUND FROM *1620* UP TO *1685*. SOMEWHAT RARE AT THE EARLIER DATE

THE USUAL PLAIN TYPE OF THE SEVENTEENTH CENTURY. SCRATCH-MOULDED, BUTTED AT JOINTS AND CHAMFERED AT BASE

AN OAK BOOKCASE OR CABINET, THE WORK OF A MAKER OF PANELLING RATHER THAN OF A CABINETMAKER

HEAVILY MOULDED FRAMING, THE MOULDINGS TRULY MITRED. THE LATE SIXTEENTH CENTURY TYPE AS AT HADDON HALL

ARRANGEMENT OF VERTICAL AND LAY PANELS AS AT BROMLEY-BY-BOW PALACE. EARLY SEVENTEENTH CENTURY

CHAPTER VI

Panelling and Interior Woodwork: The Large Panel

ONLY during the closing years of the seventeenth century does a remarkable change take place in English panelling. Apparently insignificant as this is, being merely a change from the small panel to the large, there lie, behind this trifling alteration of detail, certain events of far-reaching importance. Hitherto, the craft of the woodworker had been vested in the carpenter and the joiner, who were responsible both for design and for workmanship. There were definite and fast-bound traditions of the trade and certain precautionary methods which were seldom, if ever, ignored. Before even timber could be used at all, it had to be subjected to the scrutiny and approval of certain of the officers of the Guild, the "Serjaunts of the Mayes." These officials had plenary powers regarding oak which was incorrectly cut, or improperly seasoned. There are many entries to be found in the records of the Carpenters' Company such as "Paid to the Serjaunt of the Mayes for restynge of stuffe, iiij.s.," which means that the "Serjaunt" received four shillings for seizing improper timber.

If we take down a flank of wall-panelling of the early Stuart type and examine it from behind, we shall find, as a rule, that the oak, especially in the panels, is riven, not sawn. The panels are of uneven thickness and smoothed up on the face side only. If this were invariable (which it is not) one might be tempted to enquire whether the saw was, at this date, a tool of the carpenter or of the joiner. We know, however, that saws were used in very early times. Riving, or splitting with the wedge and the "beetle," leaves the natural cleavage face on oak; the "riving-iron" follows the grain of the timber, and riven oak stands better than sawn, as park palings and shingles manifest. Even at the present day these are split, not sawn.

It is one of the striking characteristics of the early craftsmen that they followed right methods, often by instinct or tradition (which is the trade-name for much the same thing) rather than by ascertained experience, even when the traditional way entailed additional labour. One of the reasons why very early, oak woodwork has persisted in England to the present day is that the wood was split instead of being sawn.

During the closing years of the seventeenth century a marked change took place in woodworking. The woodworker had steadily lost status for nearly one hundred years; he was no longer the creator; he was only a workman, and with the rise of the architect (beginning with Inigo Jones) he assumed a subordinate position. The architect began to design, not only buildings—his proper field—but interior woodwork and even furniture, and the carpenter and the joiner merely executed what the architect designed. Throughout the whole of the eighteenth century we find this false position pertaining, of the architect dominating the cabinetmaker, and certain of the latter—Batty and Thomas Langley, or W. & J. Halfpenny, are instances—style themselves "architects" in the design books which they published. Yet, although the architect commanded the woodworker, the former learned continually from the latter. At a later stage in this enquiry, we shall see the spectacle of a masterful architect, Robert Adam,—one with the largest practice enjoyed by any architect, before or since—employing the famous cabinetmakers of his day, yet learning from them practical methods which revolutionised his later designs and caused him to seriously modify his early drawings; the teacher learned from his pupils.

The functions of the architect being confined, properly, to marble, stone or brick, it is only natural, perhaps, that he should meddle with timber. Knowing little or nothing of the possibilities—or the limitations—of the strange material (to him) he designed with absolute disregard of the prevailing traditions. He sketched large panels, which did not permit of riving, and which demanded jointing in sections, a practice which the early woodworker had steadily refused to countenance. The art of jointing was known, as the panels on which pictures of the school of Van Eyck are painted, will bear witness, as early as the late fourteenth century. It was not that the carpenter did not know how to edge-joint panels; he preferred to run no risks, and, in consequence, he remained faithful to the small panel. He is the dominant factor, both as executant and as designer, in the early years, but, after the architect had attained prominence, the joiner, against his better judgment and his trade traditions, had to saw and to joint.

If "fools rush in where angels fear to tread," sometimes foolhardy people achieve results which the sober-minded have not dared to attempt. The large panel is a case in point. The joiner found, probably to his own amazement, that oak could be sawn, and could be edge-jointed in large panels, and yet persist without cracking, shrinking or warping, and so, from the ignorant, came wisdom—and the large panel in English woodwork.

It was on the fifth day of February, in the year 1674, that a certain John Penhalow, a Cornish gentleman, acquired a set of chambers at No. 3, Clifford's Inn, within the precincts of the City of London, hard by Temple Bar. Later, he secured an additional set, for the space of three lives "in consideration of the outlay to which he had been put." The wonderful little room which is illustrated in this chapter shows how he spent his money. He lived to enjoy his panels for twenty-eight years. Benjamin

Penhalow followed him in possession, and in 1722 the third "life," John Rogers, succeeded, and the lease then was determined. Fleet Street, upon which Clifford's Inn abuts, was very different in 1674 to what it is at the present day. Bazalgette's Embankment was undreamed of, and on the south side, dingy lanes gave on to the muddy Thames below. It is possible that John Penhalow, from the windows of his chambers in Clifford's Inn, may have gazed on mercantile shipping, as vessels were of light draught in those days, although Old London Bridge, with its street of houses on the bridge itself, must have barred any "tall ships" from adventuring any higher than the Pool. The houses on the south side of Fleet Street would hardly obstruct the view of one perched up high in Clifford's Inn, as many must have been in the process of rebuilding, in consequence of the Great Fire of 1666.

This Clifford's Inn room is not the pioneer of the large panel, although it is among the earliest. It is not until fourteen years after John Penhalow had entered into peaceful possession of his room and chambers that the Earl (afterwards the Duke) of Devonshire employed Robert Owen and Henry Lobb, the "London joyners," in the large-panelled woodwork at Chatsworth. Samuel Watson, a Derbyshire man, executed much of the fine carvings in soft lime-tree, in the great chamber, and in the style of Grinling Gibbons, whereas Penhalow's enrichments are in Barbados cedar. Watson was still carving at Chatsworth thirteen years after John Penhalow had surrendered one of his "lives," namely, his own. If the dining room at Ham House may be said to be panelled in the new, large manner (the panels are of comparatively small area compared to those at Clifford's Inn) then the latter is not the earliest by some ten years. Still, it must have been something new, and even epoch-marking, at the time when it was done, and there is nothing as fine in quality at Ham House. Who the architect was we do not know, but it is certain that Penhalow's panelling must have been designed by one. Whether Wren, busy in schemes for the re-building of St. Paul's, and obstructed, in most irritating fashion by the Duke of York (afterwards James II) acted in an advisory capacity, we have no means of knowing, but Christopher Wren and Grinling Gibbons undoubtedly inspired this Clifford's Inn woodwork. The former —who was hoisted, in a basket, every week, to the top of St. Paul's, endangering life and limb for a paltry fifty pounds a year—could hardly have had the dominating influence in 1674 which his fellow architect, Robert Adam, possessed less than one hundred years later. But Wren's prestige was just as great and he over-topped Adam, immeasurably, before he died. Yet his reward, in money, was scanty indeed, nor did succeeding generations of architects ever confess how much they owed to the man who designed more than one-half of the churches in the City of London. Thus the lesser have borrowed from the greater, since the dawn of man, and often without acknowledgment.

The era of the large panel in oak was comparatively short-lived. Oak, to stand without warping or shrinking, demands quarter-cutting, and, in consequence, narrow boards with many joints. The red, or Memel deal, imposes no such restrictions; consequently it soon replaced the harder timber. The taste of the day was for lighter rooms, which necessitated painting. Even the oak panelling of the Clifford's Inn room had many coats, which had to be pickled and stripped, when it came into the possession of the Victoria and Albert Museum, at the price of £606:7:6. (How far would $3,000 go towards its purchase today?) Again comes in the accidental discovery; deal is not a picturesque wood and was never intended to be left in its natural state. But lead-painted for generations and then stripped, the wood takes on a lovely faded pencil cedar colour, utterly uncontemplated at the date when the first coat was applied. The first stripping was intended solely for educational purposes, to show the natural timber and the construction. But out of this has arisen the present-day fashion for these stripped deal rooms, many of which were growing timber long after the date of the Clifford's Inn room. Demand creates supply; that is only natural.

The use of the large panel in English woodwork inevitably engendered a new style. The architect turned that style in the classical or Palladian direction, and we got the boldly-projecting skirting and surbase mouldings and classical cornices with their entablatures, now a part of the wall, and, therefore, of the room, and not of the ceiling, as with the older work. The room was then constructed with the panelling, not merely with the walls clothed with woodwork, as a mere decorative adjunct. The constructive appearance was still further enhanced by the use of pilasters, not as simple features of the wainscoting, as in the instance of the Exeter room, but fulfilling their proper purpose in supporting something, such as the entablature of a room, the shelf of a mantel or the cornice of a window. Here is a return again to the constructive thoroughness and purity of principle which we find, nearly always, in new styles. Designing, also, had to follow fixed principles and laws; a badly-proportioned treatment of a classical room would no longer pass for designing idiosyncrasy; everything had to be correct. That this was recognised at the time is evident from the fact that every design book of this period commences, as a matter of course, with the Five Orders, and diagrams giving the correct proportions of mouldings, columns and pilasters. The projecting chimney-breast, which is a rarity in houses of the Stuart period or earlier, became a feature, and was treated decoratively with breaks and mitres. The usual cornice copied that of a classical building, and the dado—the combination of surbase and skirting, with the plain or panelled space between—was treated as a base to the room—as it should be. Doors also assumed a dignity and an importance they had not hitherto possessed. Above the mantel was often an elaborate frame containing either a picture or a mirror; more often the former. Perhaps one of the most charming of the features of these classical, architect-designed rooms is the treatment of corners with open niches, such as the example from Bristol, illustrated here. Decorative china was now coming into vogue, chiefly oriental, brought back from the East in the tea clippers or the argosies of "John Company."

The houses of this period, if lacking much of the earlier home-like character, were more convenient, in some ways, running less to outhouses and to odd corners. As an offset, they were usually four stories or more in height (which meant flights of stairs for the unfortunate domestics, as they worked in the bowels of the earth and slept just under the stars) and the basement had become a settled and abiding institution. The entrance door to the house took on a large dignity, overshadowing all other external details, whereas, in the house of the carpenter, the door was one of several openings to the interior and otherwise comparatively inconspicuous. Many of these early eighteenth century doorways are exceedingly fine in character, and to me, the houses of this period appear to suggest, in every way, the development away from the communal life of the earlier days, and to intensify the ever-widening gulf between the two classes, those (in the words of Heine) born with saddles, as compared with others born with spurs. It is not that England was growing wealthier, simply that its wealth was becoming more centralised, getting into fewer hands. The status of the working classes was steadily becoming lower and lower, until, during the first years of the nineteenth century, the first Poor Law Act (since known as the Speenhamland Act) was passed for the relief, not of the out-of-work, but for the artisan, as it was found—to the utter surprise of the "governing classes," naturally—the wages paid in nearly every trade were so miserably inadequate that workmen were literally starving at their benches. At the same time, commodities of every description were ruinously dear. Yet there are people, even at the present day, who maintain that wages follow prices! Still, the houses of the wealthy were fine and the interiors magnificent, even if, well out of sight, were hovels in which the makers of these fine houses "lived"—and died, the latter rather frequently, it is to be feared. Behind the victorious army, there must be many graves, however. That is a necessary corollary of victory.

THE CLIFFORD'S INN ROOM. OAK PANELLING, DOOR-CASES AND MANTEL PUT IN ABOUT *1686-8*

CARVED DEAL MANTEL AND PANELLING, *1750-60*, AT 5 GREAT GEORGE STREET, WESTMINSTER, LONDON

MANTEL IN THE CLIFFORD'S INN ROOM WITH COAT OF ARMS ABOVE

ONE DOOR AND DOOR-CASING IN THE CLIFFORD'S INN ROOM

ONE OF THE TWO DOORS IN THE CLIFFORD'S INN ROOM

TYPICAL MID-EIGHTEENTH CENTURY CARVED DEAL DOOR

26 HATTON GARDEN. CARVED DEAL CHIMNEY-BREAST, *c. 1730*

26 HATTON GARDEN, LONDON. DOOR AND PANELLING, *c. 1730*

26 HATTON GARDEN, LONDON, E. C. DEAL ROOM IN SITU, BEFORE REMOVING. ALL THE WOODWORK HAS INNUMERABLE COATS OF PAINT, *c. 1730*

26 HATTON GARDEN, LONDON, E. C. DEAL ROOM IN SITU, PAINTED, *c. 1730*

DUDLEY HOUSE, PARK LANE, LONDON, W. MORNING ROOM PANELLED IN STRIPPED DEAL

26 HATTON GARDEN, LONDON, E. C. DEAL ROOMS IN SITU, PAINTED, *c. 1730*. SHOWING CLASSICAL TREATMENT OF ORNAMENT

MID-EIGHTEENTH CENTURY DEAL CLASSICAL "CONTINUED" MANTEL WITH PILASTERS AT SIDES SUPPORTING THE CORNICE

ELABORATE AND MONUMENTAL DEAL ARCHITECTURAL CHIMNEY-PIECE WITH IONIC COLUMNS SUPPORTING THE ENTABLATURE. SCHOOL OF JAMES GIBBS, EARLY EIGHTEENTH CENTURY

DEAL "VENETIAN" WINDOW IN SOHO SQUARE. CLASSICAL TREATMENT OF PILASTERS SUPPORTING WINDOW CORNICE. NOTE PROJECTION OF SURFACE AND SKIRTING. EARLY EIGHTEENTH CENTURY

CASSIOBURY PARK, WATFORD, HERTFORDSHIRE, A SEAT OF THE EARL OF ESSEX. THE LIBRARY WITH CARVINGS BY GRINLING GIBBONS, EARLY EIGHTEENTH CENTURY

CASSIOBURY PARK, WATFORD, HERTFORDSHIRE. THE INNER LIBRARY. LIME-TREE CARVINGS BY GRINLING GIBBONS. EARLY EIGHTEENTH CENTURY

18 CAREY STREET, LONDON, W. C. EARLY EIGHTEENTH CENTURY ENTRANCE DOORWAY OF HOUSE

DEAL NICHE CORNER CUPBOARD FROM BRISTOL. THE ARMS IN THE COVING ARE THOSE OF THE HICKS FAMILY

ABINGDON HOUSE, WRIGHT'S LANE, KENSINGTON, LONDON, E. MID-EIGHTEENTH CENTURY DEAL DOORWAY

CARVED PINE MANTEL. SCHOOL OF GIBBS. *c. 1730.* 5 FT. 5 INS. WIDE BY 5 FT. 2 INS. HIGH. OPENING 4 FT. 6½ INS. BY 4 FT. 0 INS. HIGH

CARVED PINE MANTEL. SCHOOL OF GIBBS AND HAWKSMOOR. *c 1730-5.* 6 FT. 0 INS. WIDE BY 5 FT. 0½ INS. HIGH. OPENING 4 FT. 11½ INS. BY 4 FT. 0 INS. HIGH

CARVED PINE MANTEL. STYLE OF JAMES GIBBS. *c. 1735.* 6 FT. 9 INS. WIDE BY 5 FT 6 INS. HIGH. OPENING 5 FT. 5½ INS. BY 3 FT. 10 INS. HIGH

CARVED PINE MANTEL. *c. 1745.* 6 FT. 1½ INS. WIDE BY 5 FT. 2¼ INS. HIGH. OPENING 4 FT. 5 INS. BY 3 FT. 1 IN. HIGH

CARVED PINE MANTEL. SCHOOL OF CHIPPENDALE. *c. 1760.* 5 FT. 6 INS. EXTREME WIDTH, 5 FT. 9 INS. TOTAL HEIGHT. OPENING 4 FT. 0¼ IN. BY 3 FT. 7½ INS. HIGH

CARVED PINE MANTEL. *c. 1745-50.* 5 FT. 7½ INS. WIDE BY 4 FT. 10 INS. HIGH. OPENING 4 FT. 4½ INS. BY 3 FT. 8¼ INS. HIGH

PINE AND COMPOSITION MANTEL. SCHOOL OF ADAM. *c. 1765.* 7 FT. 3½ INS. WIDE BY 5 FT. 8 INS. HIGH. OPENING 4 FT. 6 INS. BY 4 FT. 5½ INS. WIDE

CARVED PINE MANTEL WITH CARVED BACKBOARD. *c. 1770.* 5 FT. 5½ INS. WIDE BY 4 FT. 10¼ INS. HIGH. OPENING 3 FT. 9¼ INS. BY 3 FT. 6½ INS. HIGH

CARVED PINE MANTEL AND OVERMANTEL. THE INFLUENCE OF THE FRENCH LOUIS XVI. *c. 1785-1790.* 4 FT. 11 INS. WIDE BY 7 FT. 3 INS. TOTAL HEIGHT. OPENING 4 FT. 2¾ INS. BY 3 FT. 11 INS. HIGH

PINE MANTEL. *c. 1755.* 5 FT. 11½ INS. WIDE BY 5 FT. 2½ INS. HIGH. OPENING 4 FT. 3 INS. BY 4 FT. 1½ INS. HIGH

CARVED PINE MANTEL. *c. 1780.* 5 FT. 3¾ INS. WIDE BY 5 FT. 2¾ INS. HIGH. OPENING 3 FT. 11½ INS. BY 3 FT. 11 INS. HIGH

CHAPTER VII

Oak Furniture

THERE ARE TWO WAYS in which English oak furniture may be considered: on broad and general lines or in full detail. From the first point of view there are certain uniform characteristics; from the second the subject presents a bewildering variety. It is not so much that changes take place from time to time—although this is true in a measure—but that fashions vary considerably, in different districts, at the same period. To enter into this field, and to give evidences for the ascription of this piece to one locality and that to another (the alternative is merely to make empirical statements which do not help the student) would take far more space than is available here, and would only repeat much which was written in an exhaustive work on the same subject.§

Having dealt, at some length, with English woodwork, and having carried the enquiry up to the middle of the eighteenth century, we are compelled to retrace our steps to the early Tudor period. We have already seen that cultured Gothic furniture, from early times up to the dissolution of monasteries, is practically non-existent in England at the present day. Solitary examples, such as the Guild chair in St. Mary's Hall at Coventry and the great tables at Penshurst, in their isolated character, serve only to emphasise this fact.

After the great monasteries had been dissolved, and, incidentally, all the culture of England scattered abroad, to haunt forest and thicket as outlaws, or to emigrate to other countries where intolerance did not proceed as far as despoiling churches, and after things had settled down in England into something like order, English oak furniture began to diverge into two distinct paths. On the one hand, the superior craftsman adopted the new style, the Renaissance, re-inforced and probably instructed by foreign workmen well acquainted with the new manner. Then we get such examples as the choir stalls at Christchurch in Hampshire and the woodwork in King's College Chapel at Cambridge, both dating from the actual period when the demolition of the great monasteries was in active progress. The Renaissance really begins, in England, with the accession of Henry VIII in 1509, and some of the examples from Devonshire may be earlier than this.

On the other hand, we have the inferior craftsman, who is post-dissolution, exclusively, unacquainted with the Renaissance and possessing neither knowledge nor

§"EARLY ENGLISH FURNITURE & WOODWORK" by Herbert Cescinsky and Ernest R. Gribble. Routledge. London.

culture. His furniture is crude in design and with little or no constructive science. This crudity has led many writers on the subject of English furniture into grave errors. The prevailing idea, hitherto, has been that immaturity is an irrefutable indication of early date. The arguments adduced in support of this contention are apparently sound. If we admit a certain stage of artistic and constructional development at a given period, how can we account for immature work produced subsequently? The reply is two-fold. To accept this proposition, we would have to place much of this post-dissolution furniture back in the thirteenth century, if not earlier. Many details, such as in the crudely-pierced or chip-carved chests which have been described as "Gothic," in so many books, negative any such early date conclusively. Yet the later we place them the greater is the difficulty to fit them into the evolutionary scheme. Secondly, if we suppose the culture of England to have been either clerical or directly inspired from church sources (as we know it was up to the end of the fifteenth century) and as we know that the homes of this culture were either razed or despoiled and the teachers driven abroad, is it not natural that inferior craftsmen, the arkwrights or *huchiers*, no longer under clerical guidance, should produce Gothic furniture of a very primitive kind? They knew little of the Gothic, it is true, but they knew less of any other style. This theory fits all the known facts; the older one agrees with none. It is more than probable, therefore, that much of this so-called fifteenth-century furniture has been ante-dated by nearly one hundred years.

If we examine such examples as the chip-carved oak chest illustrated in this chapter, several details will soon become apparent. The man who made it knew how to frame timber; witness the ends, but he constructed the front from a slab, battened and pegged. Why? Simply because framing was a trouble to him; a difficult operation. Then why frame the ends? Because this chest was made to be slung between sumpter mules for transport from place to place, and the ends had to bear all the weight of the chest and its contents. There are signs that the top framing-rail, at each end, has been strained in this way. Now examine the front. The chip-carving bespeaks a want of skill in the use of the carver's gouge and an equal absence of facility in the designing of free forms. The entire pattern may be produced with the compass or the divider, and has been so outlined, if the accuracy of the lines, compared with the crudity of the remainder, be any reliable criterion. True, much of the Gothic at its zenith is designed with the compass, but the skill with which purely geometrical forms are used is in striking contrast to the pattern of this chest-front.

The second example has a framed front with open-pierced and carved panels of a primitive Gothic type. There is tradition here, of a kind. The use of the wheel of St. Catherine complete with spikes (or cusps) implies a certain degree of knowledge of legend, as St. Catherine was supposed to be the patron saint of philosophy, and this chest may have been intended for college use. On the other hand, the Guild of St. Mary, at Coventry, as we have seen, had St. Catherine as one of its patron saints, and there is no apparent connection between philosophy and a guild of cloth-workers.

The third example, which is also geometrical and copies Gothic fenestration, is unbelievable, in its primitive character (if this be the criterion of date) at any later period than the middle of the thirteenth century, but this the style of the ornament absolutely interdicts. The fourth, a side table, is late in type and in its piercing, although early in every other respect. But we are compelled to date by the latest characteristic which a piece exhibits, not by the earliest, and this for obvious reasons which need not be laboured here.

Examples of this post-dissolution Gothic could be multiplied *ad lib.*, but enough has been illustrated here to show that this work is ignorant and late; not crude and early.

If we accept this disparate character of the sixteenth-century furniture and woodwork in England, certain mature examples fall into place, naturally, without distortion either of date or of idea. Thus, the so-called Nonsuch chests may be referred to the period between 1560 and 1600, and placed side by side with examples which are immeasurably below them in quality, knowledge and design. One of these chests is illustrated here, which may be taken as typical of others, as they are all very similar, varying only in trifling particulars. The old Palace of Nonsuch, built near Cheam for Henry VIII, hardly needs detailed reference here, although every trace of it has disappeared long since. That there was such a palace is an historical fact, and Hofnagle's drawing gives us some idea of its general appearance, but whether it was taken as the basis for the design of these chests is doubtful. The palace had ceased to be Crown property in 1555, and these Nonsuch coffers are as late, if not later, than this; and as its royal builder died in 1547, there seems no reason for the sudden popularity of the palace at this late date. There may be other causes to account for the number of these inlaid chests which still exist, to say nothing of the many which may have been destroyed since the sixteenth century. These reasons may be given here, briefly, although they involve a description of a method which belongs to a much later stage in our enquiry.

These inlaid chests are often styled as "marqueterie," a description which is technically incorrect. Marqueterie is an inlay of various woods, cut into a veneer, the complete pattern, in its veneer, being "laid" or glued to its bed, with the caul or the veneering hammer. These Nonsuch chests are inlaid by quite another method, known as "parqueterie." A number of pieces of wood, combined to form a pattern, often of various colours and textures, are pieced together, and, in practice, are assembled in a thickness of one inch or more, and then cut into lateral slices with the saw. The entire front is neither made nor laid as one complete whole, but is put together in sections. The later equivalent of the same method is the well-known "Tonbridge ware," used in the eighteenth century for the decoration of work-boxes and similar small articles. The important point here is that the inlay is produced in multiples of the one pattern, according to the original thickness of the pieces and the number of cuts with the saw. The obvious result would be to use up the inlay on a number of articles, and this may account for many of these Nonsuch chests of nearly the same design. The method would allow of some variation in the pattern, which would not be the case with true marqueterie.

If important factors, on careful examination, lose much of their apparent significance, there are others which may easily pass unnoticed, which have the gravest bearing on our subject. The foremost of these is the prevalence and influence of fashion. Once a definite taste in furniture can be established, it is reasonable to suppose that the unfashionable thing would be made only in the most exceptional instances. Made "for stock" it would sell only with the greatest difficulty, and then, probably, at a loss, whereas, if definitely commissioned, the person ordering would have to face the same circumstances in the event of later disposal. As a general rule, once a defined fashion exists, everything made at that time conforms to the mode of its period. It must not be assumed, however, that fashions always had this paramount character. For example, while walnut superseded oak as the English furniture wood shortly after the Restoration of 1660, oak pieces continued to be made, and of the highest quality. Witness the oak chair from Thorpe Arch Hall, illustrated here, which is dated 1682, and is, therefore, right in the walnut years. This is not a cottage piece, by any means; it is a fine important chair. We find, also, walnut used for Chippendale furniture, especially for chairs, when mahogany had apparently ousted walnut entirely. Had fashion decreed that mahogany was the exclusive timber for furniture at this period, walnut would not have been used, as no one would make a chair, for example, from the latter wood if to do so would mean that it would lose value out of all proportion to the comparative cost of the two timbers, which could have been only slight. Conversely, we find dominant fashions existing at other periods, often succeeding each other with bewildering rapidity, where such matters would be stringently enforced, and, in consequence, we can date the furniture in these manners within as narrow a margin as a single decade. This subject will be referred to again, and in detail, at a later stage. For our present purpose it may be stated, definitely, that once the Renaissance had submerged the Gothic in England, no defined fashions can be traced from 1550 to 1660, in the sense used above; and even after the Restoration we do not find arbitrary mandates until more than fifteen years later.

With Tudor and Stuart oak, therefore, design is an inadequate, unsafe indication of date. The well-known bulbous leg used on tables or as balusters to cupboards or bedsteads, can be found as early as 1595 and as late as 1680, and there are no intrinsic indications of the one period or the other, in this detail, considered by itself. It is well known how dated pieces upset theories; the chair from Thorpe Arch Hall is a case in point. One assumes too lightly and easily that once a fashion has departed, everyone turns automatically to a new manner. At no period, even when fashions are absolutely dominant, is this a fact. The change from oak to walnut and from walnut to mahogany requires both an alteration of technique and of tradition, to say nothing of a revolution in the lumber yard, and this in periods when timber was seasoned for seven years or longer. The change in technique alone is greater than one would imagine; carved oak is usual; carved walnut is exceptional. Oak is never veneered; solid walnut, other than for chairs, is very rare. The early mahogany marks a return to the older method of solid construction, a very radical change considering that it entailed the scrapping of such implements as veneering presses and screws, and other tools incidental to veneering. Marqueterie, also, implies patterns, prickings and stocks of coloured veneers; and fret-cutting necessitates a number of "rubbings," to say nothing of fret-saws, all of which the cabinetmaker would not easily discard. Only a powerful and popular fashion would compel him to turn to an utterly different manner.

Dating is important; we wish to know when each particular piece was made, if possible, but to lay down rules based upon incorrect premises, especially in a book which purports to be authoritative, is not only misleading, but immoral. If a writer does not know, then he has no right to impose upon his readers with dubious information. An incorrect statement travels fast, is seldom overtaken, and one ignoramus begets many others.

English oak, whether of the sixteenth or of the seventeenth century, varies little, if at all; certainly there are no variations which indicate any definite period. Details, as we have seen, are hardly less illusive guides. There remain only construction and proportion, both of which are of the highest importance. The former is not apparent in a photograph, and camera distortion, the use of a short or a long focus lens may, apparently, alter the latter entirely. One is confined, therefore, to empirical statements, more or less. It is also curious that we can often tell the place of origin of much seventeenth century oak more certainly than we can ascribe a definite date to it.

True Elizabethan oak furniture is much more rare than many writers imagine. It has been the custom to style as "Elizabethan" many pieces which belong to the seventeenth century, and are often as late as the end of the reign of Charles I, if not still later. Again, we have the puzzling factor of the subsequent copying, as with the "stick-back" chairs, those made entirely by the wood-turner on the pole-lathe. We know that these chairs were made, originally, in the sixteenth century, as they figure in inventories of the time as "turneyed chairs" but I have never seen an example which could definitely be referred to that period. Copies made in the seventeenth century, on the other hand, are not unusual, and it is interesting to trace the development of the stick-back chair from the early years of the reign of James I right up to Chippendale in *circa* 1760. The seventeenth century chairs are nearly always made from fruit-woods, pear, apple, plum or damson, all hardwoods which take a good friction polish and age with a fine patina. The eighteenth century stick-back chair is usually from yew-tree or ash, with a seat of elm. A full range of examples is illustrated.

The most instructive way to trace the development of English oak furniture is to take each type separately. We have seen that the secular chair is a late arrival; that it remains for a long time as a seat of dignity or for personal use, and that, up to the close of the sixteenth century, it remains in the form of a panelled box, with back and arms. The alteration from this form to another, where legs are substituted for the box, in other words, where the back is mounted on a stool, almost coincides with the dawn of the seventeenth century; and the English chair then retains this form from that time onwards. To anticipate, it will be found that the stretchering of legs is general in the oak period, remains so, in fact, until the later days of the reign of Anne (some fifty years after the introduction of walnut) and then disappears until the middle of the eighteenth century, when the fashion again is revived, in the hands of the later craftsmen, Chippendale, Hepplewhite, Sheraton and their schools.

Oak chairs differ considerably, one from another, but the distinction is rather of locality than of date. No wood persists like oak, throughout the history of English furniture. The well-known cottage dressers of the late eighteenth century (the type itself is not early) are always of oak, with inlay or bandings of fruit-woods. Oak clock-cases and bureaux are found right up to the commencement of the Napoleonic wars, and without a break in continuity in the country districts of England. It is merely an old timber tradition persisting.

Stools and forms develop side by side with chairs, changing from the box or the end-trestle form to the four-legged type. The former remains, as the usual seat at meals, until the Restoration, if not later.

Tables change in much the same way, but here the development is much earlier. Unlike the chair or the stool, the sixteenth century table usually has legs; it is much earlier that end-trestles and bracing stretchers are used. At all times, during the oak period, tables are not plentiful; once made, they must have been retained for an indefinite time, in spite of changes of fashion.

Perhaps the most striking development is that of the chest, which evolves into the standing cupboard some time during the early sixteenth century, yet never loses its own identity, persisting as a chest, side by side, with the new form, but now being reserved for linen, vestments, fabrics and the like, for the containing of which it possesses advantages over the cupboard. The latter, however, with its doors and shelves, permits of orderly arrangement of silver, brass, pewter or glass, which the chest denies. In the early days of the seventeenth century, also, cupboards were made in several tiers, and with drawers, to combine the functions of cupboard and chest. We get the well-known Court cupboard, and, at the same time, the open buffet, intended for display only, and at the other end of the century a further evolution takes place, from the chest with lid to the chest with drawers, and from the cupboard to the bookcase and the cabinet. But by that time walnut has superseded oak for fine furniture, the latter remaining merely as the wood for cottage pieces. The later developments will be traced in succeeding chapters.

DIAGRAMS BELOW SHOW THE METHOD OF QUARTERING OAK

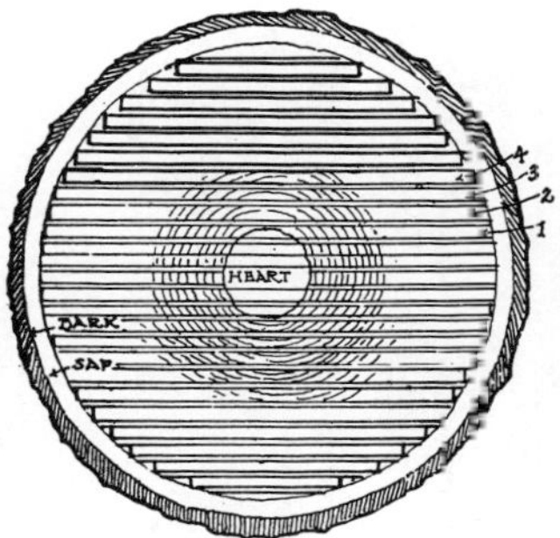

A

SECTION OF TRUNK, SHOWING THE CUTTING OF BOARD RIGHT ACROSS. BOARDS CUT IN THIS WAY WILL WARP (SEE C)

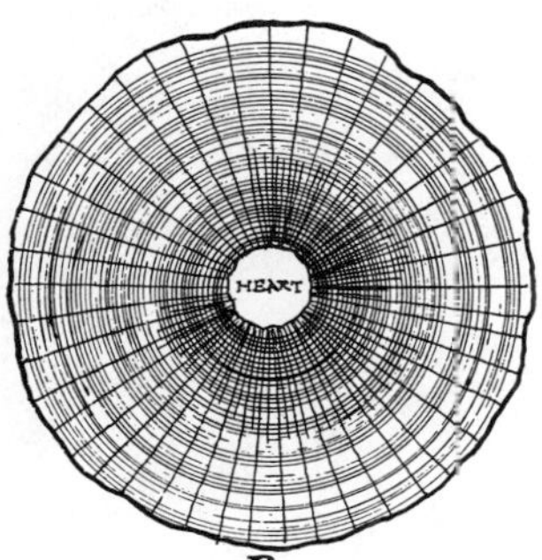

B

SECTION ACROSS TRUNK SHOWING THE ANNULAR RINGS AND THE MEDULLARY RAYS

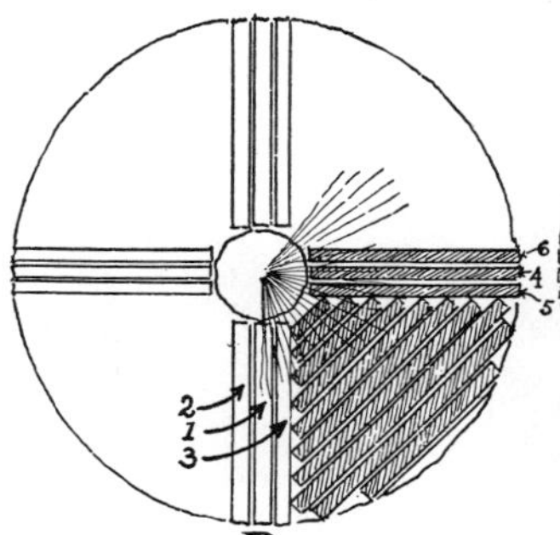

D

QUARTERING. BOARDS CUT IN THIS WAY ARE WITHOUT FIGURE

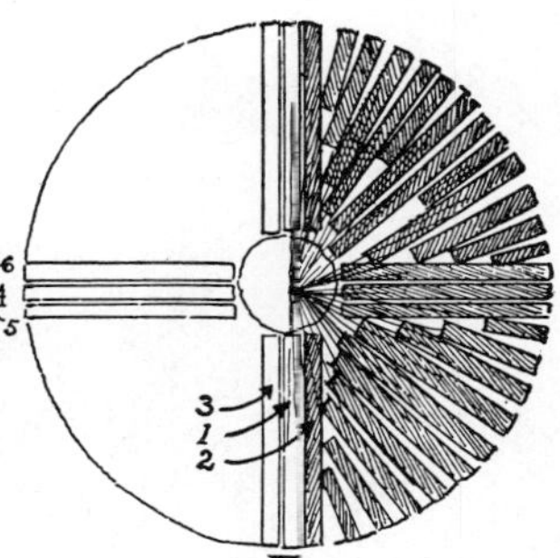

E

TRUE QUARTERING. HERE EACH BOARD IS CUT ALMOST PARALLEL TO THE MEDULLARY RAY, AND THE MAXIMUM FIGURE IS OBTAINED. CUT IN THIS WAY, ALSO, THE WOOD STANDS WITHOUT WARPING OR SPLITTING, AS THE NATURAL CLEAVAGE LINES ARE FOLLOWED

C

A BOARD CUT RIGHT ACROSS, SHOWING HOW THE ANNULAR RINGS CAUSE THE BOARD TO WARP

MID-SIXTEENTH CENTURY OAK CHEST. THE FRONT IS A SOLID BOARD, CHIP-CARVED IN CRUDE IMITATION OF GOTHIC FENESTRATION

MID-SIXTEENTH CENTURY OAK CHEST. THE FRONT IS FRAMED, AND THE PANELS PIERCED WITH THE DEVICE OF THE WHEEL OF ST. CATHERINE

MID-SIXTEENTH CENTURY CHIP-CARVED CHEST. NOTE THE ENDS ARE FRAMED FOR GREATER STRENGTH IN TRANSPORT; THE FRONT IS A SINGLE BOARD BATTENED AT THE ENDS. THE ORNAMENT HAS BEEN DRAWN ENTIRELY WITH THE COMPASS

MID-SIXTEENTH CENTURY OAK SIDE TABLE. DOOR IN THE CENTRE. NOTE THE CRUDITY OF THE CONSTRUCTION AND THE PIERCING IN A PIECE LATE IN TYPE

OAK INLAID NONSUCH CHEST. THE INLAY SAID TO HAVE
THE PALACE OF HENRY VIII, NEAR CHEAM, LONG SI

MID-SEVENTEENTH CENTURY CHEST OF EAST ANGLIAN TYPE

CARVED OAK MARRIAGE COFFER INSCRIBED: "THIS IS ESTHER HOBSONNE CHIST, *1637*." HOME COUNTY ORIGIN

MID-SEVENTEENTH CENTURY OAK CHEST. THE FINELY DESIGNED FLAT CARVING OF THE HOME COUNTIES

CARVED OAK CHEST, MID-SEVENTEENTH CENTURY. THE ARCADED TYPE OF WARWICKSHIRE OR DERBYSHIRE

OAK CHEST, CARVED AND INLAID, WITH TWO DRAWERS BELOW.
MIDLAND COUNTY ORIGIN, *c. 1660*

OAK CUPBOARD OR CREDENCE; LATTER HALF OF THE SEVENTEENTH CENTURY.
MIDLAND, *c. 1660*

LATE SEVENTEENTH CENTURY CARVED OAK CUPBOARD-CHEST. MARKING THE DEVELOPMENT FROM THE CUPBOARD AND CHEST TO THE CHEST OF DRAWERS. *c. 1680*, MIDLAND TYPE

MID-SEVENTEENTH CENTURY OAK CHAIR. YORKSHIRE TYPE. A DUPLICATE, BUT SMALLER, WAS MADE FOR THE MISTRESS OF THE HOUSE

A SEVENTEENTH CENTURY OAK CHAIR OF MIDLAND TYPE, PROBABLY FROM DERBYSHIRE OR WARWICKSHIRE

OAK CHAIR FROM THORPE ARCH HALL, DATED *1682*, RIGHT IN THE WALNUT YEARS. VICTORIA AND ALBERT MUSEUM, LONDON

A SIXTEENTH CENTURY CHAIR OF BOX TYPE WITH TWO CARVED DECORATIVE PANELS. TORONTO MUSEUM

JAMES I OAK ARMCHAIR. SEAT COVERED WITH COARSE NEEDLEPOINT KNOWN AS "TURKEY WORK"

MID-SEVENTEENTH CENTURY OAK CHAIR OF EAST ANGLIAN TYPE

A SEVENTEENTH CENTURY OAK CHAIR, LANCASHIRE TYPE

OAK CHAIR IN BARKING CHURCH, SUFFOLK, LATE SIXTEENTH OR EARLY SEVENTEENTH CENTURY. PEDIMENT AND VASES AT TOP ARE LATER AND SOME OF THE INLAY HAS BEEN RESTORED

MIDLAND TYPE, PROBABLY CHESHIRE, SEVENTEENTH CENTURY OAK CHAIR

A SEVENTEENTH CENTURY COPY OF THE SIXTEENTH CENTURY STYLE STICK-BACK CHAIR

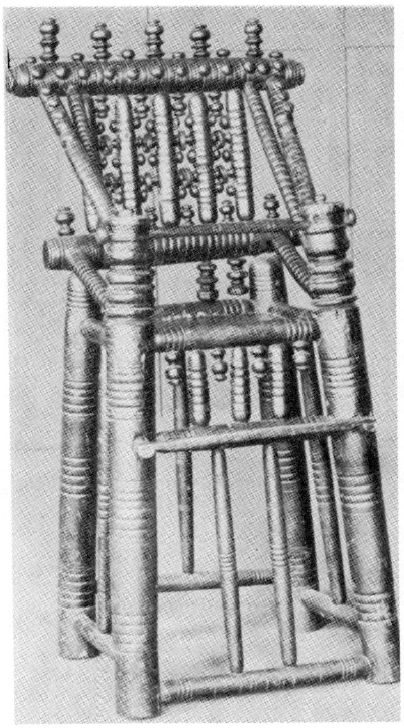

THE DEVELOPMENT OF THE STICK-BACK CHAIR. AN EXAMPLE WHICH MAY DATE FROM THE LATE SIXTEENTH CENTURY

A SEVENTEENTH CENTURY STICK-BACK, "TURNEYED" OR "THROWN" CHAIR FROM BROWSHOLME HALL, NEAR CLITHEROE, YORKSHIRE

THREE SEVENTEENTH CENTURY "JOYNED" STOOLS OF SIMPLE TYPE

RARE TYPE OF EIGHTEENTH CENTURY STICK-BACK CHAIR WITH "EARS" OR SIDE WINGS

OAK STOOL OF FIFTEENTH CENTURY TYPE WITH TRESTLE ENDS

A SEVENTEENTH CENTURY STOOL OF ORNATE TYPE

THE USUAL TYPE OF YEW-TREE WINDSOR STICK-BACK CHAIR WITH PIERCED CENTRAL SPLATS. THE EXAMPLE ON THE LEFT IS KNOWN AS A "WHEEL-BACK" AND IS RARE

YEW-TREE STICK-BACK OR WINDSOR CHAIR OF THE CHIPPENDALE PERIOD. *c. 1750.* NOTE CENTRAL SPLAT

VERY RARE WINDSOR STICK-BACK CHAIR WITH CABRIOLE LEGS. CHIPPENDALE TYPE OF SPLAT IN BACK

OAK TABLE, PROBABLY LATE SIXTEENTH CENTURY, IN THE DRAPERS' CHAPEL OF COVENTRY CATHEDRAL (ST. MICHAEL'S PARISH CHURCH). THE SPLAY FEET ARE NOT ORIGINAL, AND THE WHOLE TABLE HAS A PRONOUNCED FOREIGN CHARACTER

OAK TABLE OF JAMES I PERIOD IN THE MAYOR'S PARLOUR IN ST. MARY'S HALL, COVENTRY, FORMERLY IN THE POSSESSION OF THE FAIRFAX-LUCY FAMILY OF CHARLECOTE. THIS TABLE IS ABSOLUTELY ORIGINAL, EVEN TO ITS TUSK-TENONS. THE BASES OF THE FEET ONLY HAVE WORN UNTIL THE STRETCHER RAILS NOW REST ON THE FLOOR

MID-SEVENTEENTH CENTURY OAK FLAP TABLE WITH "GATE-LEG." TOP OF OCTAGON FORM. STRONG FRENCH INFLUENCE IN THE ARCADING BETWEEN THE LEGS

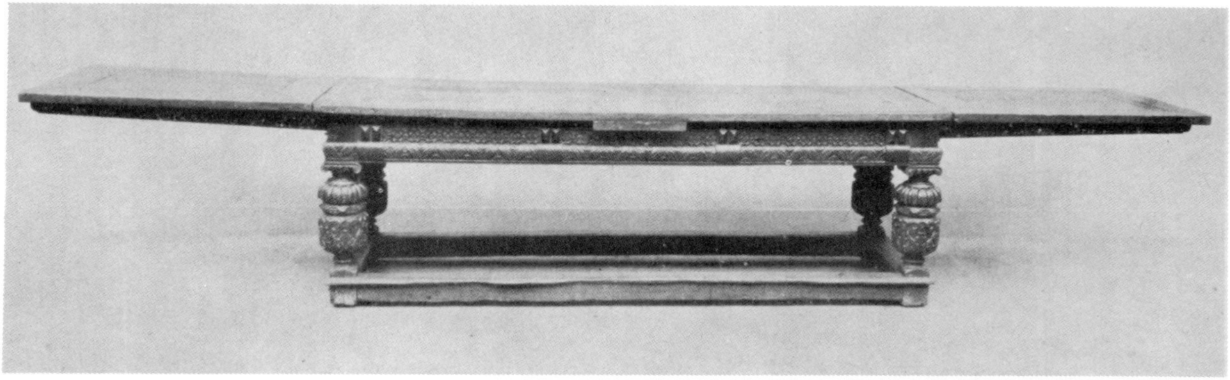

OAK "DRAW-TABLE" WITH EXTENSION FLAPS PULLED OUT TO SHOW THE "LOPERS" UNDERNEATH

OAK REFECTORY TABLE WITH MOULDED STRETCHER FRAMING

MID-SEVENTEENTH CENTURY OAK TABLE. HAS BEEN CUT IN LENGTH AND WIDTH TO ADAPT AS AN ALTAR TABLE. THE GRACEFUL TURNING OF THE BULBOUS LEGS INDICATES AN EAST ANGLIAN ORIGIN (NORFOLK OR SUFFOLK). *c. 1650*

LATE SIXTEENTH CENTURY OPEN BUFFET OF OAK AND WALNUT. THE USE OF WALNUT AT THIS DATE IS VERY EXCEPTIONAL AS THE WOOD MUST HAVE BEEN IMPORTED. COMPARE THE SIMILAR CHARACTER OF THIS BUFFET WITH THE CHAIR IN BARKING CHURCH

AN OAK CHARLES I (*c. 1630*) BUFFET ON TWO STAGES. IN UPPER STAGE, CENTRAL DOOR AND TWO FLANKING PANELS CARVED AND INLAID. CARVED BULBOUS BALUSTERS AT CORNERS

AN OAK CHARLES II (*c. 1665*) TWO-TIER CABINET OR CUPBOARD. THREE HEAVILY MOULDED PANELS ABOVE, INLAID WITH MARQUETERIE OF BONE. TWO DOORS FLANKING A CENTRAL PANEL WITH SPLIT BALUSTERS BETWEEN, ON TWO HEAVILY-CARVED BULBOUS LEGS AND THUMB-MOULDED SHELF FRAMED UNDERNEATH

A RARE SIXTEENTH CENTURY (*c. 1590*) OAK INLAID BUFFET; ABOVE, UNDER A BROAD FRIEZE, TWO DEEPLY-RECESSED, CARVED AND INLAID DOORS, WITH CENTRAL CARVED CARYATID AND CARVED CHIMERAE AT ANGLES; BELOW, A CENTRAL FRIEZE IN TWO STAGES, THE UPPER ONE INLAID, THE LOWER CARVED WITH A RUNNING LEAF PATTERN ON A BOLD CUSHION MOULDING. LOWER STAGE WITH LARGE BULBOUS SUPPORTS AND HEAVY PLATFORM; *54½* INCHES WIDE

OAK TWO-TIER OPEN BUFFET. THE UPPER STAGE SUPPORTED ON HERALDIC LIONS HOLDING SCROLLED SHIELDS. *50* INCHES WIDE. JAMES I, *c. 1610*. PROBABLY ONE OF THE FINEST EXAMPLES IN EXISTENCE

OAK CARVED AND INLAID CABINET ON STAND WITH PLATFORM BELOW; GUILLOCHE-CARVED CENTRAL FRIEZE WITH DRAWERS. CARVED TRUSSES BETWEEN UPPER PANELS. CHARLES I, *c. 1635*

AN OAK COURT CUPBOARD OF CHARLES I (*c. 1630*) UPPER STAGE WITH TWO FRAMED DOORS AND THREE CARVED PANELS. TURNED BALUSTERS AT CORNERS AND GUILLOCHE-CARVED FRIEZE. BELOW, TWO FRAMED DOORS AND THREE PLAIN PANELS. FROM HILL HALL, ESSEX, ENGLAND

CARVED OAK COURT CUPBOARD; BALUSTERS WITH IONIC CAPITALS, AND CARYATIDS DIVIDING DOORS IN UPPER PART. EAST ANGLIAN, *c. 1670*

OAK STANDING CUPBOARD OF IMPORTANT SIZE (THE STUMP FEET ARE LATER). *c. 1660-70*

EARLY SEVENTEENTH CENTURY OAK ANGLE-BUFFET. SO CALLED FROM THE SPLAYED SIDES TO THE CUPBOARD ABOVE

OAK OPEN BUFFET WITH TWO DRAWERS OF *c. 1650*. THE REFINED EAST ANGLIAN TURNING, WITHOUT CARVING, SHOULD BE NOTED AS IT IS REPRESENTATIVE OF FINE WORK OF THESE COUNTIES

MID-SEVENTEENTH CENTURY OAK COURT CUPBOARD WITH THE SLENDER BALUSTERS OF LANCASHIRE TYPE

EARLY SEVENTEENTH CENTURY LIVERY OR DOLE CUPBOARD. THE FRAMEWORK IS OF PINE, PAINTED IN BLACK WITH FLORAL DESIGNS AND MASKS, AND THE DOOR PANELS WITH ARCHITECTURAL MOTIVES. THE DOORS ARE OAK, CARVED, THE BORDERS INLAID WITH A CHEQUER OF HOLLY AND BOG-OAK; THE SPINDLES OF TURNED PEAR-WOOD. *c. 1620*

OAK TWO-TIER CUPBOARD, THE FRAMING OF THE UPPER DOORS INLAID WITH A CHEQUER OF HOLLY AND BOG-OAK. *c. 1650*

CHAPTER VIII

Walnut Furniture of the Seventeenth Century

THE INTRODUCTION of a new wood must be an event of the highest importance in the history of a nation's furniture, especially when it has a strong tendency to modify not only design but constructive methods as well. The replacement of oak by walnut as the fashionable timber for furniture, which may be said to coincide with the restoration of the monarchy in 1660, revolutionised both design and processes.

It is probable that chair-making and cabinetwork had become distinct and separate trades earlier in the seventeenth century; it is certain that this disparate character existed shortly after 1660, and that both processes and designing differ, in many respects, with the chairmaker, from those usual with the cabinetmaker. One striking distinction is that the former uses the new wood in the solid, something which the latter seldom, if ever, does. Walnut furniture, with the exception of chairs and kindred pieces, of the later Stuart and Jacobean years, is really oak carcase-work veneered with walnut, the solid wood being used only for mouldings and cabriole or turned legs or feet.

English walnut, *Juglans regia*, is really a true native of Persia and Hindostan, and appears to have been first planted in England, at Wilton Park by the Earl of Pembroke and Montgomery, some time during the middle of the sixteenth century. The wood had been sparingly used, both for furniture and for panelling, early in the seventeenth century, but there is little doubt that the timber, at this date, was imported. Of the varieties known in Europe, we have the English, the French, the Dutch or German, the Spanish and the Ancona or Italian, each variety possessing marked differences in texture, colour and figure. In America there appear to be two distinct kinds, the *Juglans nigra* or black walnut and the curly-figured Pennsylvanian, which seems never to have been used outside of that state.

Oak, with its open grain, makes a good bed for laying veneer, but it is harsh for delicate carving detail. The well-known Restoration chairs, however, were often made from the older wood; it is only for the more ornate examples that walnut was used. This, however, was the practice for a short time only. The new wood soon inaugurated a rapid development in style, and shortly after 1670 we find details from Spain, Portugal, France and the Low Countries in chair models, all introduced in a marked and original manner. The Spanish curled foot and bow stretcher, the Portuguese bulb (which develops rapidly into the inverted cup) the French palmette and Palmer's shell, and the Flemish C- and S-scrolls, are all found, often in the same example.

It is exceedingly difficult to summarise the furniture of any given period without being inaccurate, by reason of omission rather than by actual false statement. A full enquiry would—and should—take cognizance of every model which was made at any stated time, and then, after eliminating the sporadic (which would only confuse an issue) the remainder would have to be taken into account, in arriving at any decision, no matter how many pre-conceived notions were upset by so doing. In all these investigations, the easy road is always dangerous or deceiving. *Facilis est descensus Averni.* Seventeenth century makers of furniture did not consider difficulties of twentieth century investigators or writers, possibly for the same reason as the man who declined to have any regard for posterity, on the plea that posterity had never done anything for him.

We have to seek for broad and general rules (with certain large exceptions, of course) but we have to be sure that the exception is not the rule. One can prove anything by segregation, as pointed out before in these pages. If we except chairs for the moment, and concentrate on the oak furniture veneered with walnut or marqueterie, or decorated with applied lacquer, it may be fairly stated that the general fashion, from 1670 to 1695 was for box-like pieces, enriched only with figured veneer, inlay or lacquer. In the detail of mouldings alone there is significant indication of the influence of architects in these late seventeenth century pieces. Classical sections are almost unknown in Jacobean or Stuart oak, which was, obviously, joiner-designed. They give to the walnut a refined appearance which is absent in the oak, and this is especially noticeable in high-grade, long-case clocks of this period. Many of these could not have been designed by the cabinetmakers of this period, even those of Dutch extraction, as so many were during the last years of the seventeenth century.

There is little doubt that much, if not all, of the inspiration of these early walnut pieces of furniture came directly from the Low Countries. Charles II had been brought back from exile in Holland (Samuel Pepys was one of the escorting train) and it is more than probable that many Dutchmen and Flemings came with him. It is difficult to imagine that English cabinetmakers would turn to an entirely new manner—and a new method, which is much more important—merely because a new king had ascended the throne. Even then, had they adopted a Low Country style, as a compliment to the country which had afforded asylum to the English king, how can we account for Spanish and Portuguese details being used at the same time? When we recollect that Catherine of Braganza was the consort of Charles II, and that designers from the Peninsular would be encouraged in England, in consequence of this alliance, the mystery begins to clear up.

We have to look, also, for new types, pieces which are original in purpose as well as in design; from such pieces we gain invaluable knowledge. Thus, an Elizabethan wardrobe, a James I day-bed, or a Queen Anne sideboard are all impossible; neither the wardrobe, the day-bed nor the sideboard existed, as an article of furniture at these respective periods. There are cupboards, settles and dressers, but these are not the same; to assume otherwise would be to confuse prototype with descendant.

Subject to slight exceptions, the spiral twist in turning belongs to the Restoration period. Prior to this date, the twisting had been done by hand, but after 1660 the slide-rest comes into use, as an adjunct to the lathe. The cabinet-on-stand, with doors and with drawers behind, the elongated chair known as a day-bed, and fixed upholstery (ignoring the examples at Knole Park, Sevenoaks, which are distinctly in advance of their period) are all either of late Stuart inception, or else they became general then, whereas they were exceedingly rare before. Similarly, the cabriole leg marks the dawn of the eighteenth century in England, although this feature, in embryonic form, exists in the Orange period.

To trace the development of English furniture during the years from 1660 until nearly 1700 it is necessary to make certain divisions, and to deal with each separately. Plain walnut, marqueterie, lacquer, and lastly, chairs, stools, settees and similar pieces, are not only distinct from each other in design-evolution, but they also involve separate trades and processes, and, therefore, demand individual treatment. There is some over-lapping in each, which is inevitable. Thus, the chairmaker often makes tables and similar small articles, and both marqueterie and lacquer are sometimes mere added decoration, as distinct from pieces specifically designed and made for such work. These "bridge-pieces" must be ignored, in the present enquiry, but we must always bear in mind that they exist, and, in certain circumstances, may acquire a considerable importance.

In the forty-two years, from the accession of Charles II to that of Anne, the craft of the chairmaker was the most advanced in design, in method and in rapidity of evolution. Fashions succeed each other, often within the space of a few years, and we get several distinctive types even in the four years' reign of James II. That Netherland influences should predominate under his successor, William of Orange, one can readily understand, but, actually, these foreign influences are even more marked in the reign of the last of the Stuarts.

The typical Restoration chair, with twisted legs and balusters, carved cresting, front stretcher, and caned seat and back, is too well known to need extensive illustration here. The first change is in the introduction of the Flemish curves, the C- and S-scrolls. As with all new motives, in the early models these Flemish curves are introduced wherever possible, but in those of slightly later date, they are used more sparingly, as occasional details. The second stage in the progression is that in which the front stretcher, instead of being tenoned between the front legs, is placed lower down, between the cross-rails which tie the front and back legs together. In the third stage the entire stretcher is placed flat, uniting all four legs in the form of a wavy X. This again disappears in the early days of Anne, if not somewhat before, being replaced by simple turned rails, until about 1710 the stretcher is abolished entirely from fashionable chairs and is never again found associated with the cabriole leg. Chippendale reintroduces it in his square-leg models, and Hepplewhite follows him with the tapered leg, which is so general with his chairs. This is anticipatory, however.

Between lacquer and marqueterie there are basic differences. The former is purely an added decoration, the latter involves many processes which demand some explanation. Lacquer, also, is not evolutionary; good and bad work were done at all periods, from 1670 to 1740 (the period of true lacquer-work in England) and there are no reliable indications of date in the work itself, although the design of the pieces which are lacquered may give some imperfect indication. Marqueterie, on the other hand, does evolve in a certain defined way, and, in addition, in the actual methods employed, both in the cutting and in the laying, there are some significant indications of period which will be considered later. It is as well to remember, however, that lacquer and marqueterie run side by side with plain walnut veneered pieces, although the separate consideration of each (which is obligatory in any book arranged on a systematic plan) may give a contrary idea.

It is only at the very close of the seventeenth century that walnut wall-furniture (i. e., as distinct from chairs, tables and the like, which, for convenience, may be called "floor-furniture") begins to take on a definite design-form. This is noticeable in the shaping of pediments and cornices, the glazing and latticing of doors and the use of shaped mouldings. There are earlier exceptions to this, of course, but they are rare. The later Jacobean and the Orange periods were the age of sporadic production, and it is difficult, and unwise, to postulate as to what was or was not made during those years. In addition, to attempt to differentiate between the work of an English cabinet-maker trained by a foreigner, that of a foreign workman domiciled in England, or, say, of a Dutch artisan working to the order of an English maker (such as Thomas Tompion, with his clockcases) in the English manner, and, possibly, with English timber, involves an assumption of knowledge which no one can possibly possess at the present day.

We get a clean-cut line, more or less, with the dawn of the eighteenth century, especially in the instance of the complete, smooth cabriole leg, but the subject of the later walnut furniture must be deferred to a later chapter. There is a gap between the work of the marqueterie-cutter, which demands attention at some length, and in considerable technical detail, before the Queen Anne and early Georgian walnut can be reached.

WALNUT RESTORATION CHAIR, *c. 1665-70,* WITH FLEMISH TYPE OF FRONT LEGS

WALNUT RESTORATION ARMCHAIRS FROM RAYNHAM HALL, GOOD REPRESENTATIVES OF THE *1660-70* PERIOD. THE SEATS AND BACKS WERE ORIGINALLY CANED

WALNUT CHARLES II CHAIR OF ELABORATE TYPE. NOTE THE CRESTING RAIL IS TENONED BETWEEN THE OUTER BALUSTERS OF THE BACK, AND THE CARVED STRETCHER IS PLACED BETWEEN THE FRONT LEGS

BEECH "FARTHINGALE" CHAIR SHOWING THE BOBBIN-TURNING OF THE LATE CROMWELLIAN PERIOD, *c. 1650*

WALNUT CHARLES II ARMCHAIR WITH THE FLEMISH CURVES IN THE BACK AND THE FRONT STRETCHER, *c. 1670*

WALNUT CHARLES II CHAIR (FROM BOND'S HOSPITAL, COVENTRY) SHOWING THE INTRODUCTION OF THE FLEMISH CURVE IN THE FRONT LEGS AND ARM SUPPORTS, *c. 1670-5*

WALNUT CHARLES II CHAIR WITH THE FLEMISH CURVE AND THE LOW COUNTRY OUTWARD THROW OF THE ARMS, *c. 1680*

LATE STUART WALNUT CHAIR WITH THE FLEMISH C SCROLL. A MODEL FROM LYME PARK, CHESHIRE, *c. 1680*

WALNUT JAMES II ARMCHAIR, *c. 1685*

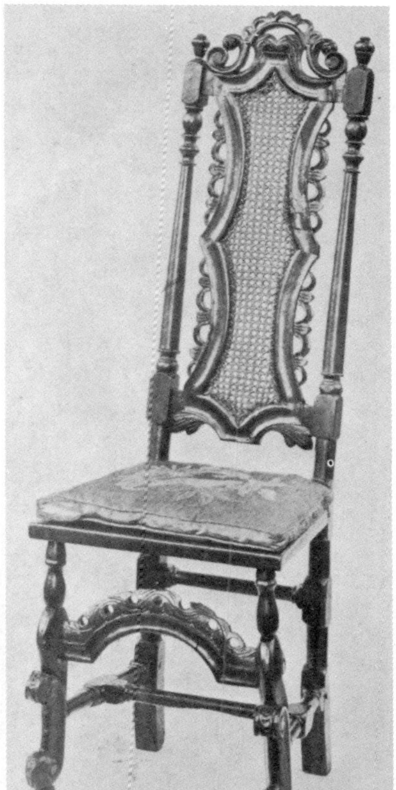

WALNUT JAMES II CHAIR WITH THE SPANISH CURVE IN THE FRONT STRETCHER AND THE BACK FRAMING, *c. 1685*

RARE FORM OF LATE CHARLES II STATE CHAIR. *c. 1680.* CARVED WALNUT, THE EARLY RESTORATION STRETCHER RETAINED. IN RUBY VELVET AND TASSELLED FRINGE OF THE PERIOD

WALNUT ARMCHAIR OF JAMES II PERIOD. *c. 1685-9.* THE USE OF THE DOUBLE C SCROLL AND THE FLEMISH CURVE, ALSO THE FLAT SECTION OF THE LATHE TWIST

TYPICAL WALNUT ARMCHAIR OF JAMES II AND WILLIAM III PERIOD BRIDGING. *1685-90.* AN EARLY USE OF THE FLATTENED STRETCHER RAIL TYING THE FOUR LEGS

TYPICAL TRIPLE-SPLATTED ARMCHAIR OF THE WILLIAM III PERIOD. *c. 1690,* WITH CUP-TURNED LEGS AND WAVED STRETCHERS

WALNUT CHAIR, BRIDGING JAMES II AND WILLIAM III PERIODS. FRAMED BACK WITHOUT OUTSIDE BALUSTERS, INVERTED CUP-TURNING, WHORLED SPANISH FOOT AND FLEMISH STRETCHERS, *c. 1690-5*

WALNUT ARMCHAIR OF ELABORATE TYPE, SHOWING STRONG FLEMISH INFLUENCE SUPERIMPOSED ON CHARLES II DETAILS, *c. 1680-5*

LACQUERED BEECH CHAIR, SPANISH FRAMED BACK AND FOOT, PORTUGUESE BULB ON FRONT LEGS AND STRETCHER, *c. 1690*

WALNUT ARM AND SIDE CHAIR, SHOWING THE TALL BACK OF THE JAMES II PERIOD (*1685-1689*) WITH GRACEFUL LINES, BUT TOP-HEAVY AND LIABLE TO FALL BACKWARDS. THE CRESTING RAIL OF THE BACK IS NOW PEGGED ON THE TOP OF THE BALUSTERS

WALNUT JAMES II ARMCHAIR OF FINE TYPE. NOTE THE SINGLE AND DOUBLE C SCROLLS INTRODUCED EVERYWHERE, *c. 1685-9*

WALNUT ARMCHAIR OF JAMES II PERIOD, *c. 1685*, MARKING THE TRANSITION FROM THE CHARLES II TO THE JAMES II WITH VERY LITTLE USE OF THE FLEMISH MOTIVES

WALNUT CHAIR WITH THE ELABORATE PIERCED AND CARVED BACK OF THE *1695* PERIOD. NOTE THE STRETCHER SET BACK BETWEEN THE CROSS RAILS. THE TOP RAIL IS NOW TENONED ON THE OUTER BALUSTERS INSTEAD OF BETWEEN THEM

WALNUT CHAIR OF LATER ORANGE YEARS SHOWING CHANGE FROM THE CUP-TURNING OF FRONT LEGS AND EVOLUTION OF CENTRAL SPLAT IN BACK. THE FLEMISH APRON-PIECE, SPANISH FOOT AND FLAT, WAVY STRETCHER PERSIST, *c. 1700*

WALNUT ARMCHAIR OF *c. 1695*. THE ELABORATE PIERCED AND CARVED BACK IS IN THE FRENCH STYLE. NOTE INVERTED CUP-TURNING OF THE FRONT LEGS AND THE SHAPED FLAT STRETCHER OF THIS PERIOD

WALNUT SIDE CHAIR WITH ELABORATE BACK. ONE OF A PAIR IN THE CHANCEL OF BIDDENDEN CHURCH, KENT. THE FRONT STRETCHER HAS THE FLEMISH CURVE, AND IS TENONED BETWEEN THE FRONT LEGS IN THE EARLIER MANNER, *c. 1690*

ELABORATE WALNUT ARMCHAIR IN PETIT-POINT NEEDLEWORK. NOTE THE FLAT, WAVY X STRETCHER TYING ALL FOUR LEGS. *c. 1090-5*

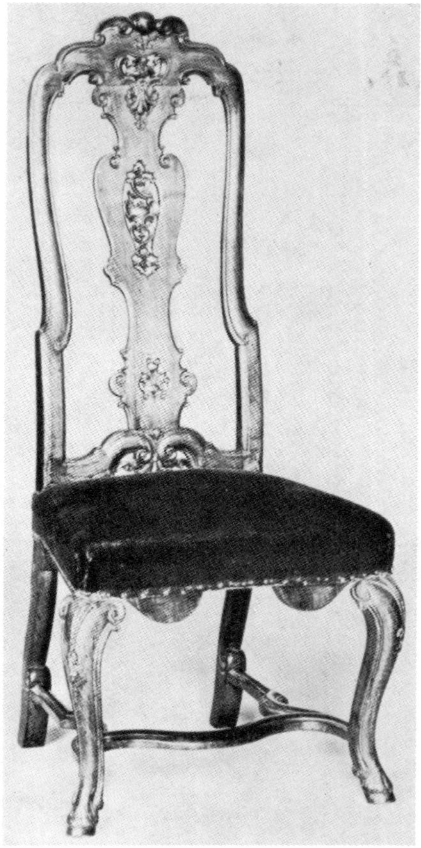

WALNUT SIDE CHAIRS OF WILLIAM III PERIOD, *c. 1695*, SHOWING THE EARLY DEVELOPMENT OF THE CABRIOLE LEG IN EMBRYONIC FORM, ALSO THE BEGINNING OF THE HOOP-BACK WHICH BECOMES SUCH A FEATURE OF THE QUEEN ANNE CHAIRS. NOTE THE FLAT STRETCHER SET BACK BETWEEN THE CROSS-RAILS

EASY CHAIR OF WALNUT COVERED WITH "HUNGARIAN-STITCH" NEEDLE-POINT. PERIOD OF JAMES II (*1685-9*), THE PROTOTYPE OF THE EASY OR WING CHAIRS OF THE EIGHTEENTH CENTURY

WALNUT ARMCHAIR OF EARLY ORANGE PERIOD, *c. 1690*. NOTE THE PORTUGUESE BULB IN THE FRONT LEGS AND ARM BALUSTERS, AND THE WAVY X STRETCHER

WALNUT TWIST-LEG TABLE OF CHARLES II PERIOD, *c. 1670.* THE TOP IS VENEERED WITH "OYSTER-PIECES" OF LABURNUM AND BANDINGS OF CROSS-GRAINED OLIVE WOOD

WALNUT TABLE OF WILLIAM III PERIOD WITH CUP-TURNED LEGS AND FLAT, WAVY STRETCHER

WALNUT SPANISH TABLE, MID-SEVENTEENTH CENTURY. THIS TYPE MAY HAVE INSPIRED MUCH OF THE CHARLES II SPIRAL-TURNED FURNITURE

VERY RARE TYPE OF PEDESTAL DESK OF *c. 1695*. VENEERED WITH POLLARDED ELM AND INLAID WITH "HERRING-BONE" STRINGING. HANDLES AND LOCK-PLATES ARE ALL ORIGINAL

WALNUT TABLE WITH OPEN DOUBLE-TWISTED LEGS SHOWING SKILLFUL USE OF THE SLIDE REST. THE PLACING OF THE SIX LEGS SHOWS FRENCH INFLUENCE. *c. 1670-80*

RARE TYPE OF WALNUT DESK ON STAND OF *c. 1695*. THE TWO INNER FRONT LEGS PULL OUT AS A "GATE" TO FORM A SUPPORT FOR THE WRITING BED

WALNUT BUREAU ON STAND. *c. 1695.* CUP-TURNED LEGS AND FLAT, WAVY STRETCHERS.
Courtesy of the Kent Gallery

CHEST OF DRAWERS ON STAND. *c. 1695-1700.* FRONTS VENEERED WITH OYSTER-PIECE WALNUT BANDED WITH CROSS-CUT LABURNUM. ALL MOULDINGS CROSS-BANDED

WALNUT BUREAU CABINET OF *c. 1700.* NOTE THE DETACHED TYPE OF DESK ON ITS CHEST STAND. THE GLASS IN THE UPPER DOORS, AND THE CROSS-LATTICE ARE NOT ORIGINAL

WALNUT FALL-FRONT SECRETAIRE OF *c. 1700.* THESE WRITING CABINETS WERE MADE ONLY DURING THE YEARS FROM *1695* TO *1710.* THE CLASSICAL CORNICE AND FRIEZE SHOULD BE NOTED AS INDICATING THE ARCHITECTURAL INFLUENCE. THE "CUSHION" FRIEZE CONTAINS A WIDE, SHALLOW DRAWER

WALNUT BUREAU CABINET OF THE LATE WILLIAM III PERIOD, *c. 1700*

"MAZA-WOOD" CABINET SHOWING ITS ORIGINAL, BRILLIANT, CUT SILVERED GLASSES IN THE DOORS. SEE FOLLOWING PAGE FOR INSIDE VIEW

HOOD OF LONG-CASE CLOCK IN EBONY BY THOMAS TOMPION, "THE FATHER OF ENGLISH CLOCK MAKING." PROBABLY ONE OF HIS LATEST PRODUCTIONS, *c. 1709*. THE CASE ILLUSTRATES THE INFLUENCE OF THE ARCHITECT IN CLOCK-CASE DESIGNING

THE SEVENTEENTH CENTURY TYPE OF BUREAU WITH BUN FEET. THE UPPER PART IS IN THE FORM OF A SEPARATE DESK ON A CHEST-STAND

THE EIGHTEENTH CENTURY TYPE OF BUREAU WITH STRAIGHT SIDES AND BRACKET FEET

BUREAU CABINET OF THE LATE ORANGE PERIOD, *c. 1700.* THIS PIECE IS VENEERED WITH POLLARDED OLIVE-WOOD, KNOWN AS "MAZA-WOOD" AT THE TIME. NOTE THE ELABORATE INTERIOR OF THIS PIECE AND ALSO THAT THE SMALL DRAWERS ARE "BLOCK-FRONTED" IN THE MANNER OF NEWPORT AND RHODE ISLAND. THE DETAIL IS VERY RARE IN ENGLISH FURNITURE. THIS PIECE IS SHOWN CLOSED ON THE PRECEDING PAGE

CHAPTER IX

Marqueterie Furniture

MARQUETERIE, considered as an art, neither originates nor evolves in England; it comes from Italy, Germany and Holland, fully-developed, perhaps with technical methods imperfectly understood by English workmen, and it is in these methods and processes only where definite evolution does take place. Style in marqueterie also undergoes certain changes shortly after the art is introduced into England; in fact, the typical Dutch inlay is never literally copied. The distinction between the work of the two countries is immediate and apparent. Before considering this development in style, which is rapid, it may be as well to point out what marqueterie really is.

Marqueterie implies an inlay, but inlay is not necessarily marqueterie. The idea of inlaying one wood in another is ancient, but the method consisted in chopping one or more woods into a solid ground. In England, as early as during the reign of James I, we find oak pieces inlaid in this manner, and in Germany and Italy intarsia work is much earlier still. In addition, the inlay is actually cut with the fine marqueterie saw, but it is in the chopping into the solid ground that inlay differs from true marqueterie.

The laying of small veneers, inlaid with patterns in various coloured woods, presents no great technical difficulties to the maker of furniture at any period, and in Stuart oak cabinets and chests, where the inlay is cut into the solid, small areas such as the beds of pilasters or the panels of doors or the backs of chairs are often veneered in true marqueterie fashion. The unknown art consisted in the laying of large sheets, such as the tops of tables, and these were seldom, if ever, attempted prior to about 1670. The following account of the processes of cutting and laying marqueterie will show the nature of these difficulties.

The marqueterie-cutter begins with a carefully drawn design, in line, without shading or colouring. This design, when completed, is "pricked," that is, the lines are finely perforated with an instrument having an action similar to that of a modern sewing machine. This perforated design is the "master pricking," and is carefully preserved. To duplicate from it, a sheet of white paper is placed underneath and the master pricking is lightly dusted with a "pounce" consisting of fine bitumen powder tied up in a rag, the powder escaping through the rag when the pounce is thus beaten, and also through the perforations of the pattern, printing off on the white paper below. The next stage is "burning in." The powdered replica would wipe off, in the ordinary way, if rubbed; to prevent this happening, the sheet is laid on a plate and heated to just below scorching point, when the bitumen powder burns into the paper and becomes permanent. Several of these pouncings are taken, one for the veneer ground, the others for cutting up according to the number of coloured pieces used for the inlay.

The marqueterie-saw being extremely fine and thin, is held in a wide bow frame, the farther-end travelling backwards and forwards in a guide-rod. Veneers, either for ground or inlay, are usually cut in layers of four, with two outer, or waste pieces, to take up the "rag" of the saw. All the layers are temporarily secured together by headless nails, known as veneer pins, hammered in outside the design, of course, and the cut-up portion of the pounced design is pasted on the face, as a guide to the cutter. Unlike other shaping operations, where the saw follows the line and the wood remains stationary, the marqueterie-saw has only the backward and forward action, and the wood has to be moved so that the design may be followed. To hold the wood rigid, and to prevent splintering, the packet of veneers is secured in a vice or "chops," which may be opened or closed by the action of the foot. Complete with its sitting bench, the whole apparatus is known as the marqueterie-cutter's "donkey."

The size of the pieces which may be cut being limited by the length of the saw-bow, a table-top, say of three feet by two, cannot be cut at one operation. If we examine a top of this size it will be found that the design has been so arranged that the ground may easily be cut in separate sections, in halves or in quarters, at one operation, in layers, and then put together. This, obviously, necessitates a balanced design.

After ground and inlay have been cut, the next operation is putting together, which involves only a following of the original master pattern. To keep the whole in place (the pieces are assembled jig-saw-puzzle fashion and may only be edge-glued) so that the sheet may be handled without falling to pieces, paper is pasted on the *face* side of the complete veneer. In some examples of marqueterie there is another operation, that of sand-burning or shading, which must precede the putting together. Above a fire, usually a gas-ring, a flat tray filled with silver sand is placed, and into the hot sand the tips of the pieces to be shaded are inserted. These pieces must be of light coloured wood, such as holly or box, otherwise the shading will not be evident. At the point of contact with the sand, the yellow wood will be scorched to a deep brown, which shades off into the natural colour of the wood. A laurelled banding, thus shaded, such as is found on many of the examples here illustrated, gives a remarkable appearance of relief.

The complete veneer, with its inlay, when thus finished, is handed over to the cabinetmaker, whose province it is to glue, or "lay" it to its bed. Before following this next operation, there is one point in connection with the actual cutting which is interesting, as showing a natural technical evolution; and in such an art progress in method must be some indication of date, as the 'prentice efforts would certainly be the earlier. Ground and inlay being cut from patterns pounced from the same pricking, should fit each other exactly, if cut precisely to the lines, but human error is against such exactitude, and in the earliest work this close fit is not found. With the passage of time and the gaining of facility in cutting, English marqueterie improves in this particular, and then, quite suddenly, we find exact fit, coupled with apparently careless cutting, with scrolls ill-shaped and lines distorted. One must assume that something of premier importance, the master-pattern, would be both drawn and pricked with extreme care; it is the cutting which goes astray. But in this later marqueterie, if the lines of the inlay are cut in this slovenly fashion, so are those of the ground, and to exactly the same degree, so that one fits the other. How has this happened? The cutter has simply discovered the secret that if ground and inlay are cut at the one operation, any inaccuracy in the one must have its counterpart in the other. To make this quite clear, draw out a pattern on a sheet of white paper, place a black sheet behind, and, at the same time, cut out both with scissors. No matter how carelessly the pattern has been followed, the black inlay must fit the white ground precisely, and we obtain, in the pieces which fall out, a reverse pattern, (known as a counterpart) of white inlay in a black ground. It is advisable to remember that this counterpart, or reverse, the marqueterie-cutter does not throw away.

If a pattern be cut in four thicknesses, four counterparts must remain; if it is cut in four quarters, making one complete design, then one counterpart only will exist. It is curious, with the old work, from as early as the first years of the eighteenth century, especially in the trunk-panels of long-case clocks, that one finds, quite often, one the reverse of the other; the first an inlay of walnut in holly, for example; the second of holly in walnut. It is surprising, also, how this counterchange of colour alters the appearance of the design. Two cabinets are illustrated here, the marqueterie of the one the exact counterpart of the other, but close attention is required to reveal that fact.

The cabinetmaker taking charge of the marqueterie top or panel, has to prepare it for laying, and the first operation is "toothing" to give a key for the glue. This is done by a plane with a vertically-pitched iron, the edge of which is serrated like a saw, known as a "toothing-plane." This scratches the surface of the veneer in a series of shallow parallel grooves. The next operation is the laying, and here are secrets which would not be readily discovered and were evidently unknown in the early work, as certain manifestations attest. Glue will stick only when it is hot, and the first idea would be to use hot glue for the laying of veneers. This is the initial error of inexperience. The heat will cause the veneer to expand instantly, and, as it contracts very slowly, it is put down in a state of strain, as it will stick before the contraction has taken place. The inevitable after-contraction will cause the veneer to split, and early marqueterie is always found in this condition, with a later filling of the cracks. The proper method is a later discovery; to use the glue cold, to lay the veneer, and then to apply a hot caul which is hand-screwed into position before the veneer has had time to expand. The heat from the caul penetrates the veneer and liquefies the glue beneath.

Shaped surfaces are laid with the hammer (a tool similar to an axe with the head fixed transversely) or with the sand-bag, which takes up any irregularities of surface. With the first method, the veneer expands and contracts again during the actual operation; with the second, as with the flat caul, it is not allowed to expand at all.

The marqueterie, glued in position, is put aside for a week, at least, as the actual drying of the glue is very slow, being imprisoned under the veneer and partly protected from the atmosphere. The outer layer of paper is then scraped off (it must not be soaked to remove it) the surface cleaned up with the scraper followed with fine glass-paper, and then the final polish or varnish is applied. Original surfaces always consist of an initial coating of varnish with subsequent waxing and friction. Modern shellac or "French" polishing is unknown before about 1820.

English marqueterie may be resolved into classes, but these are by no means infallible indications of date. We cannot accept the early cases of grandfather clocks as examples, as there are many evidences to prove that these were made in Holland, to the order of English clock-makers, and, therefore, do not properly belong to English furniture at all. The typically Dutch cases are those with fan-and-star inlay. Probably the earliest English marqueterie is that in which the jessamine flowers are used in white ivory, with the leaves in the same material but stained green. All-over patterns, or those in separate panels appear at all periods and were, obviously, merely an alternating fashion. It may be stated, with reasonable approximation to the truth, that as English marqueterie develops, it becomes quieter in tone. The taste for gaily coloured woods and white and stained ivory soon departs, and we get a more subdued assortment of woods, with the carnation as the predominant flower. The next, and final stage, which shows greater skill in execution, but less in decorative design, is the fine scrolled marqueterie, often mis-described as "seaweed," which it in no way resembles.

There is another finishing process, that of engraving, which is never found in the early work. To save the trouble of veining with the saw (all the seventeenth century work was done in this way) the finished piece is first coated with shellac or varnish and is then engraved with a small V-tool or graver. After this is done black wax is rubbed into the engraved lines and the work is then polished. It is during the later years of the eighteenth century that this engraving of marqueterie is extensively practised; it is never found before about 1780, and it is doubtful whether the process was known before that date.

Had the art of the marqueterie-cutter originated in England there is little doubt that it would have passed through definite evolutionary changes in progressive order. Instead, it is imported as a fully-developed fashion, if not as a technical practice, from Holland, brought over by the artisans from the Low Countries. In England, therefore, the older evolutionary stages are merely copied with certain modifications incidental to a change of country; and each new importation, whether of pieces or of workmen, must have resulted in additional models for copying. The inception of the French Boulle- or Buhl-work, an inlay of brass or pewter in tortoise-shell, must have occurred in much the same way. Italy and the Rhine Provinces were the pioneers in the art, and the inlay of coloured compositions in marble (which is a much older art than the inlay of woods, in Europe) may have suggested wood inlay; and thence to true marqueterie would be only a step. This seems to prove the truth of the old adage, that there is nothing new under the sun.

LATE STUART OAK STANDING CUPBOARD, *c. 1660*, INLAID WITH MARQUETERIE PARTLY IN VENEERS AND PARTLY CHOPPED INTO THE SOLID WOOD

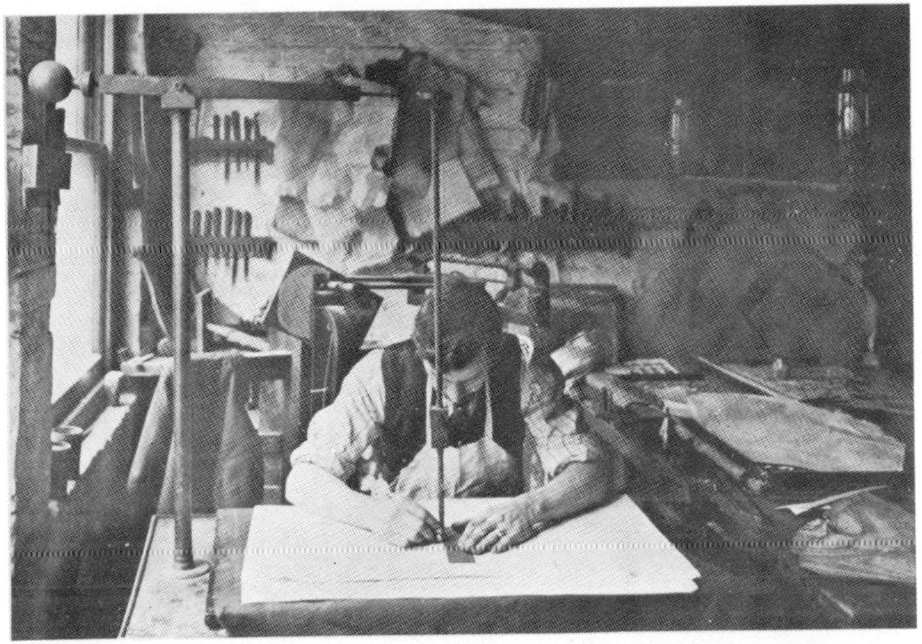

PRICKING THE MASTER PATTERN IN MARQUETERIE CUTTING. ON THE RIGHT ARE THE LEAVES OF VENEER

CUTTING THE MARQUETERIE INLAY ON THE "DONKEY"

PIECING TOGETHER MARQUETERIE CUTTINGS. BEHIND HANGS A MASTER-PRICKING AND IN FRONT IS THE SAND TRAY CONTAINING THE SHADED PORTIONS OF THE DESIGN

SHADING THE PIECES OF INLAY IN HOT SAND

ORIGINAL AND COUNTERPART MARQUETERIE. THE INLAY OF THE ONE CABINET IS THE EXACT COUNTERPART OF THE OTHER AND HAS BEEN PUT TOGETHER FROM THE WASTE PIECES FROM THE CUTTING OF THE FIRST. THE "OYSTER-PIECE" FILLING BETWEEN THE PANELS IS NOT A PART OF THE MARQUETERIE DESIGN

CABINET OF OAK AND WALNUT, VENEERED WITH WALNUT OYSTER PIECES AND INLAID WITH FLORAL MARQUETERIE OF WHITE AND STAINED IVORY, AND VARIOUS WOODS. *c. 1670*

CABINET ON STAND VENEERED WITH AN ELABORATE MARQUETERIE OF LABURNUM OYSTER PIECES WHERE THE SAP IS RETAINED FOR GREATER EFFECT. *c. 1680*

OAK TABLE VENEERED WITH LABURNUM AND EBONY AND INLAID WITH MARQUETERIE OF COLORED WOOD AND WHITE AND GREEN-STAINED IVORY. THE INLAY OF THE COLUMN-LEGS IN BRITTLE IVORY, IS A TRIUMPH OF FINE CRAFTSMANSHIP. THE CAPITALS AND BASES TO THE LEGS ARE IN ALMOND WOOD. *c. 1685*

TABLE OF OAK, VENEERED WITH WALNUT AND INLAID WITH FLORAL MARQUETERIE. THE LEGS HAVE THE LONG TWIST CHARACTERISTIC OF THE LATE CHARLES II PERIOD, *c. 1680.* IN THE TABLE TOP NOTE THE PREDOMINANCE OF CARNATIONS IN THE FLORAL MARQUETERIE, ALSO THE SAND-BURNING OF THE BORDERS

TABLE WITH FINE SCROLLED MARQUETERIE IN PANELS, THE BED VENEERED WITH WALNUT OYSTER PIECES. THE CUSHIONED HEADS AND THE SCROLLING LEAF BELOW, TOGETHER WITH THE FEET AND PATERAE ARE GILT. *c. 1690-5.* EACH PANEL OF THE TOP IS CUT EITHER IN TWO HALVES OR FOUR QUARTERS AT THE ONE OPERATION, AND THEN PIECED TOGETHER

A CHARACTERISTIC MARQUETERIE TABLE TOP; THE CENTRAL OVAL OF HOLLY CUT IN A LAURELLED PATTERN; THE BED VENEERED WITH WALNUT OYSTER PIECES. *c. 1690*

WARDROBE OR HANGING CUPBOARD ELABORATELY INLAID WITH MARQUETERIE IN THE DUTCH MANNER OF DANIEL MAROT. THIS PIECE WAS MADE FOR WILLIAM III AND BEARS HIS CIPHER. *c. 1695*

TABLE VENEERED WITH WALNUT AND INLAID WITH FLORAL MARQUETERIE OF HOLLY, BOX AND OTHER WOODS. NOTE THE FLEMISH SCROLL PERSISTING IN THE DESIGN OF THE LEGS. *c. 1690*

WALNUT CHEST OF DRAWERS ON STAND. *c. 1690.* INLAID WITH MARQUETERIE OF VARIOUS WOODS IN PANELS OF HOLLY

WALNUT CABINET ON C-SCROLLED STAND. *c. 1695.* INLAID WITH FINE SCROLLED MARQUETERIE OF HOLLY

CABINET VENEERED WITH WALNUT OYSTER PIECES AND INLAID WITH FLORAL MARQUETERIE. *c. 1690.* NOTE THAT THE BACK OF THE DOORS AND THE INTERIOR DRAWERS ARE AS ELABORATELY TREATED WITH MARQUETERIE AS THE EXTERIOR

CABINET ON STAND VENEERED WITH WALNUT AND LABURNUM OYSTER PIECES AND INLAID WITH FLORAL MARQUETERIE OF VARIOUS WOODS. THE PLAIN LEGS ARE NOT ORIGINAL BUT HAVE BEEN ADDED TO PREVENT SAGGING. A FINE EXAMPLE OF INTRICATE VENEERING. *c. 1690*

BUREAU (OPEN AND CLOSED) VENEERED WITH ALMOND WOOD AND INLAID EVERYWHERE WITH FINE SCROLLED MARQUETERIE. EACH MARQUETERIE PANEL HAS BEEN CUT IN TWO HALVES AND THEN PUT TOGETHER. THE ENDS ARE INLAID IN THE SAME WAY. NOTE THE SEPARATE CHARACTER OF THE DESK. *c. 1690*

FALL-FRONT SECRETARY INLAID WITH FLORAL MARQUETERIE IN PANELS. THE CENTRAL PANEL OF THE FALL IS CUT IN TWO HALVES. THE GROUND OF THE FLORAL INLAY IS MACASSAR EBONY. *c. 1695*

THUYA, WALNUT AND OYSTER-PIECE CABINET. *c. 1695.* THE USE OF OYSTER-PIECE MARQUETERIE. THE OUTSIDE FACES ARE VENEERED WITH THUYA, BANDED WITH WALNUT, AND FRAMED WITH CROSS-CUT HALF-ROUND WALNUT BEADS. INSIDE THE CENTRAL CUPBOARD IS A SECRET SLIDING PARTITION WITH DRAWERS BEHIND

WALNUT, FALL-FRONT SECRETARY. *c. 1690-1700.* INLAID WITH CURIOUS TYPE OF MARQUETERIE IN PANELS OF PLANE TREE

EARLY MARQUETERIE PANELS OF FINE QUALITY IN A WARDROBE OF LATER DATE

WRITING CABINET VENEERED WITH PALE WALNUT, BY SAMUEL BENNETT. SEE ILLUSTRATION TO RIGHT FOR INTERIOR VIEW

INTERIOR OF WRITING CABINET SHOWN AT LEFT. NOTE THE SIGNATURE AT THE BASE OF THE INLAID PILASTERS ON THE INSIDE OF THE DOOR AND THE ELABORATE INTERIOR BUREAU. THE ORNAMENTATION OF THE PEDIMENT IS ESPECIALLY NOTABLE. *c. 1690*

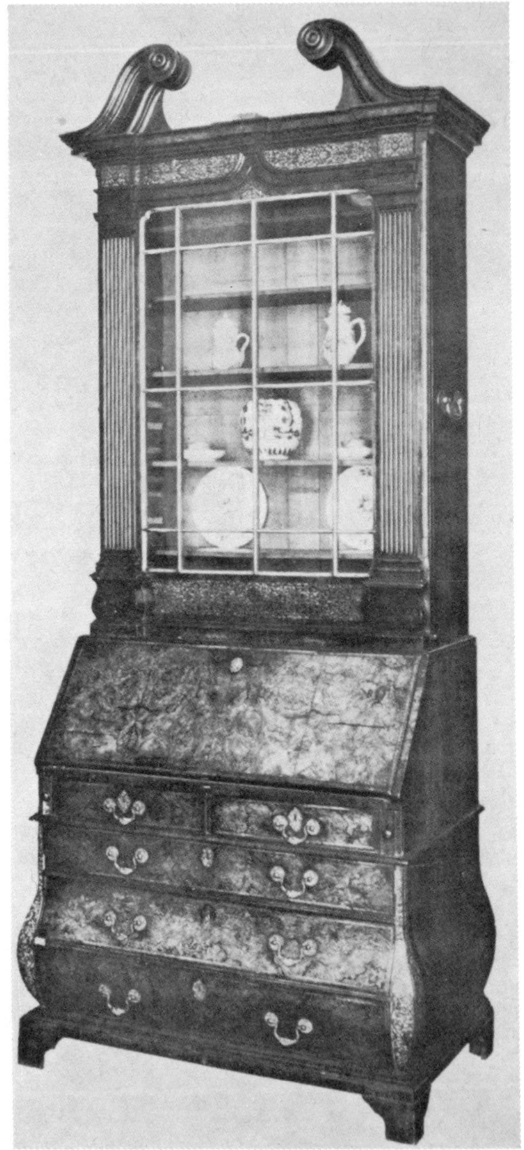

CHINA CABINET VENEERED WITH BUTT ELM AND INLAID WITH MARQUETERIE. SIGNED "SAMUEL BENNETT. LONDON FECIT." *c. 1690*

CHAPTER X

English Needlework

It is inevitable, in dealing with the subject of English furniture, that there should be certain side issues or ramifications which demand some attention. The initial difficulty, where to stop, immediately presents itself. Needlework is used, to a great extent, for covering furniture during the seventeenth and eighteenth centuries, but the same may be said, in a lesser degree, of appliqué, embroidery and tapestry. To deal with all these adjuncts, in anything like an adequate manner, would involve a far greater space than is here available, and would carry our enquiry much beyond its projected scope. At the same time, some technical knowledge of these allied arts is necessary if the subject of English furniture is to be properly understood. It is proposed, here, to treat of tapestry, embroidery and appliqué in the briefest possible manner, and to concentrate, at greater length, on needlework, or "needlepoint," to use the term current in the United States.

Tapestry is a wide term, and has been used to describe wall-hangings or furniture coverings in the most indiscriminate way. Tapestry is really a material with a ribbed or rep surface, woven either on a vertical or on a horizontal loom, by the treadle or by power, the design being woven in various coloured wools in these lateral ribs as the work proceeds. Old tapestry is, of course, hand-woven; modern tapestry is usually made by machine or power looms. The subject is so wide that to venture beyond this brief account would carry us far beyond the sphere of this book.

Appliqué, as the name implies, is the super-position of one material upon another—velvet on damask, for example—the design being cut out from the one and sewn down upon the other. The usual way is to border the pattern either with a "roping" of floss silk—which is button-hole stitched both to the pattern and to the ground—or to edge the ground with a sewn bullion thread.

Embroidery is a pattern formed by stitchery, on a ground material, in silks, wools, or metal, usually of differing colours, the pattern being disposed at intervals, leaving a certain amount of the background visible. A pattern entirely covering the underlying material, or nearly so, would be described as needlework, although the distinction between the two is quite arbitrary, and is employed more for convenience than for accuracy. Where the ground is entirely hidden, it is evident that to use any material of value would be sheer waste. In needlework a canvas of varying degrees of fineness, is used, according to the pattern and the size of the stitches.

If we except embroidery, appliqué, crewel-work and similar varieties of the needleworker's art, we may divide our subject into two main classes, point and stump-work, the flat and the raised, respectively. According to the number of stitches to the inch, in the former, it is known as either gros-point or petit-point. Anything above eighteen stitches to the inch is petit-point; less than twelve stitches is commonly known, from 1650 to 1710, as "Turkey-work." The old English wool carpets are really large panels of this "Turkey-work." The smaller the stitch the more enduring is the work. Petit-point of over twenty-four stitches has a life far exceeding even that of a fine velvet, and tapestry is, perhaps, even longer wearing. In needlework, long wear is conditional on two things: that no silk be used for the stitchery and that no spurious appearance of age be imparted to the fabric by using acids or bleaches. When fancy stitches are introduced the work is not so lasting, and warp-threads of canvas will have a tendency to cut silk yarn. Petit-point, executed with well-dyed wools and in a texture of twenty-eight or more stitches to the inch, will last, with ordinary care, for hundreds of years. In the old work, for the delineation of faces and similar fine details, silk was often used, and there the work is usually found perished or abraded.

Before proceeding with a description of the processes and stitches in needlework, a brief account should be given of the raised, or "stump-work," which, compared with the true petit-point, is merely doll-making with the needle. An immense amount of time must have been lavished on these Charles II mirrors and panels or pictures (stump-work is almost exclusively a Restoration art) as all the textures are made by the needle, no ready-made fabrics being used anywhere, with the exception of the base (generally a cream satin) or the faces of the figures, for which a plain silk is used, with the features pencilled in. All the costumes and draperies are pure stitchery, and the stitch-variety is amazing. In these old pictures one often finds tiny seed pearls used for the necklets or bracelets the female figures wear, incredibly minute, as one may well imagine, yet industriously threaded together in true pearl fashion.

It is most probable that this stump-work was purely an amateur, or home art, although there are evidences to show that the Carolean ladies were taught by migrating teachers or professors. It is impossible, otherwise, to account for exactly the same details figuring in places as far distant as the northern and the home counties. That it was an occupation of an uncommercial character, where time was not reckoned at any value (like the modern crochet tea-cloth or mat) is shown by the fact that many of these stump pictures have been raised and completed over an underwork of petit-point, which the later stumping entirely hides. I have found this underlying stitchery quite finished in itself, on many stump panels which I have had the opportunity of examining in a dilapidated condition, before being restored. In the stumping, where actual relief is attempted, hands, feet and faces are generally carved from wood (I have had one example in which ivory was used for this purpose) sometimes, but not invariably, silk-covered and outlined with the bitumen pencil. So much for stump-work; the illustrations here will complete this brief explanation.

If we take a piece of canvas and a needle with thread or wool, and over-sew each thread, it will be obvious that the stitch may be made in one of four ways; vertically, horizontally, and diagonally in two directions. Now, using the needle for vertical stitching, we may miss one or more threads of the canvas and get larger stitches, and we may alternate these again, in Morse dot-dash fashion, and the same may be done horizontally or diagonally. Leaving pure stitchery, we may obtain other effects by knotting or button-hole stitching, and if we alternate with a tight yarn, a loose wool, and a floss silk, other varieties of texture may be obtained with the same stitches. Again, we may criss-cross, in what is known as herring-boning, and the crewel and chain stitches permit of further variation. It would be hopeless, here, to attempt to describe all the stitches known to the needle-worker or to the embroiderer; detailed explanations with illustrations of the actual stitches and the finished results, in each case, would be necessary. The subject is a wide one, and Lewis F. Day, in his "Art in Needlework," has already written an invaluable handbook on the subject. As usual with all these home-arts—and some others—terms are used with a false meaning. One of these is "tent-stitch" which really means that the stitchery takes only one warp-thread at a single stroke. There is also "Hungarian-point," "Congress-stitch" and "Burgundian-point," all terms which might have a descriptive value if each were used always to mean the same thing, which is not the case

The only reliable indications of date, in nearly all this unpedigreed petit-point needlework, is that of costume, which nearly always coincides with the period of the actual work itself, or of the date at which it was commenced. It is a mistake to imagine that each piece or panel was begun and carried to a conclusion straightway; it is by no means uncommon to find unquestionable evidences of the work having been put aside, sometimes for many years, and then taken up again. This would not apply, of course, to such an example as the large panel illustrated here, from the Sheldon Looms at Barcheston. With the domestic work one often finds over-stitching (that is, the further elaborating of a finished piece with fancy stitches applied over others) which shows that needlework was never really accepted as completed. On the other hand, there is the method known as "voiding," where the bare canvas is left unworked, deliberately, to obtain a particular effect, which must not be regarded as unfinished on this account alone. There was also no defined fashion regulating the style of this needlework; it was purely the work of leisure time, and of ladies so circumstanced that they had both the time and the leisure.

Perhaps the best examples of petit-point and stump-work are to be found on the caskets and work-boxes of the later Stuart period; the nature of the articles themselves suggests that they could not have been made to sell, at the time. Their making must have been what the Victorian ladies used to term a "bottom drawer" pursuit, and, no doubt, there was considerable fashionable female rivalry, at the time, to possess the finest work-casket. On the other hand, such examples as the wonderful needlework cabinet illustrated here (which came from Barlaston Hall in Staffordshire) must have been definitely commissioned; it bears obvious signs that it was not a home-made affair.

There are other little-known industries which could be bracketted with this needlework, such as straw-work and scrolled paper, to which considerable space could be devoted, perhaps with questionable advantages. Together they form an interesting side-avenue from the main stream of the development of English furniture, and, in common, they possess one supreme advantage to the intelligent student, that of the unregulated and the unexpected. There is the greatest temptation to be discursive, here, and to enter into a vast and absolutely unexplored subject, that of the peasant arts in wood, in England, where in such things as coffee and snuff mills, love-spoons, wassail bowls, standing salts, nut-crackers and numerous other articles, wood was used in place of the lordly silver, and many articles were produced of supreme artistic merit, which, like Gray's "mute inglorious Milton," remain, more or less, unknown, and certainly unappreciated by nearly all. Here is virgin ground for the collector of the future, where the prizes have no great commercial value but where the quarry is difficult to find and still more difficult to stalk.

A REMARKABLE CABINET COVERED WITH APPLIED NEEDLEWORK ON A GROUND OF CREAM SATIN. EVERY STITCH KNOWN TO THE NEEDLEWORKER IS REPRESENTED ON THIS CABINET. THE COAT OF ARMS ON THE LEFT-HAND DOOR IS THAT OF THE LONDON BREWERS' COMPANY; THAT ON THE RIGHT IS UNRECORDED. *c. 1680.* SEE OTHER VIEWS FOLLOWING

"PEACE" WITH DOVE AND SPRIG OF MYRTLE (SIDE PANEL)

FIGURE OF "PLENTY" WITH CORNUCOPIA (SIDE PANEL)

THE TOP OF THE CABINET, WITH FIGURES OF "PLENTY" AND "JUSTICE." FRAMED IN EBONY

THE CENTRAL PANEL OF INSIDE DOOR IS OF FINE PETIT-POINT, *48* STITCHES TO THE INCH

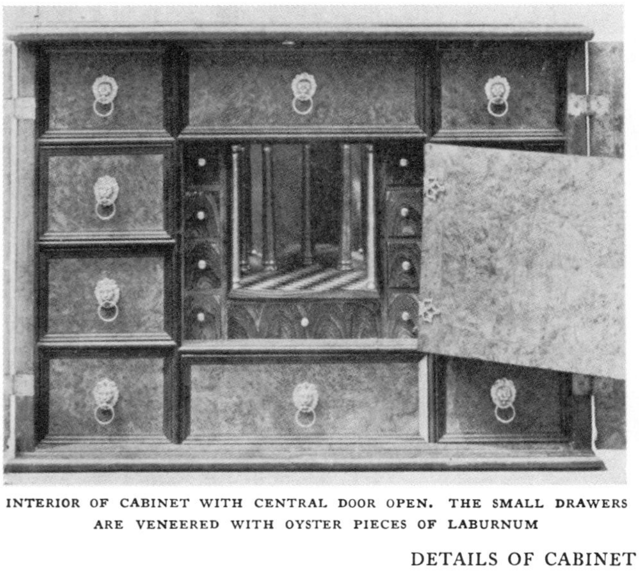

INTERIOR OF CABINET WITH CENTRAL DOOR OPEN. THE SMALL DRAWERS ARE VENEERED WITH OYSTER PIECES OF LABURNUM

THE INSIDE OF THE CABINET SHOWING THE FINE PETIT-POINT PANEL OF THE CENTRAL DOOR. THE WOOD IS POLLARDED ELM, FRAMED IN EBONY

DETAILS OF CABINET ON PRECEDING PAGE

STUMP AND NEEDLEWORK MIRROR. CHARLES II, *c. 1670*. THE FIGURES ARE IN HIGH RELIEF, IN COSTUMES OF THE PERIOD, ALL MADE WITH THE NEEDLE IN SILKS AND WOOLS. THE FACES ARE OF WOOD, CARVED, OVERLAID WITH SILK AND PENCILLED. EVIDENTLY MADE AS A MARRIAGE GIFT, AS THE FIGURES CRUDELY REPRESENT ACTUAL PERSONAGES

STUMP AND NEEDLEWORK MIRROR. CHARLES II, *c. 1670*. THE CLOSE RESEMBLANCE BETWEEN THESE MIRRORS, CASKETS AND PICTURES AND THE VARIOUS POINTS OF DIFFERENCE SUGGEST THAT THERE MUST HAVE BEEN SOME COMMON SOURCE OF INSTRUCTION, POSSIBLY BY TRAVELLING TEACHERS WHO VISITED FROM HOUSE TO HOUSE, LEAVING DETAIL PATTERNS BEHIND THEM

TWO STUMP-WORK PICTURES IN HIGH RELIEF, OBVIOUSLY MADE TO COMMEMORATE MARRIAGES, *c. 1670*, TIME OF CHARLES II. THE COSTUMES IN THESE PICTURES ARE ALWAYS TRUE TO THE PERIOD IN WHICH THEY WERE MADE, EVEN WHEN ANCIENT OR BIBLICAL SCENES ARE REPRESENTED

SETTEE WITH INSET PANEL IN THE BACK IN FINE PETIT-POINT WHICH IS A COPY OF THE PICTURE BELOW BY PETER BREUGHEL. THE PANEL, BEING MAINLY IN TONES OF BLUES AND GREENS, HAS THE APPEARANCE OF BEING AN ADDITION, CONTRASTED WITH THE RUBY GROUND OF THE COVERING, BUT IT IS CONTEMPORARY, HAVING BEEN WORKED AT THE SAME TIME WITH A NARROW GOLD BORDER ON THE RUBY GROUND, WHICH DOES NOT GO UNDERNEATH THE PANEL

ANOTHER SETTEE WITH THE PICTURE BELOW BY PETER BREUGHEL
FROM WHICH THE CENTRAL NEEDLEWORK PANEL IS COPIED.
THE FRAMEWORK IS CARVED AND GILDED

ONE OF A REMARKABLE SET OF SIX CHAIRS AND TWO SETTEES IN GILT GESSO OF GEORGE I PERIOD. THE COVERINGS ARE OF FLOWERS, SPRAYS AND RIBBONS WORKED WITH THE NEEDLE ON A RUBY GROUND (ALENTOUR) IN CONGRESS-STITCH ON THE TAMBOUR FRAME

A REMARKABLY FINE MAHOGANY CHAIR OF THE LION PERIOD, *c. 1735,* FROM A SET COMPRISING TWELVE CHAIRS AND ONE SETTEE IN FINE PETIT-POINT WORK IN WOOL AND SILK, THE DESIGN OF EACH BEING DIFFERENT. COMPLETE WITH ORIGINAL BORDERS

A PAIR OF MAHOGANY CHAIRS OF THE LION PERIOD, *c. 1735,* UNUSUAL IN HAVING THE LION MASKS ON ALL FOUR LEGS. EACH HAS ITS ORIGINAL COVERING OF GROS-POINT NEEDLEWORK. THE PROPERTY OF FRANK STEPHENSON VOSS OF NEW YORK

TAPESTRY FROM THE ROYAL LOOMS AT WINDSOR, ABOUT *1880*, ILLUSTRATING SCENE FROM TENNYSON'S "IDYLLS OF THE KING"

PETIT-POINT NEEDLEWORK PANEL OF SIXTEENTH CENTURY FROM THE SHELDON LOOMS AT BARCHESTON, *9* FT. *4* IN. WIDE BY *5* FT. *5* IN. HIGH, REPRESENTING THE THREE MAGI, MELCHIOR, GASPAR AND BALTHAZAR APPEARING BEFORE HEROD. NOTE THE STAR IN THE HEAVENS. BORDER WOVEN WITH JUSTICE, FAITH AND OTHER EMBLEMATICAL FIGURES, SPHINXES, MYTHICAL MONSTERS, CUPIDS AND FLOWERS

PETIT-POINT PANEL. PASTORAL SCENE. *c. 1720.* THE WINDOWS OF THE HOUSE ARE FORMED FROM MICA INSET TO REPRESENT GLASS

PETIT-POINT PANEL, "CAIN SLAYING ABEL." EARLY EIGHTEENTH CENTURY

PETIT-POINT PANEL, "DANIEL IN THE DEN OF LIONS," *c. 1700*

PETIT-POINT PANEL, "THE VISIT OF SOLOMON TO THE QUEEN OF SHEBA." EARLY EIGHTEENTH CENTURY

PETIT-POINT PANEL, EARLY EIGHTEENTH CENTURY

PETIT-POINT PANEL, "THE VISIT OF THE QUEEN OF SHEBA TO SOLOMON," *c. 1690*

Courtesy of the Kent Gallery

LARGE PICTURE OF PETIT-POINT NEEDLEWORK PICTURING DAVID AND BATHSHEBA. *c. 1680.* THE SUBJECTS OF THESE NEEDLEWORK PANELS ARE NEARLY ALWAYS SCRIPTURAL

THE TOP OF THE NEEDLEWORK CHEST

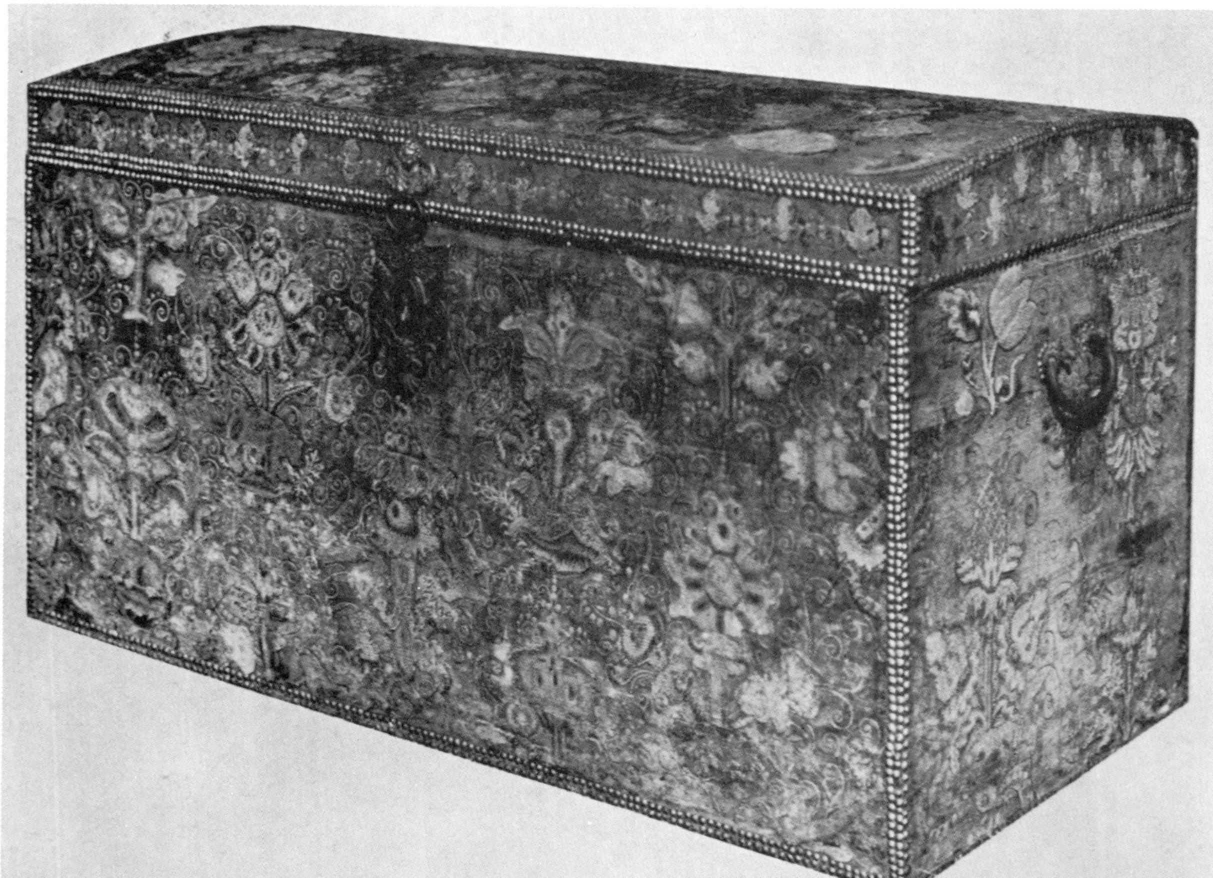

AN EXAMPLE OF NEEDLEWORK APPLIQUÉ CASKET OR CHEST. *c. 1680-90.* COVERED WITH RED VELVET, FINISHED WITH CLOSE BRASS NAILING. APPLICATION OF NEEDLEWORK IN VARIOUS STITCHES, AND EMBROIDERY. LOCK-PLATE AND FURNITURE OF FORGED IRON

HEAD-BOARD OF BED. *c. 1690-1700.* CROCHET-WORK AND NEEDLE-TRIMMING ON A GROUND OF PLAIN AND QUILTED SATIN

TESTER OR ROOF OF COVERED BED, SHOWING BULLION THREAD SEWN DOWN TO BORDER THE PATTERNS

CHAPTER XI

Queen Anne Walnut Furniture

THE WALNUT FURNITURE of the eighteenth century differs from that of the seventeenth in certain important particulars. With the wall furniture there is a strong tendency to depart from the older box-like forms, which had been so popular in the marqueterie years and during the first age of veneering, and to give to the piece itself some decorative outline. Thus we get several types of pediments, the single and double-dome, the complete and broken-arch, the scroll and the portico, both with akroteria, sometimes furnished with a surmounting bust or vase, more often, without either. The doors of cabinets are no longer flush-veneered, but are panelled, with the panels either projecting or recessed. Silvered glass begins to come into fashion, and to replace wooden panels in the doors of cabinets and bureau-bookcases. The subject of this glass, which demands special treatment here, will be considered in detail in the next chapter, when the wall mirrors of the Queen Anne and early Georgian periods will be dealt with in their chronological order.

With floor furniture, and especially with chairs, the innovations are very marked in the first years of Anne—if not slightly earlier. Perhaps the most important of these are the two details of the smooth cabriole and the ball-and-claw foot. The smooth cabriole really belongs, exclusively, to the eighteenth century, although it is found, in embryonic form, shortly after 1695. To comprehend what the making of the cabriole leg entails, it is necessary to enter into technical detail.

To make a cabriole leg, the first requisite is the pattern, which is marked out on a thin flat board, and then cut to shape. This is known as a template and is used, in turn, for marking the block of wood, from which the leg is to be cut. It is obvious that the first cutting produces the shape only the one way. To lay this flat on the bench for the cutting in the opposite direction, the pieces which have fallen out from the first cutting, have to be replaced to act as "saddles." When the second cutting is finished the cabriole leg is complete, cut all four ways, but in square section. If the illustrations to this chapter be examined carefully, it will be found that, in some examples, the leg has been so left, in this square-sectioned form. In others, the shape is left square at the top, or "knee," and is rounded below, down to the foot, the junction between the square and the round being marked by a moulded "collar." There is a very definite reason why the early legs were made in this way. With the four-way cutting, the work is done to pattern, and if the cutting be accurate, one leg will be the exact counterpart of others to follow. To round the shaft is not difficult, but to round the entire leg, up to the knee, entails a complete departure from the pattern, and the eye of the workman becomes the only guide. It is akin to pushing out from a known port into an uncharted sea.

The rounding is done with a tool known as the spokeshave, and is finished with the rasp, file and glass-paper. The first thing which goes is the profile which the saw has left, and, in fact, in the smooth cabriole, there is very little of the original pattern which remains after the leg is finished. With tables, with rectangular framing, the square section of the knee is retained, but with chairs where the seat rail is rounded at the corners, no template can assist. That is why a really perfect cabriole is so conspicuously rare.

With the feet of the early walnut pieces, the first—and, perhaps, the most satisfactory—is the club or pad-foot, which, in its simplicity, has a charm peculiarly its own. It will be found, in the entire study of English furniture, that carving often hides a multitude of imperfections. There are variations of these club feet, where the foot is clothed by a leaf, or where the leg finishes in a scroll on the floor. Examples of all are illustrated here. The next in order, and in date, is the well-known ball-and-claw, a detail said to have been borrowed from the Chinese dragon-foot grasping a pearl. The detail is certainly to be found on many of the porcelains of the K'Hang H'si and the Kien Lung periods.

The ball-and-claw, like many other details, in English furniture, commences in a vigorous and perfect fashion, and soon degenerates into something bald and meaningless. It will be noticed, in the illustrations of this chapter, that in all the early examples the claw is powerful, and without webbing, almost the entire surfaces of the ball being visible. In those of somewhat later date, the ball is partly hidden by the webbing between the claws. The first, in fact, is the Chinese dragon's claw, the second is that of a bird, and one of no particular genus.

The treatment of the knee also undergoes a rapid evolution. Apart from the uncarved smooth cabriole—which is really the most perfect development—the earliest ornamentation is the escallop or Palmer's shell. This passes through many stages until we reach the acanthus decoration which persists right into the period of Chippendale. The earliest cabriole appears to be planted under the seat-rail with little or no connection, but in the later examples the top of the leg is crested over the rail itself, in a kind of scrolled finish which is adopted in many chairs and tables of the early Georgian period.

The stretcher under-railing, which was such a general feature in the Orange chairs, soon disappears in those of the Queen Anne years. Occasionally, we find a reversion to the original type, and this even as late as during the mahogany period, after 1725. In the hands of Chippendale and Hepplewhite the under-railing is revived again, but only in chairs with straight or tapered legs. There is another change which is just as striking. The chair-back is now defined, into side balusters and central splat, which are, nearly always, unconnected. Very rarely we find a strapping which ties the central splat to the outer balusters, but such examples are distinctly exceptional. The splat itself, in the early chairs, is broad, in shape something akin to a violin—hence the common name of "fiddle-splat"—unpierced, and generally veneered. This fashion soon changes in the direction of solid construction (the veneering of a dished splat is something of an ordeal) and then the splat begins to be pierced. Almost simultaneously with this development begins another, in which the hoop-back—the joining of the side balusters and the top rail of the back to each other, in one unbroken line—gives way to the flattened top rail, which is tenoned to the side balusters as a distinct thing, as a capping rail. While the entire back of the early Queen Anne chair is veneered, with the flattened top rail, in its many forms, solid construction is the rule.

To trace the further development of the walnut chair carries us into the early mahogany years, and there it is difficult to find a line of demarcation. We are compelled to make one, which is easier to do in text than in illustration. Fashions, especially in chairs, succeed each other with such bewildering rapidity, in the years from 1715 to 1745, and these fashions overlap and persist to such a remarkable extent, that classification becomes almost impossible, yet the attempt must be made if the subject is to be presented in an orderly fashion.

If the walnut years may be said to extend from 1690 onwards, then the bureau belongs to that period. Generally, but not invariably, the seventeenth century bureau is, in form, like a desk placed on a chest of drawers, and divided from it by a bold moulding. Shortly after 1700 this is replaced by a straight, flush-sided form; desk and chest are united. The knee-hole belongs to the eighteenth century, almost exclusively.

Not the least of the distinguishing characteristics of this Queen Anne walnut furniture is the use of walnut veneers of fine grain and texture. The wood is usually of lighter shade than in the Orange pieces, and there is some evidence to show that much of this early walnut must have been imported from Holland or Germany; with the later pieces, the timber is English, unmistakably. The foreign walnut does not bleach nor fade like the English. The latter takes on a beautiful golden shade if exposed to sunlight, and this is assisted by the fine clear varnish which was used on many of the Queen Anne pieces, similar to that on the back of a fine violin. It is doubtful whether this fading is not in the varnish rather than in the wood itself; it is certainly impossible to replace the old colour once the original varnish is removed. I possess the doubtful credit of having tried the experiment in the days, now more than thirty years ago, when all original surfaces were scraped, as a matter of course, when pieces were sent for "restoration."

In some of this Queen Anne furniture the influence of the architect is very noticeable, especially in the sections of mouldings. There is a fine sense of detail and proportion in many of these, which one can hardly believe was possessed by the cabinetmaker. In the case of chairs the influence of the architect may be dismissed, as either negligible or as greatly to the detriment of English chair-design. William Kent—that versatile genius who appeared to be equally at home with architecture, furniture or ladies' dresses, and never wholly successful with any of the three—did try his hand at chairs, but they may be dismissed as absolute failures, more worthy of execution in stone rather than in wood. Chairmaking is an art possessed only by the chairmaker; it is one entirely foreign even to the cabinetmaker or the joiner.

While on the subject of this walnut furniture, due credit must be given to the cabinetmaker for the subtle and effective use made of cross-grained wood (known as cross-banding, if using the word in a dual sense is permissible) and the piecing of burl and other freaks of timber grain to produce the utmost richness of effect. The ability with which the "eyes" of walnut burls are joined with the marqueterie saw is often truly amazing; taste and skill of a high order are displayed. All effects are produced by quiet and refined means; the age of gaudy marqueterie had departed during the early years of Anne. Construction had degenerated, and ornament had become paramount. But for this defect in constructive principle, this walnut furniture might be acclaimed as the finest in the entire history of English furniture. For sheer refinement, it has never been equalled, before or since. Unfortunately, veneering is an art to which dampness is a formidable enemy, and when, to flat veneering, shaped surfaces, such as the dishing of splats, shaping of seat rails, the bombé carcases—more usual in Dutch than in English furniture—are added, furniture of this kind must be evanescent. It is regrettable to find many of the broad-splatted chairs of this period in which the veneer has fallen off and disappeared. Veneer, laid on the one side only, and often on a bed of soft wood—deal or pine—will not stand. In the damp climate of England, the error is not so serious, perhaps, but in America, with its dry atmosphere—and especially with its domestic steam heating—this walnut furniture falls to pieces after a short space of time. I regard it as an artistic error when I see this Queen Anne or Orange walnut furniture in American homes. When it cracks, warps and blisters it is sent to be "reconditioned," as if such "re-conditioning" could replace the old glory of faded varnish and lovely golden shade which the years, and kind treatment, both by people and climate, have produced. It may be contended that a man may do what he desires with his own. I am free to admit it, but I cannot help the feeling that, with everyone of these "re-conditioned" wrecks which I see, in my peregrinations in the United States, something of the domestic history of England has departed, and forever. Perhaps I have learned, in my later life, to love things more than persons; who knows!

WALNUT CHAIRS OF THE FIRST YEARS OF THE EIGHTEENTH CENTURY, INLAID WITH MARQUETERIE. INLAID CHAIRS OF THIS PERIOD ARE VERY RARE AND INDICATE THAT IN MARQUETERIE DECORATION THE CHAIRMAKER DID NOT FOLLOW THE CURRENT FURNITURE TASTE OF THE TIME, *c. 1700-5*

VERY RARE ARMCHAIR FROM BROWSHOLME HALL, CLITHEROE, YORKSHIRE, ENGLAND. PERHAPS THE FINEST EXAMPLE EXTANT OF ITS PERIOD, *c. 1720*

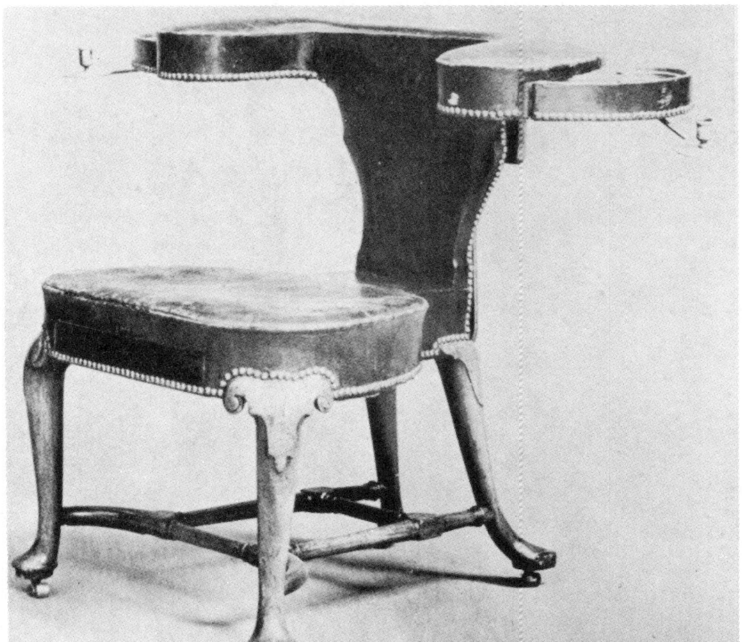

WALNUT SMOKER'S CHAIR, CONSTRUCTED FOR STRADDLING, OR SITTING HORSE-FASHION. IT IS FITTED WITH A READING DESK, SWING-OUT BOXES AND PAIR OF CANDLE SCONCES, *c. 1705*

WALNUT SIDE CHAIR, *c. 1705*. THIS TYPE, WITH THE WIDE CENTRAL SPLAT BRACED TO THE SIDE BALUSTERS IS COMMONLY KNOWN AS A "HOGARTH" CHAIR

WALNUT CHAIR WITH TALL BACK. THE EARLY TYPE OF CABRIOLE LEG, SQUARE IN SECTION AT THE KNEES, WITH HOOF-FEET AND SHAPED CROSS-RAILING UNITING THE LEGS, *c. 1700*

QUEEN ANNE CHAIR OF *c. 1705*

QUEEN ANNE CHAIR OF *c. 1705*

WALNUT SETTEE OF EXCEPTIONAL FORM, WITH THE EARLY TYPE OF CABRIOLE LEG WITH CLOVEN KNEE AND CROSS-RAILING UNITING THE LEGS, *c. 1705*

A VERY RARE WALNUT SETTEE OF *c. 1710*, WITH CENTRAL SPLATS DETACHED FROM THE TOP RAILS AND BRACED TO THE SIDE BALUSTERS IN A VERY PECULIAR MANNER

WALNUT SETTEE AND SIDE CHAIR OF THE LAST YEARS OF QUEEN ANNE. NOTE THE STRONG GRIP OF THE CLAW FEET, THE DEEP SEAT RAIL AND THE BROAD SPLAT IN THE BACK OF THE SETTEE, *c. 1710*

WALNUT SETTEE AND SIDE CHAIR FROM AN IMPORTANT SET FROM THE MASTER'S HOUSE, PETERHOUSE, CAMBRIDGE, ENGLAND. THE NEXT DEVELOPMENT FROM THE PLAIN CABRIOLE LEG OF THE QUEEN ANNE PERIOD, *c. 1715*

SIDE CHAIR WITH THE EARLY TYPE OF BALL-AND-CLAW WITHOUT WEBBING BETWEEN THE CLAWS, *c. 1710*

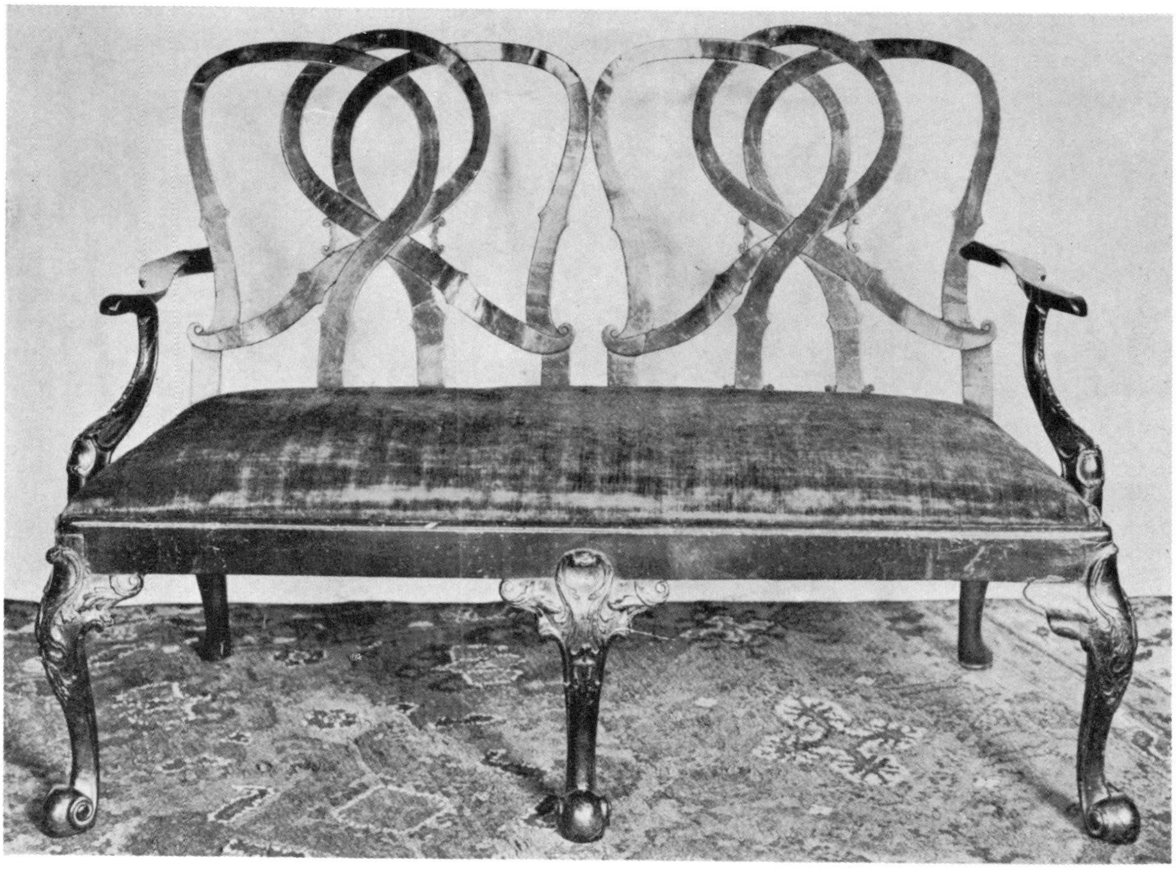

VERY RARE TYPE OF WALNUT SETTEE, WITH INTERLACED BACKS. THIS PATTERN UNDOUBTEDLY SUGGESTED THE LATER RIBBON-BACK OF THE CHIPPENDALE SCHOOL, *c. 1715*

WALNUT SETTEE FROM DUDLEY HOUSE, PARK LANE, LONDON, ENGLAND. THE DEVELOPMENT IN THE BROAD-SPLATTED BACKS TO CURLING OR SCROLLING, WHICH AFTERWARDS DEVELOPS IN THE EARLY MAHOGANY FURNITURE, *c. 1715-20*

NOTE THE IDENTICAL FORM OF TASSELLED BACK IN A MAHOGANY CHAIR OF ABOUT FIFTEEN YEARS LATER THAN THE TWO CHAIRS BELOW. ALSO THE CABRIOLE LEGS CARVED AT THE KNEES AND THE PAW FEET, *c. 1730*

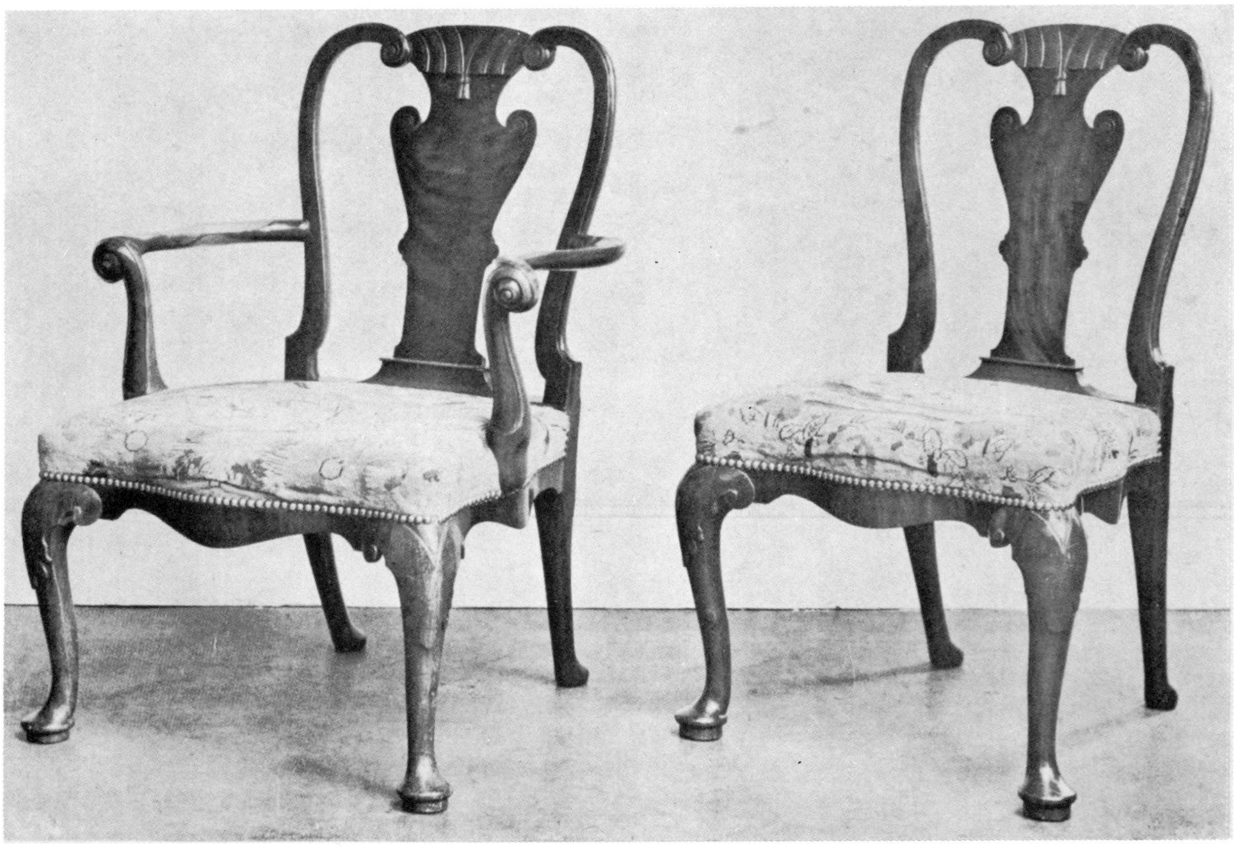

ARM AND SIDE CHAIR IN WALNUT, WITH PLAIN CABRIOLE LEGS AND CLUB FEET. THE TYPE OF *1715*

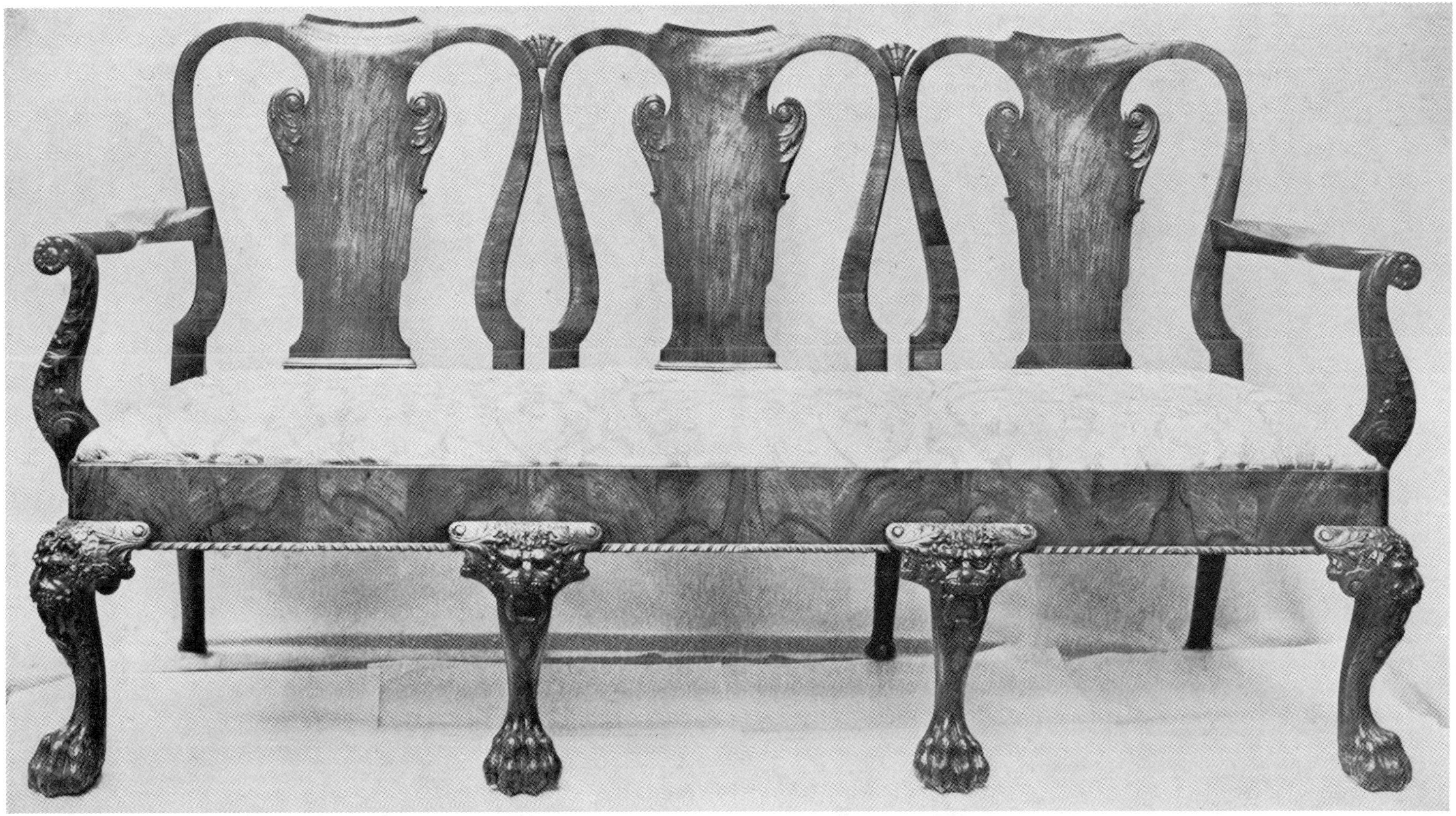

WALNUT SETTEE OF THE LION YEARS (*1730-5*) WHEN MAHOGANY HAD LARGELY REPLACED WALNUT FOR FINE FURNITURE. THE EARLY HOOP-BACK OF THE QUEEN ANNE PERIOD IS RETAINED IN THIS PIECE. SETTEES OF CHAIR-BACK FORM, WITH THREE BACKS, ARE VERY RARE

WALNUT CHAIR OF *c. 1700.* SMOOTH CABRIOLE LEGS SET SLIGHTLY UNDER A SHAPED FRAMING TO THE SEAT APPLIED OVER THE NEEDLEWORK. COMPARE CHAIR BELOW

WALNUT WING CHAIR OF EARLY TYPE. THE CABRIOLE HERE IS NOT FULLY DEVELOPED, AND IS OF SQUARE SECTION WITH THE ORANGE TYPE OF FLAT SHAPED STRETCHER, *c. 1695*

WALNUT WING CHAIR COVERED WITH FINE NEEDLEWORK. NOTE THE APPLIED FRAMING TO THE SEAT RAIL. COMPARE WITH THE SIDE CHAIR ABOVE. *c. 1700*

WALNUT WING CHAIR WITH UNDEVELOPED CABRIOLE OF SQUARE SECTION, THE TYPE WHICH IMMEDIATELY PRECEDES THE SMOOTH ROUNDED CABRIOLE OF THE FIRST YEARS OF EIGHTEENTH CENTURY, *c. 1695*

WALNUT WING CHAIR OF THE SMOOTH CABRIOLE YEARS, *c. 1705.* NOTE HERE THE STUMP-BACK LEG WHICH IS SUCH A GENERAL FEATURE IN PENNSYLVANIA CHAIRS OF *c. 1750-60*

WALNUT WING CHAIR COVERED WITH NEEDLEWORK. THE CABRIOLE LEGS, SHELL-CARVED ON THE KNEES, AND WITH PROJECTING EARPIECES IN THE FORM OF EAGLES' HEADS, IS THE FASHION OF *1710*

WALNUT WING CHAIR COVERED WITH PETIT-POINT NEEDLEWORK. THE FRONT LEGS, OF CABRIOLE FORM, DECORATED ON THE KNEES WITH THE REVERSED ESCALLOP SHELL, AND ON THE FEET WITH THE CLUB-AND-CUSHION ARE IN THE FULL MANNER OF *c. 1715*

WALNUT WRITING CHAIR OF *c. 1705.* VERY FINELY DESIGNED

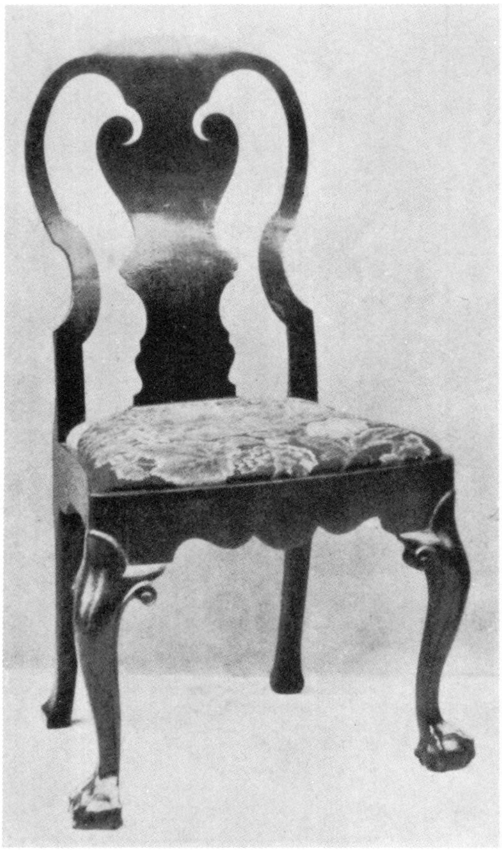

WALNUT SIDE CHAIR OF *c. 1705*, WITH SHAPED SEAT RAIL. THIS IS THE ENGLISH TYPE WHICH INSPIRED SO MANY OF THE PHILADELPHIA CHAIRS OF FIFTY YEARS LATER

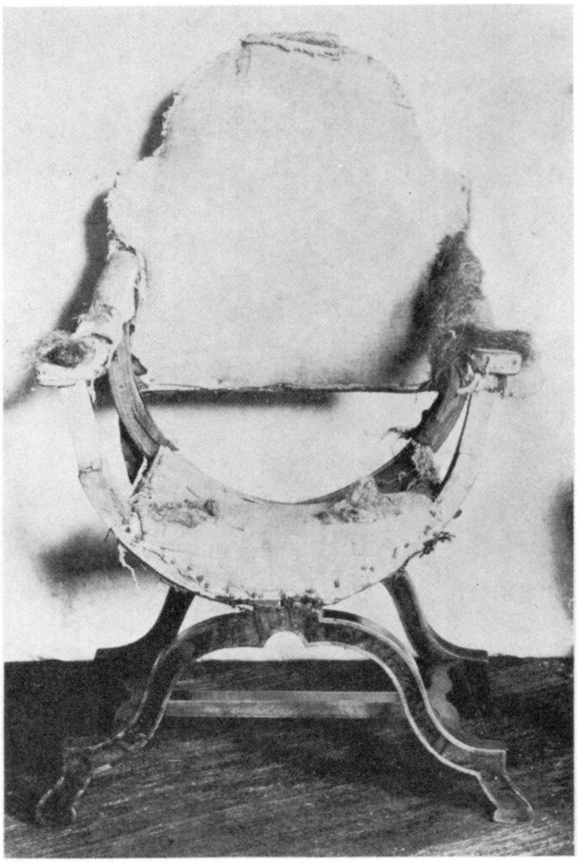

WALNUT X CHAIR OF RARE FORM. THE FRAMING IS CROSS-BANDED AND EDGED WITH HOLLY. *c. 1705*

TWO RARE WALNUT HALL CHAIRS FROM LYME PARK, DISLEY, CHESHIRE. THE ONE ON THE LEFT HAS THE BACK SLIGHTLY CARVED AND INLAID WITH THE DISLEY RAM. *c. 1705*

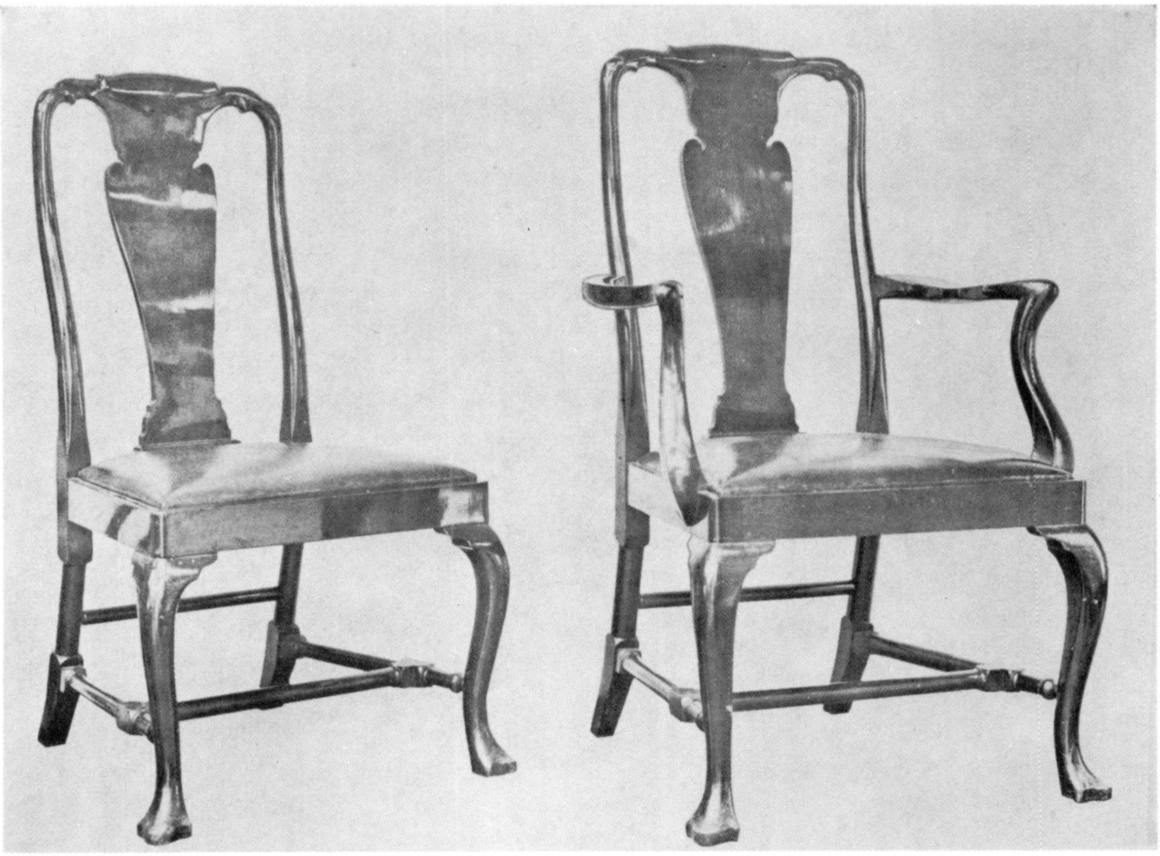

WALNUT ARM AND SIDE CHAIRS OF *c. 1705*

TWO CHAIRS OF GOLDEN WALNUT, PARCEL GILT. THE HOOF-FOOT, WITH PEARLED RING ABOVE, IS IN THE MANNER OF *c. 1715*. THE DOUBLE TOP RAIL SHOULD BE NOTED AS THIS IS ANOTHER FEATURE OF THE YEARS IMMEDIATELY FOLLOWING THE DEATH OF ANNE IN *1713*

WALNUT ARM AND SIDE CHAIRS OF THE GEORGE I PERIOD, *1713-27*. THE EAGLES' HEADS TO THE ARMS ARE AN EARLIER FEATURE THAN THE FULLY DEVELOPED CABRIOLE LEGS, CARVED AT THE KNEES AND WITH BALL-AND-CLAW FEET, WEBBED BETWEEN THE CLAWS

RARE TYPE OF WALNUT SETTEE WITH ARMS FINISHING IN SCROLLED PELICANS' HEADS, AND EAGLES' HEADS INTRODUCED INTO THE CENTRAL SPLATS, *c. 1715*

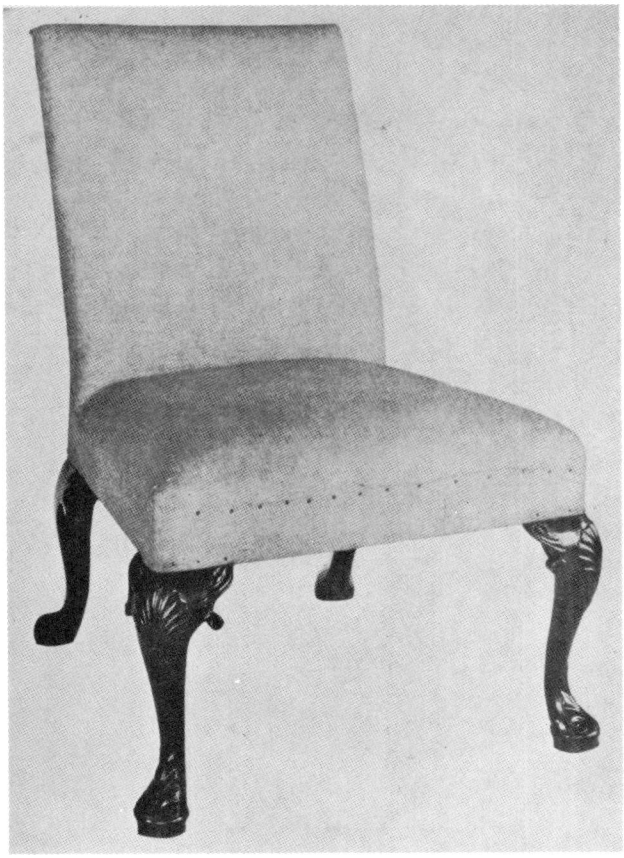

WALNUT SIDE CHAIR OF THE LATER YEARS OF QUEEN ANNE. THE CARVING OF THE CLUB FEET IS EXCEPTIONAL, *c. 1710-15*

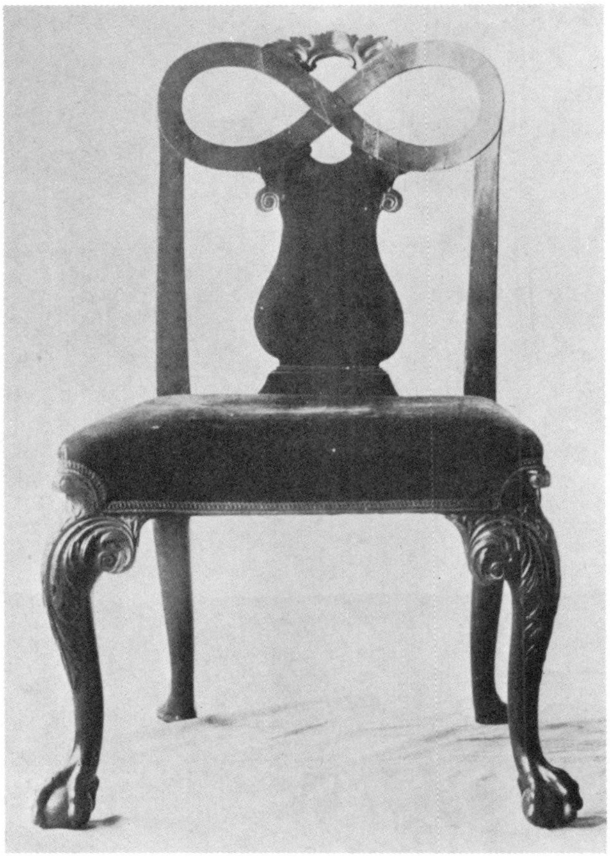

UNUSUAL WALNUT CHAIR WITH INTERLACED TOP RAIL. NOTE THE CRESTING OF THE LEGS OVER THE SEAT RAIL, ANOTHER DEFINED FASHION OF THE TIME, *c. 1720*

WALNUT SETTEE ILLUSTRATING THE DEVELOPMENT AWAY FROM THE QUEEN ANNE HOOP-BACK TO THE FLAT-TENONED TOP RAIL OF THE EARLY MAHOGANY YEARS. THE SMOOTH CABRIOLE LEG IS STILL RETAINED, *c. 1725*

A FINE EXAMPLE OF A WALNUT SIDE CHAIR IN THE EARLY MAHOGANY YEARS, ILLUSTRATING THE FASHION OF PAPER-SCROLLING THE JUNCTIONS OF TOP RAIL AND SIDE BALUSTERS, AND THE CRESTING UP OF THE LEGS OVER THE SEAT-FRAMING

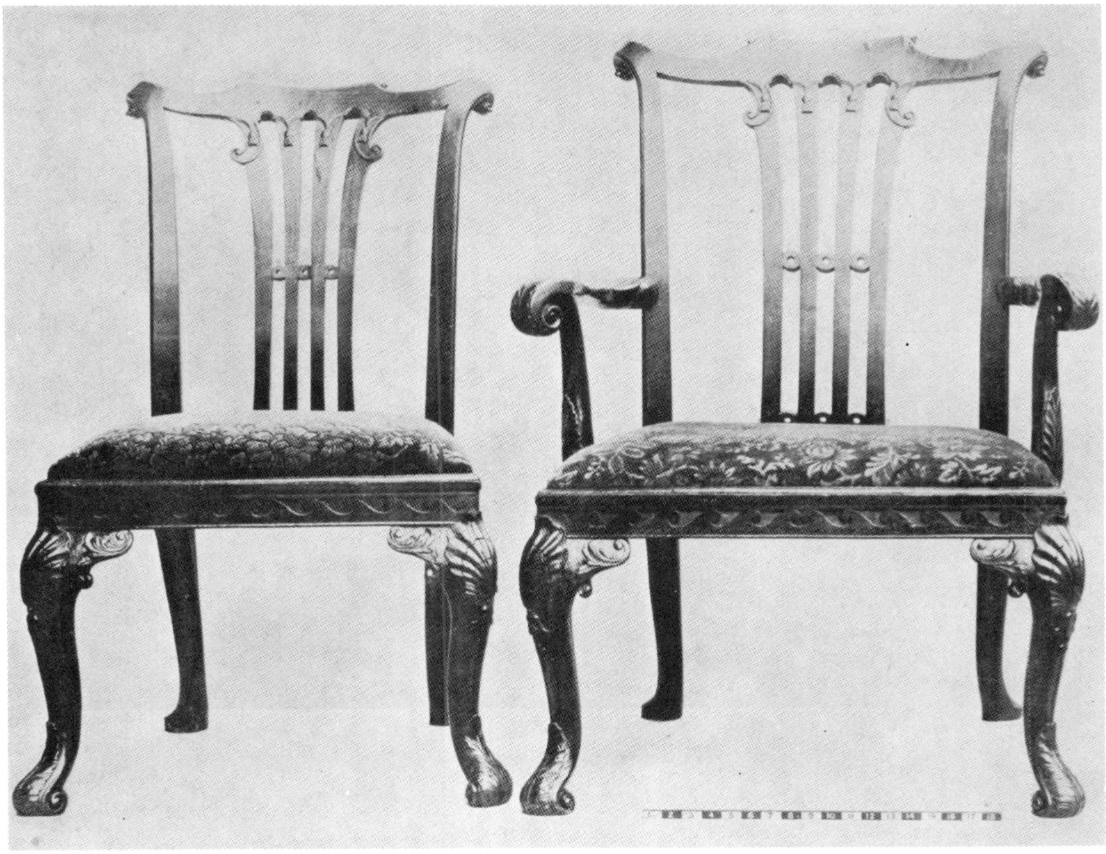

WALNUT CHAIRS OF *c. 1720*, SHOWING THE PASSING OF THE HOOP-BACK AND THE DEVELOPMENT OF THE FLATTENED TOP RAIL. THE USE OF THE SCROLL, AT THE JUNCTIONS OF THE TOP RAILS WITH THE BACK BALUSTERS, IN THE SPLATS AND ON THE FEET OF THE FRONT LEGS, SHOULD BE NOTED, AS THIS SCROLLING MARKS AN IMPORTANT FASHION OF THE TIME

RARE TYPE OF WALNUT SETTEE ALMOST IN THE MAHOGANY YEARS, WITH PECULIAR ROPED TOP RAILS TO THE BACKS, SCROLLED OVER AT THE ENDS. THIS PIECE IS IN QUITE A DEFINITE FASHION IN SPITE OF ITS RARE FORM, *c. 1720*

THE BEGINNING OF THE FLATTENED TOP RAIL OF THE MAHOGANY YEARS. THE CENTRAL SPLAT IS NOW PIERCED, BUT THE EARLY TYPE OF CABRIOLE IS RETAINED WITH THE LEAF-AND-SCROLL FOOT. *c. 1725*

MAHOGANY ARMCHAIR IN THE SCROLL FASHION OF *1725*. IT IS INTERESTING TO NOTE HOW EXTENSIVELY THE SCROLL IS USED IN THIS DESIGN. THE COLLARED LEAF-CARVED CLUB FOOT IS EXCEPTIONAL

ELABORATE ARMCHAIR SHOWING THE QUEEN ANNE HOOP-BACK RETAINED IN THE MAHOGANY YEARS, IN SPITE OF THE CHANGE OF FASHION TO THE FLATTENED TOP RAIL. *c. 1725*

AN ORIGINAL CASTOR SHOWING THE WHEEL OR "BOWL" MADE FROM FOUR LAMINATIONS OF LEATHER

QUEEN ANNE WALNUT CARD TABLE WITH ORIGINAL NEEDLEWORK TOP
c. 1710
Courtesy of the Kent Gallery

WALNUT TRAY-TOP CENTRE TABLE. *c. 1705.*
SIMPLE BUT FINE TYPE

TRAY-TOP CENTRE TABLE OF WALNUT AND CHERRY. *c. 1700-5*

SIDE TABLE OF OAK AND CHERRY-WOOD. *c. 1700-5*

CHERRY-WOOD TABLE. *c. 1715*

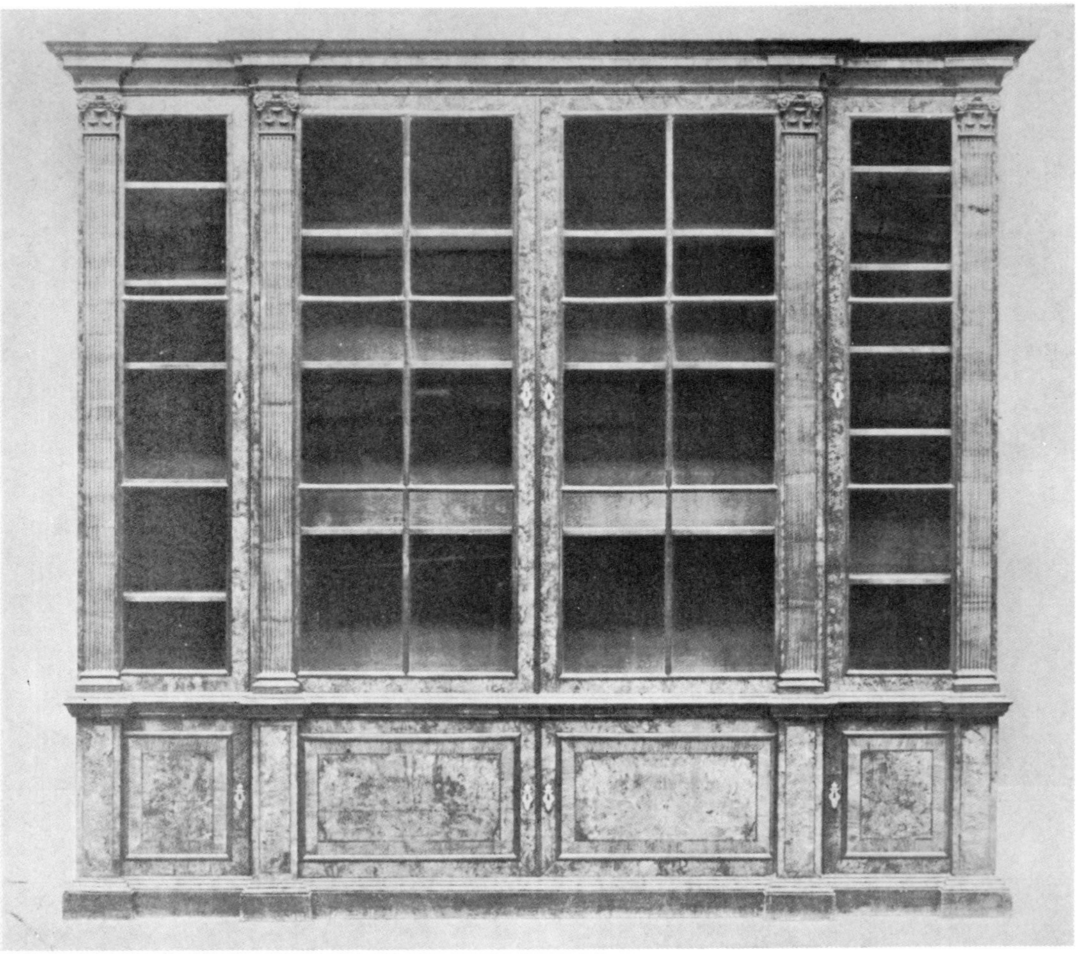

WALNUT BOOKCASE, *c. 1710.* HERE IS AN EXAMPLE OF A CABINETMAKER USING ARCHITECTURAL DETAILS AS DISTINGUISHED FROM A CABINETMAKER WORKING TO AN ARCHITECT'S DESIGN

WALNUT CORNER TABLE, *c. 1730.* TABLES OF THIS TYPE, IN WALNUT, AND OF THIS QUALITY, ARE EXCEEDINGLY RARE

WALNUT BUREAU ON CABRIOLE LEGS, *c. 1710.* VENEERED WITH FINELY FIGURED ENGLISH WALNUT. THESE BUREAUX ON SEPARATE STANDS MARK THE PROGRESSION FROM THE BUREAU ON PLINTH TO THE WRITING TABLE ON LEGS. ORIGINAL PIECES OF THIS KIND AND QUALITY ARE EXCEEDINGLY RARE. THE HARDWARE ON THIS BUREAU IS ALL ORIGINAL

CHEST OF DRAWERS ON STAND, *c. 1700.* THE FRONT VENEERED WITH STRIPED WALNUT WITH BROAD INLAID CHEQUERED LINES. NOTE THE EMBRYONIC TYPE OF CABRIOLE LEG

WALNUT CHEST OF DRAWERS ON STAND, AN EXAMPLE WHICH IS TRUE TO ITS PERIOD

WALNUT BUREAU CABINET, *c. 1705.* DOUBLE SERPENTINE TOP MOULDINGS ALL CROSS-BANDED

WALNUT BUREAU CABINET, *c. 1705.* THE DOORS WITH SILVERED GLASS PANELS WITH FLAT BEVELS

BUREAU CABINET, VENEERED WITH GOLDEN WALNUT, WITH BUREAU FALL AND UPPER DOORS OPEN. THE MOUNTS OF THE COLUMNS AND PILASTERS ARE OF GILT BRASS. *c. 1710*

BUREAU CABINET SHOWN OPEN ON PREVIOUS PAGE. THE DOORS HAVE THE ORIGINAL VAUXHALL PLATES. THE FIVE FIGURES ABOVE ARE OF GILT WOOD

WALNUT BUREAU CABINET WITH INTRICATELY MITRED CORNICE IN THE LOW COUNTRY MANNER. THIS PIECE IS ORIGINAL THROUGHOUT, *c. 1700*

WALNUT DOUBLE-DOME BUREAU CABINET OF THE MORE USUAL ENGLISH TYPE, *c. 1710*

WALNUT BUREAU CABINET WITH PULL-OUT WRITING SLIDE, *c. 1710*

WALNUT ARCH-PEDIMENT BUREAU CABINET (OPEN AND CLOSED) OF VERY FINE QUALITY. THE INTERIOR OF THE UPPER PART IS BLOCK-FRONTED. THE GLASS SPINES ARE ORIGINAL, *c. 1705*

BUREAU VENEERED WITH POLLARDED WYCH-ELM, *c. 1700*. HANDLES AND LOCK-PLATES ARE ORIGINAL

WALNUT BUREAU (OPEN AND CLOSED) VENEERED WITH RICHLY-FIGURED WOOD. ALL THE HARDWARE IS ORIGINAL. *c. 1705*

KNEEHOLE BUREAU VENEERED WITH BLEACHED BURL WALNUT. *c. 1700*

WALNUT KNEEHOLE BUREAU WITH NARROW PEDESTALS, *c. 1700*. THE VENEERS ARE VERY PALE, BLEACHED BY LIGHT

WALNUT BUREAU SHOWN OPEN ABOVE

WALNUT DRESSING TABLE ON CURIOUS BRACKET-PLINTHS, *c. 1700*

CHAPTER XII

English Wall Mirrors

MIRRORS, whether of polished or of plated metal, or of silvered glass, have always been regarded as prized possessions, from very early times. This esteem may be due to to three causes, each of which is considered below.

Silvered glass, from its introduction into England in the beginning of the seventeenth century, up to about 1845, was prohibitively expensive. This was due, in part, to the cost and difficulties of manufacture, especially in large sheets, but more to the heavy duties which were imposed in 1695, repealed in 1698 (at the instigation of the Duke of Buckingham, of whom more later) re-imposed in 1745, and finally taken off by Sir Robert Peel in 1845.

The first of the three causes, referred to above, is this expense. It is only natural that the costly thing should be highly valued; the terms are almost synonymous. Even at the present day, when silvered glass has become a commercial product, the old superstition has survived, that ill-luck attends the one who breaks a mirror. Superstitions generally have some historical basis in fact, and this one dates, undoubtedly, from the days when a broken glass was a serious loss to the owner.

The second reason for popular esteem was that to possess a "looking-glass" implied wealth; to own a large pier-glass indicated great means, indeed. For example, in 1769, Thomas Chippendale, only ten years before his death, and therefore, towards the end of his business career, contracted with the Earl of Mansfield, Premier Earl of Scotland, and Lord Chief Justice of England, to procure, for Kenwood at Hampstead, two silvered "French Plates" 74 inches by 44 inches, at £69:10:0, each. When it is remembered that, at this date, money had more than four times its present purchasing power (the carved gilt frames for these glasses were priced at only £16) the enormous cost of silvered glass may be comprehended. Thomas Chippendale had to have the money advanced, beforehand, for the glass, and he entered into a contract so to do; his security was William France, another cabinetmaker of the time.

The third reason is, that for a plate of silvered glass, of large size, there is no substitute. It reflects with a clarity which no polished metal can do; and if the glass be good and even, and the silvering properly done, it does so without either distortion or discolouration. Its use considerably enlarges the apparent size of a room; for dressing table purposes it is quite indispensable. Eighteenth century beauty, in England and in

France, and also in Italy, spent much time before the mirror (much more than was spent in the bath, it is to be feared). In many paintings of the time the mirror is depicted as noteworthy.

Quoting from one of my books of nearly twenty years ago—which I trust may be permissible: "As considerable confusion has often resulted from an imperfect understanding of the various processes of making glass, the slight digression necessary to describe these may be allowed. Glass is formed by the fusion of mixtures of the silicates of lime, magnesia, soda, potash, alumina and lead in various proportions, according to the qualities required. These are of several kinds. Flint glass, for tableware, lustres, etc., is taken molten from the pot with a 'pontil,' an iron rod (tube) used by glass-blowers to support the metal while working, and blown or moulded into the shape required. Crown glass is taken in the same way, and is blown or whirled on the pontil until it assumes a globular form. The blowing tube is then detached, leaving a hole or boss, and the pontil, being dipped into molten glass, is applied and the globe is again whirled until it takes the form of a circular disc, adhering by the boss in the centre to the pontil. A combination of crown and flint glass is used for the manufacture of telescope lenses.

"With sheet glass nearly the same process is undergone, but the molten metal is whirled till it assumes the form of a cylinder, which is slit, longitudinally, and the sheets are heated and pressed flat.

"Plate glass is made by pouring the metal into a shallow tray, the depression being equal to the thickness required. The sheet is afterwards flattened out with a roller. It is, of course, the plate glass which was exclusively employed for silvering. Transparent glass was made in England as early as 1557, the first window tax being imposed in 1695. This tax was increased on six occasions between 1695 and 1808, reduced in 1823 and abolished in 1851, the present Inhabited House Duty taking its place."§

The term "glass-cutting" may be used in two ways; to indicate the actual severing of the sheet, (which is done with the diamond) and the so-called "brilliant-cutting," to which bevelling belongs. It may have been remarked, firstly, in the illustrations of cabinets, that glasses are made in two sections, placed together with bevels at the butt-joints, and secondly, that, in the upper section, devices such as the garter-star are cut into the glass surface. The reason for the former, especially when the upper section is shaped, is that the liability to breakage was great, and the hazard reduced, in consequence, to the smallest possible amount of glass. The latter, with the bevelling, is "brilliant-cutting," and is done with the sand-wheel. To economise labour, the bevels on the old mirrors are usually very flat, and appear to have been commenced when

§Since this was written, the Inhabited House Duty has also been abolished in England, but, as some compensation, every other tax has been increased enormously, until in this year of 1928 England is, by far, the most heavily taxed country in the world.

the plate was hot, by a species of moulding. The modern bevel is much sharper and more keenly cut.

The old glass, especially that of the early eighteenth century, is generally of a bluish tinge, and, being unevenly ground on the back, the silvering has nearly always spotted, fogged or fallen off. The original silvering was by the mercury process, which has now almost disappeared, being replaced by the "patent silvering," in which silver-foil is substituted. The result is not so good, but those who have experienced the days when the mercury process was in vogue, when the workers suffered from the frightful effects of "salivation," with teeth powdering away, decaying of the gums, painful boils and partial blindness, will appreciate, that, in this instance at least, perfection was well sacrificed.

As early as 1615 patent rights for the manufacture of looking-glasses, (i. e., the silvering of glass) had been granted to Sir Robert Mansell; but the process was not perfected until some fifty years later, when the Duke of Buckingham helped to establish a factory at Lambeth, which produced the celebrated "Vauxhall" or "Foxhall" plates. John Evelyn, the diarist, notes on September 19th, 1676, "We also saw the Duke of Buckingham's Glass-Worke, where they made huge vases of mettal as cleare, ponderous and thick as chrystal; also looking-glasses far larger and better than any that come from Venice."

It may be mentioned that the original factory of Dawson, Bowles & Co., established in 1670 under the patronage of the Duke of Buckingham, stood on the site of what is now Vauxhall Square. The factory was renowned, for many years, for its large silvered plates, and was probably the maker of the pier-glasses at Kenwood already mentioned.

A few words may be advsiable here, on the subject of gilding. This was a highly-paid trade in the eighteenth century, the pay of a gilder being usually reckoned at one penny per hour more than that of a wood-carver. Actually, this represented an advance of nearly twenty-five per cent, so the increase is considerably greater than it appears to be.

Gilding may be done by one or the other of two processes, water- or oil-gilding. For the former, the ground is prepared with whiting and size made from the boiling of parchment shavings, and brought forward in preparations of lead for the burnishing of the gold. The so-called "blue burnish" was never used for the work of this period; its presence is an infallible sign of later re-gilding or modern work. It was by no means uncommon for later gilding to be applied over the original gold without stripping, and it is often possible, with skill and care, to remove the later application and restore the original work intact.

Oil gilding is a process in which the final application is a varnish, called "gold size," to which the gold adheres. It has the advantage of rendering the gilded surface partly waterproof, but the gold cannot be burnished or toned. It is doubtful that this process was ever applied to the furniture of the eighteenth century. It was known and used for outside work, such as the gilding of signs or hatchments, even with the composition stucco of the Brothers Adam.

With water-gilding, in the way it was practised in the eighteenth century, the carving was never quite finished, the delicate details of veining and the like being left to the gilder, who cut them, with pointed sticks and water, in his final preparation. It follows, therefore, that to strip these old mirror frames to the bare wood is to destroy the finer detail. Unfortunately, this has not been appreciated, with the result that many of the best examples have been irretrievably ruined by later re-gilding. There must also have been a revulsion from gilding, at one period, as so many of the mirror frames in the finest style of Chippendale have been found painted brown. When the paint has been removed, the original gilding has been found underneath, almost intact. The painting, therefore, could not have been done to hide shabby and worn gilding.

To the eighteenth century belong the distorting or convex mirrors, which have considerable decorative value in reflecting a miniature view of the room in which they hang. The idea was borrowed from Murano and Venice, which specialised in these distorting mirrors during the seventeenth century. In many, a device was etched on the back of the glass, in such manner that it was not apparent when one stood in front of the mirror, but on moving slightly to the side, a skull or similar grim device would appear. These trick looking-glasses had a considerable vogue in England in the later Stuart period, but they are now exceedingly rare. Of the convex mirrors several illustrations are given here.

It is in designing these glass-frames that the architect begins to intrude into the domain of the cabinetmaker and the wood-carver, and both effectively and effectually. With the exception of the convex mirrors just alluded to, and those with plain cushion-moulded frames, decorated either with marqueterie or with lacquer, his hand is evident in the designing of nearly every example illustrated here. James Gibbs, William Kent, Nicholas Hawksmoor and other architects of this period not only made a speciality of glass frames, but also published books of their designs. Robert Adam made a careful study of pier-glass designing. The enormous cost of the glass they enclosed would lead to the greatest care being taken in the matter of the frames. Thomas Chippendale excelled in this field, but it is more than doubtful whether he originated many—if any—of the patterns in his book, "The Gentleman and Cabinet Maker's Director." There is strong evidence that this so-called "Chippendale Style" originated with Matthias Darly, who was also responsible for the whole of the designs in the

"System of Household Furniture" of Ince and Mayhew, published in 1763, which are "Chippendale" re-incarnated. The books of Edwards & Darly (1754), Lock & Copeland (1752), and of T. Johnson (1761), may be studied with interest and profit by those who are concerned with the authenticity of authorship of the Chippendale Style. To enter into the matter at any length at this stage, would only be to anticipate a later chapter. At the same time, if one is in New York, the opportunity of examining the original Chippendale drawings in the Metropolitan Museum should not be neglected. The history of the purchase of these, (they are nearly complete) reads almost like a modern-day romance of the auction rooms. It will be given, at a later stage, when the work of Thomas Chippendale is considered. It is necessary, however, first to give some account of the early mahogany furniture in England, which laid the foundation of the Chippendale style, if it did not actually anticipate it.

AN EARLY EIGHTEENTH CENTURY MIRROR IN FRAME OF BLACK AND GOLD LACQUER IN LYME PARK, CHESHIRE, THE RESIDENCE OF LORD NEWTON. THE DESIGN IS INSPIRED BY THE LATE SEVENTEENTH CENTURY MARQUETERIE MIRRORS, WITH THE BOLDLY-PROJECTING QUARTER-ROUND SECTIONAL FRAME

CARVED WOOD, GILT AND ETCHED GLASS MIRROR FRAME ADOPTED FROM THE MURANESE MIRRORS OF THE LATE SEVENTEENTH CENTURY, *c. 1730*. THE FRAME PANELS, AND THOSE IN THE CRESTING ARE OF ETCHED, GILT AND COLOURED GLASS

WALNUT MIRROR, *c. 1710*. THE GLASS IS IN TWO SECTIONS, THE UPPER ONE BRILLIANT CUT

CARVED WALNUT AND GILT MIRROR, WITH ORIGINAL CANDLE SCONCES, *c. 1720*

CARVED GILT MIRROR WITH ORIGINAL SCONCES, *c. 1710*

CARVED GILT MIRROR, WITH SCROLLED PEDIMENT, IN THE STYLE OF JAMES GIBBS, *c. 1720*

CARVED GILT MIRROR IN THE EARLY GEORGIAN STYLE WITH CLASSICAL PEDIMENT, *c. 1725*

CARVED GILT MIRROR, EARLY GEORGIAN STYLE. SATYR'S MASK AT TOP AND PALMER'S SHELL AT BOTTOM, *c. 1720*

CARVED AND GILT CONVEX MIRROR, WITH CANDLE SCONCES. THE CRESTING EAGLE WITH OUTSPREAD WINGS IS A FAVOURITE DECORATION ON THESE MIRRORS, *c. 1725*

AN UNUSUAL CARVED AND GILT CONVEX MIRROR CRESTED WITH A SHEAF OF WHEAT AND IMPLEMENTS OF HUSBANDRY, *c. 1730*

EARLY GEORGIAN GILT GESSO AND CARVED MIRROR, HEAD OF MEDUSA WITH PALMETTE DECORATION BEHIND, *c. 1720*

EARLY GEORGIAN CARVED AND GILT MIRROR. SCROLLED PEDIMENT WITH AKROTER AND CARTOUCHE ABOVE, *c. 1725*

GILT CONVEX MIRROR WITH TRIPLE CANDLE BRANCHES AND SURMOUNTING EAGLE, *c. 1730*

GILT CARVED AND COMPOSITION CONVEX MIRROR WITH DOUBLE CANDLE SCONCES HELD BY DOLPHINS, *c. 1760*. NOTE BALL DECORATION ON FRAME

CARVED AND GILT MIRROR, *c. 1765*

CARVED AND GILT CHIPPENDALE PIER-GLASS MADE FOR A CONSOLE, *c. 1760*

UPRIGHT WALL MIRRORS PROGRESS GRADUALLY FROM THE RECTANGULAR TO THE FLAMBOYANT. THE ADAM IS A TYPE OF THE FIRST, THE CHIPPENDALE OF THE SECOND. THE LAST HALF OF THE EIGHTEENTH CENTURY WITNESSES A GRADUAL BREAKING AWAY FROM THE SEVERELY ARCHITECTURAL TYPE, WITH WHICH THIS CLASS REALLY BEGINS

WALL MIRRORS OF WALNUT OR MAHOGANY, PARCEL GILT; OF THE EARLY EIGHTEENTH CENTURY. THE STRONG SIMILARITY OF MANY OF THESE SUGGESTS THAT THE TRADE WAS LOCALISED IN ENGLAND AT THIS PERIOD

AN IMPORTANT CARVED AND GILT CHIPPENDALE MIRROR IN DUDLEY HOUSE, PARK LANE, LONDON, THE LONDON RESIDENCE OF CAPT. THE HON. SIR JOHN H. WARD, K.C.V.O. DATE ABOUT *1755*

CARVED AND GILT CHIPPENDALE MIRROR, CRESTED WITH CHIMERAE, ***c. 1750***

CARVED AND GILT CHIPPENDALE MIRROR IN THE "CHINESE TASTE," *c. 1750*

CARVED AND GILT CHIPPENDALE PIER-GLASS. AT THE TOP IS THE PELICAN PECKING HER BREAST. THE EMBLEM OF PIETY, AND KNOWN, HERALDICALLY, AS "THE PELICAN IN HER PIETY," *c. 1750*

CARVED AND GILT CHIPPENDALE MIRROR WITH SURMOUNTING EAGLE, *c. 1750*

CARVED AND GILT CHIPPENDALE MIRROR IN THE ROCOCO TASTE, *c. 1760*

GILT WOOD, COMPOSITION AND PAINTED MIRROR IN THE ADAM STYLE, *c. 1760*

GILT CONVEX MIRROR OR GIRANDOLE OF THE ADAM PERIOD, *c. 1760*

GILT WOOD, COMPOSITION AND PAINTED MIRROR IN THE ADAM STYLE, *c. 1760*

CARVED AND GILT MIRROR OF THE CHIPPENDALE PERIOD, *c. 1755*, CRESTED WITH TWO ARGUS PHEASANTS. A VERY FINE AND RESTRAINED EXAMPLE

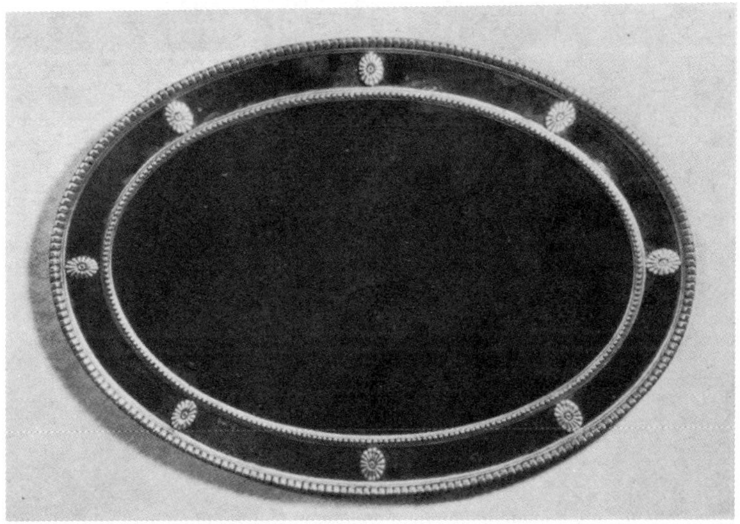

ANOTHER VARIATION OF THESE HANGING WALL MIRRORS WERE THOSE OF OVAL FORM, DESIGNED EITHER LONG OR UPRIGHT. SOME COULD BE FIXED EITHER WAY. WHEN SURROUNDED BY SCROLL WORK OR FOLIAGE, THEY WERE KNOWN AS "GIRANDOLES," BUT THE TERM WAS ALSO USED TO INDICATE BRANCHED WALL LIGHTS SIMILAR TO THOSE ILLUSTRATED AT THE END OF THIS CHAPTER

CARVED AND GILT CHIPPENDALE MIRROR IN THE CHINESE TASTE, *c. 1755*

CARVED AND PARCEL-GILT MIRROR OF THE EARLY EIGHTEENTH CENTURY

CARVED AND GILT MIRROR. AN IMITATION OF THE MANNER OF THOMAS CHIPPENDALE, *c. 1760*

A SEVENTEENTH CENTURY CARVED WOOD AND GILT FLORENTINE MIRROR SHOWING THE DEEP UNDER-CUTTING WHICH PROBABLY INSPIRED THE WORK OF THE GRINLING GIBBONS SCHOOL

CARVED AND PARCEL-GILT MIRROR OF THE EARLY EIGHTEENTH CENTURY

WALL CANDLE SCONCES OR "GIRANDOLES," AS THEY WERE OFTEN TERMED IN THE EIGHTEENTH CENTURY, REALLY BELONG TO THE SAME CATEGORY AS WALL MIRRORS. THE SCONCES WERE NEARLY ALWAYS MADE IN PAIRS, SOMETIMES WITH THE ONE AN EXACT REPLICA OF THE OTHER, BUT SOMETIMES VARYING CONSIDERABLY, WITH THE BALANCE ONLY PRESERVED. AS A RULE, THESE SCONCES BELONG TO THE ADAM PERIOD (*1755-1775*) IF NOT TO THE STYLE ITSELF, OF THE "ADELPHI"

UPRIGHT GILT WALL MIRRORS WITH COLOURED AND PAINTED GLASS PANELS ABOVE THE CENTRAL PLATE. THE TYPE WHICH WAS VERY POPULAR FROM *1770* TO *1810*, AND CONTINUED WITHOUT MATERIAL ALTERATION

CHAPTER XIII

Lacquer-Work in England

As IT WILL BE NECESSARY, at some point in this enquiry, to turn aside from the main stream of English furniture development, in order to consider the subject of lacquer-work, it may be as well to do so here, as some over-lapping will inevitably occur, even at this stage of the enquiry.

Lacquer is not a style; it is purely an adventitious decoration, applied almost indiscriminately, as an alternative to veneering or marqueterie. In England, the taste for lacquer begins with imported pieces, such as square cabinets and screens brought over the seas in the tea ships of "John Company," the cabinets being mounted on the familiar carved and gilt stands, the screens often cut up to make other cabinets or similar pieces.

The next stage in the development of the fashion in Europe, (not necessarily in England) occurs when these pieces are entirely of occidental make and decoration. At the close of the seventeenth century, in England, lacquer is applied to pieces designed in the well-known styles of the time; and the art of the lacquer-worker persists right into the Chippendale period, if not to a later date.

Any enquiry must commence with the Oriental work. This may be divided into four, if not five countries of origin. Of these only the first two or three concern us here. These countries may be placed in the following order: China, Japan, Korea, Persia and Hindostan. In these countries the art of lacquering is of considerable antiquity.

It must be understood, at the outset, that lacquer is an application of a particular varnish, either transparent or in solid or semi-solid colours, and with or without applied decoration on the lacquered ground. The term itself is ambiguous; lacquering, (or "lackering") may denote a protective coat of varnish applied to metals, to prevent tarnishing, as well as to the decoration of furniture. During the eighteenth century the usual word was "japanning," which is, perhaps, just as inaccurate, as indicating a country from which very little lacquer-work was actually imported at that time. At that date the name of "Cathay" was used to indicate some unspecified and remote Oriental country, although sometimes definitely indicating China or Manchuria.

Many names are to be found in documents, books and advertisements of the later seventeenth and the early eighteenth century, all indicating imported lacquer pieces. Thus, "Jappan" cabinets, "Bantam-work," (Bantam was the early trading station of the Dutch East India Company in Java, and "Bantam-work" usually implied incised lacquer) "India-work," "Lacker," "Coromandel-work" and "Cathay pieces." None of these names has any precise significance in distinguishing either country of origin or manner of decoration.

The true Oriental lacquer is the gum from a native tree,—Tsi—(Rhus succadanea or Rhus vernificera, both varieties of the Sumach) which is exuded from incisions in the trunk, in much the same way as rubber is procured. This gum dries on exposure to the air, and when hard, cannot be dissolved or affected by spirit of wine, which will attack all European lacquers. Both in China and in Japan the work is done in a heated and damp atmosphere, to prevent premature hardening. With all varnishes, the slower the drying the more permanent is the result.

This same protective lacquer (the gum is almost transparent) was used to preserve the wooden, paper-covered tea chests brought in the ships of the Dutch and English East India Companies.

Restricting the term "lacquer" to furniture, for the present, we may divide the subject into two principal classes, Oriental and European. As far as the surface ornament is concerned, which is a later application, of course, there are four main divisions: flat, raised, incised or "cut," and incrusted, the fourth belonging to either the second or to the third class. In incrusted lacquer the decoration, of ivory, mother-of-pearl, metals, or jade, is inset in the lacquer surface, and then carved, either in relief or in intaglio.

To give a comprehensive list of the ground-colours of lacquer, whether Oriental or European, is difficult, as some colours are exceedingly rare. At the same time, it is impossible to state, definitely, that certain colours were never used at all. Most common is black; then red, yellow, buff, green, brown, tortoise-shell or mottled (found in European lacquer only) and blue, the last being, perhaps, the rarest of all. In addition to these, in the Japanese lacquer, we find raised decoration on a solid ground of gold. The ground of the incised lacquer varies from black to green-brown or brown-green and is not easy to classify.

The ornament, whether raised, flat or incised, admits of three-fold division, into monochrome, (nearly always gold) polychrome and incrusted. The incised or "cut" lacquer belongs nearly always to the second category.

If we extend Oriental lacquer to include ornaments, as well as furniture, to vases, boxes, caskets and the like, we get further sub-divisions, such as the carved red Cinnabar or Soochow lac (the throne of Chien Lung, second Emperor of the Manchu Dynasty, now in the Victoria and Albert Museum in London, is in this Cinnabar lacquer, and I have seen the same decoration used for the bedsteads of important mandarins) the gold ground of Japan and the Chinese incrustations of jade, soapstone and other hard stones. The varieties of Chinese lacquer-work are almost infinite.

While it is not easy to differentiate between the lacquer of China, Korea and Japan, (to say nothing of the sub-divisions into the work of Soochow, Hankow, Nankin, Pekin, Swatow and Upper Manchuria, it is not difficult to distinguish Oriental from European work, if we omit those hybrid pieces made in Europe from imported screen panels or other fragments. Apart from the ground itself, the true lacquer (it is comparatively easy to distinguish between Oriental and Occidental lacquer, as nearly all of the latter is prepared with paint, varnish and shellac) Chinese or Japanese drawing is unmistakable, even in the illustrations of this chapter.

It may be pointed out here that there is one very marked difference between the Chinese and the Japanese drawing; the Chinaman sits on a stool or chair, the Japanese on the floor. There is, therefore, a viewpoint, in the one, of about four feet from the floor; in the other, of not more than two. This is a better indication of country of origin than costumes, as the Japanese frequently used Chinese figures in Chinese costumes. Had the Japanese been less of copyists, with their wonderful technical skill, their lacquer-work would now be more greatly prized than the Chinese, that is by connoisseurs who know values better than prices.

Statements have been made, in many books, (I must plead guilty myself, in my earlier years when I pinned my faith to other people's books) that pieces of furniture were made in England, sent out to China in the tea ships to be lacquered there and afterwards returned. This may have been the fact with certain French pieces which I have known; I am not qualified to judge, but I have never seen a single article of English furniture which could be said to have been made in England and lacquered in the East. I do not believe that such a piece exists, or that such a practice was ever adopted, as English-made furniture, especially if left in the bare wood—as such pieces intended for lacquering must have been—would inevitably have cracked, warped, shrunk or fallen to pieces in a climate such as that of China. I have seen how English furniture, made with every care and protected by covering varnishes or polishes, has behaved when exported to the United States—and in the mild months of the year—and I can imagine what would have happened to it in China or elsewhere in the Far East. The statement as to this dual authorship is merely another instance (not uncommon with writers of "technical" books) of an assertion, ventured at random, with the knowledge that authoritative contradiction is improbable, or may be ignored. After all, the statement has a long start, and that is one advantage to the author.

From first to last, in English or European lacquer-work, the Chinese or Japanese character is imitated, even up to the Chippendale period. Lacquer is described as "Chinese work" or in the "Chinese Taste," in every document or book in which reference is made to lacquer, and I have never seen one example, in which the ornament is of true Occidental inspiration, prior to about 1760. In fact, the Oriental character is often the only dubious distinction possible between lacquer and painting. It is difficult otherwise, to state where English lacquer ceases, as it is really only paint and varnish—sometimes only colour and French polish—and, if no line be drawn, then the painted furniture of Pergolesi, Cipriani, Zucchi, Angelica Kauffmann and the other decorative artists who were employed by the Brothers Adam, must be styled as lacquer. Even with the Adam work itself I know of examples in which the Chinese character has been used for the decoration, as at Nostell Priory and elsewhere.

Chinese lacquer depends, for its persistence, on the perfect protection which it affords, against atmospheric effects, to the wood beneath. Once this covering lacquer is fractured, the piece has no greater permanence than one made in Europe, if as much. From its extreme hardness and insolubility, Oriental lacquer is difficult to restore satisfactorily; European gum varnishes are poor substitutes for the native Tsi. The large Chinese screens, which were freely imported into England and France during the early years of the eighteenth century, are among the most decorative examples of this Oriental lacquer, and are justly prized by collectors in England. To export them to the United States, with its extremes of temperature and over-heated houses, is a dangerous practice, as they may fall to pieces after a few years. The price which Americans pay for their steam-heating, other than thinning of the blood, pneumonia and such trifles, is that they must deny themselves lacquered and marqueterie furniture; even veneered walnut should be prohibited, although I know it may be "reconditioned." They do this at their own risk, and they should not complain if they exchange furniture for fragments.

Decoratively, and used with discretion, copies of Oriental or English lacquered pieces have a decided value, but it is far better that such copies, for American consumption, should be made in that country, if the word "consumption" is not to acquire a grim and expensive meaning. The Chinese work is so infinitely varied that the possible sources of inspiration have hardly been prospected, to say nothing of being explored. If the word "inspiration" be used in its proper sense, and not to indicate mere slavish copying, the examples illustrated here should be of considerable value.

While the subject of lacquer-work should properly be confined here to English furniture, to preserve the continuity of this series, it is impossible to forget that the art owes everything to its Oriental origin. English lacquer never even approaches either the Chinese or the Japanese, decoratively or technically, even at its best. At its worst, it is merely paint, varnish and crude ornament, and, what is more unfortunate for our enquiry, at no time is quality any indication of date, in spite of what so many writers have stated, and so positively. One can even find poor lacquer on expensive pieces, and also the reverse. In the height of its fashion in England, the art abounded with charlatans, among whom, Stalker and Parker, who published a folio volume in 1688,§ may be regarded as the most portentous. It is the old, old story, that no untechnical person can write a technical book, (or one which purports to be of a practical character) without exposing himself to a real craftsman. By such, of course, Stalker and Parker had no idea of being judged, any more than the "inventor" and purveyor of pills, warranted to cure all the diseases to which the flesh is heir, has any notion of submitting his formula to a council of physicians or chemists. His concern is only with the fool-crop, which, as Carlyle caustically remarked, is perennial.

§John Stalker of "The Golden Ball" and George Parker of Oxford; "A Treatise of Japaning and Varnishing, Being the Compleat Discovery of those Arts, with The best way of making all sorts of Varnish for Japan, Wood, Prints and Pictures. The Method of Guilding, Burnishing and Lackering, with the Art of Guilding, Separating and Refining Metals, etc.; etc.;" 1688.

DETAIL OF JAPANESE LACQUER

DETAILS OF JAPANESE ORNAMENT

A JAPANESE GARDEN PARTY

JAPANESE SPRAYS OF FLOWERS

CHINESE PICTURE PAINTED ON GLASS FROM BEHIND. IN ENGLISH LACQUERED FRAME, *c. 1720*

CHINESE SIX-FOLD SCREEN, GOLD ON BLACK GROUND. EARLY EIGHTEENTH CENTURY

FUJIYAMA IN DISTANCE

ONE OF A PAIR OF GREEN LACQUER CABINETS ON CARVED AND GESSO GILT STANDS. *c. 1710.* GOLD DECORATION IN THE CHINESE MANNER. SHOWN HERE CLOSED. IN COLOUR, QUALITY AND CONDITION THIS IS PROBABLY THE FINEST PAIR OF LACQUER CABINETS IN EXISTENCE

Courtesy of the Kent Gallery

THE SAME CABINET AS ON THE PRECEDING PAGE, HERE SHOWN OPEN

ON THIS AND THE FOLLOWING PAGE IS SHOWN A TWELVE-FOLD SCREEN OF POLYCHROME INCISED LACQUER ON A SEMI-TRANSPARENT BROWN GROUND. THE REVERSE SIDE, IN CHINESE CHARACTERS, RECORDS THE

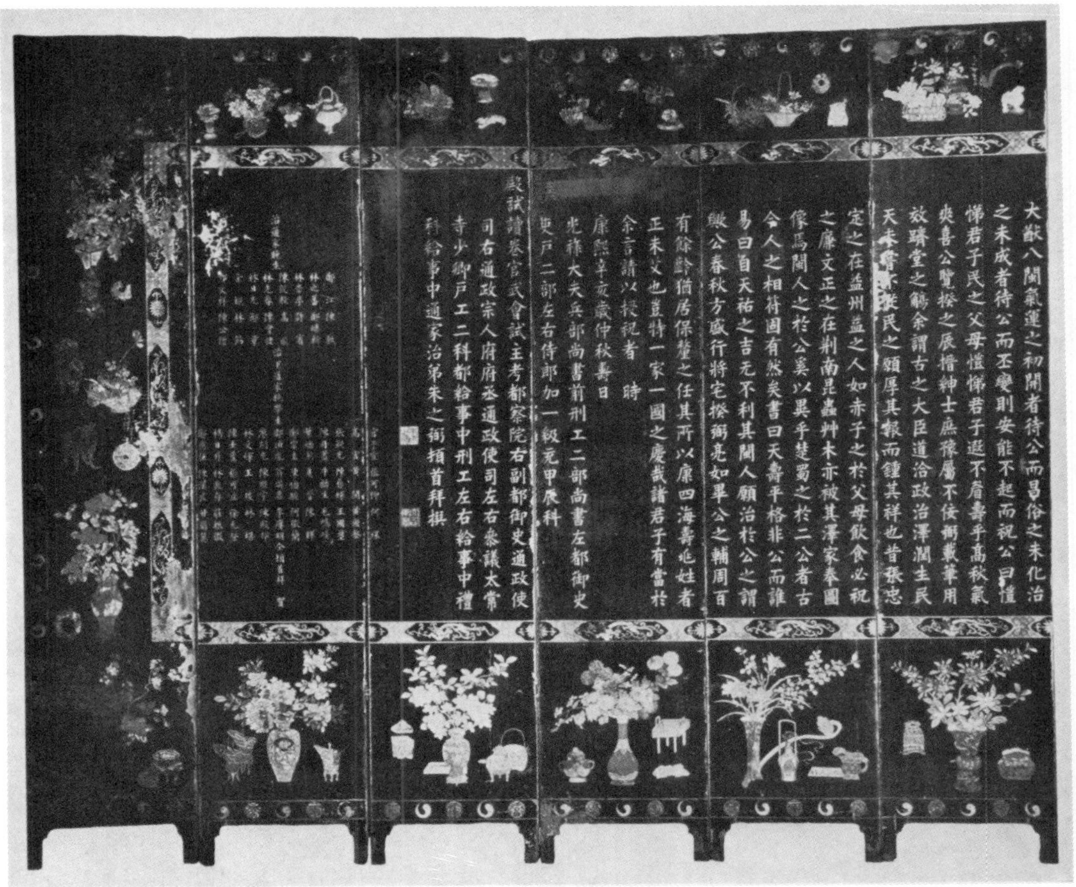

THE REVERSE OF THE SCREEN ABOVE

CIRCUMSTANCES OF THE PRESENTATION TO A CHINESE PRINCE, PROFESSOR IN AN IMPORTANT COLLEGE, BY HIS PUPILS, AND THE DATE *1671*. MANCHU DYNASTY; FINEST PERIOD OF CHINESE LACQUER

THE REVERSE OF THE SCREEN ABOVE

A SQUARE CABINET IN BLACK LACQUER ON A SILVER-GILT CARVED STAND, *c. 1670*, ENGLISH MAKE

OPEN VIEW OF THE CABINET ILLUSTRATED ON THE PRECEDING PAGE

BUREAU CABINET, GOLD DECORATION ON A GROUND OF RED LACQUER. ENGLISH, *c. 1710*

LACQUERED MIRROR FRAME; GOLD ON BLACK. ENGLISH, *c. 1700*

BLACK AND GOLD LACQUER DOUBLE CHEST ON SCROLLED-LEG STAND. GILT BRASS FINIALS AND ENRICHMENTS. ENGLISH, *c. 1720*

GOLD AND GREEN LACQUER CABINET ON CARVED GILT STAND. ENGLISH, *c.* 1720

BLACK AND GOLD LACQUERED CABINET ON CARVED GILT STAND. ENGLISH, *c.* 1730

CABINET OF RAISED GILT DECORATION ON A BLACK LACQUER GROUND. CARVED AND GILT STAND. ENGLISH, *c. 1730*

CABINET OF RAISED GOLD DECORATION ON A GROUND OF BLACK LACQUER, CARVED AND PARCEL-GILT STAND. ENGLISH, *c. 1720-5*

CABINET OF POLYCHROME. INCISED LACQUER ON CARVED GILT STAND. ENGLISH, *c. 1730*

CABINET ON CHEST STAND. GOLD ORNAMENT ON BLACK GROUND, *c. 1700*, ENGLISH WORK

CORNER CUPBOARD; GOLD ORNAMENT ON BLACK GROUND, ENGLISH, *c. 1740*

CHAPTER XIV

Early Mahogany Furniture

Mahogany begins to come into general use as the fashionable wood for furniture shortly after 1725. The change in the designing of pieces, however, is not so marked as one would suppose, considering that the early mahogany furniture is constructed almost entirely from the solid timber, whereas the later walnut is nearly always veneered. It has been pointed out before that it is easy to place a false significance on any change, by illustrating certain examples with undue prominence and ignoring others which conflict with theories or statements. There is no doubt that walnut was used, at the same time as other woods, long after mahogany had become generally accepted and was in wide demand. The new timber has many advantages over the old, which may, or may not, have been appreciated at the time. It is firmer in texture, harder in grain, yet just as easily worked, (the reference here is to the mahogany from Cuba and San Domingo, which was the only timber imported during the early years of the eighteenth century) comparatively free from sap, takes a friction or other polish much more readily than walnut; and last, but by no means least, the boards are wider —thus obviating jointing—and could be used in the solid without veneering, which meant a great saving in cost.

It might be supposed that a new wood, possessing these undeniable advantages, must have ousted all others very rapidly. Apart from the fact that the timber was heavily taxed at this time, the innate conservatism of a trade would count for a good deal, especially as the new solid construction must have involved the scrapping of veneering presses, cauls and screws, as obsolete. Perhaps this is why the era of the solid construction lasts for only a few years, and veneering is resumed again, shortly after 1740.

In the Midland districts, especially in Lancashire, even walnut had never become really popular, cherry being used to a considerable extent, and oak was at all times the favorite timber for carcase work, and even for finished surfaces, as much of the Lancashire oak dates from this early mahogany period.

It is unquestionable that certain very rapid changes do take place, in furniture design, between the years from 1725 and 1745, but one style does not replace or suppress the other, as one would suppose. Examples show that new features were incorporated with others of prior date, and from this one is compelled to date any piece by the latest detail which it exhibits. So much may be gathered from the examples illustrated here, in conjunction with the following account of the new features as they appear.

Some description of the stretchering of chairs and tables has already been given in the earlier pages, together with the positional and other changes which these stretchers undergo from 1660 to 1700. In the walnut pieces shortly after the accession of Anne these stretchers disappear entirely. At the same period the central splats of chairs become broader, without piercing, and are usually veneered. Later on this splat is again pierced, in various patterns and veneering is dispensed with altogether. The hoop-back, where the top rail joins the side balusters in one unbroken line, changes to the separate and flattened cresting-rail.

The next development is the lavish use of the "paper scroll," this being confined, almost exclusively, to chairs. Suggested probably by the classical volute, the rolling of stiff paper is deliberately imitated. Among the minor arts of the eighteenth century, not circumscribed by any particular period, is the decoration of boxes, mirrors and other small pieces with tightly-rolled paper of various colours, the rolls being glued vertically to form patterns, and afterwards etched with gold leaf. This fashion may have suggested the "paper-scrolling" of furniture. In chairs, the elaborate period of this scrolling coincides with the plain vertical piercing of back splats.

The arms of chairs and settees begin with a continuous line from back to seat-rail, but this fashion persists for only a few years, as the jointing of arm and support presents difficulties to the chairmaker.

In the succeeding manner the arm is distinct from its baluster, and finishes (a) in an eagle's head, (b) in that of a lion or other animal, and (c) in a scroll with or without leaf-carving. The feet of cabriole legs change in much the same way, but in no definite order, the club, the pad, the ball-and-claw, the paw-and-ball, the scroll and the leaf-carved feet appearing at all periods from 1720 to 1750, and in no chronological manner.

Seat-rails of chairs are first rounded at the corners (the plan of the seat being something like a truncated pear) but after 1720 the front is bowed or serpentine in shape, or straight. The usual plan-form of the early mahogany chair seat is that of a backward-tapering, straight-sided oblong.

The piercing of central splats also follows a definite line, beginning with the vase, either solid or fret-cut, then the vertical piercing like the stringing of a harp, afterwards an intricate fretting, commencing with the use of a device similar to a figure 8, repeated several times in the one design, and, lastly, an elaborate interlacing in patterns which may have been suggested by the intertwining of a flat tape. In the hands of the Chippendale School this last device again develops in two ways, in the piercing of a crude imitation of Gothic archings and in the form of a knotted and twined ribbon, the "Ribband-back" of the "Director."

The carving of the knees of cabriole legs also undergoes progressive elaboration. Commencing with the smooth cabriole, which is the most difficult of all to make, as carving can hide a multitude of errors of design—we find the escallop or Palmer's shell, then the acanthus, and, finally, the cabochon-and-leaf, which last carries us right into the Chippendale period.

One short-lived fashion, which comes in the years between 1730 and 1740, approximately, is that of the lion and satyr furniture, rare in any event, but very exceptional in walnut. The lion mask is generally used for the knees of cabriole legs, sometimes as a finish to arms, but the latter is very unusual. The lion's head on the knees is nearly always accompanied by the lion's paw for the feet, but this paw-finish persists after the fashion for this lion furniture has departed. The reason is, in all probability, that the paw-foot was cheaper and easier to carve than the claw-and-ball.

With centre and side tables the applied fret is used for friezes, some years before the date of Chippendale (to which the fret is generally supposed to belong) but the design of these early frets is either that of a running scroll (sometimes described as a "wave-moulding") or a copy of the well-known Grecian key-pattern. The geometrical or the enclosed fret is later. An enclosed fret is one in which the pattern has to be drilled in places for the insertion of the saw; the running fret is one in which the saw may enter and leave the wood without holes.

In this period, from 1725 to 1745, the first mahogany years, must be placed the fashion for gesso decoration, ornament formed by a brush and a thick medium, generally a compound of gypsum, resin and glue, partly modelled by the brush and afterwards cut by the carver's tools. Gesso, needing some disguising (as it masquerades as carving) is generally gilded.

Referring to things which are absent, as well as to others which are present, inlay of any kind is highly exceptional during these mahogany years, and veneering is used sparingly. The influence of the architect becomes very noticeable in the furniture of this period, not only in the classical sections of mouldings and in the use of pilasters with capitals and bases, but also in the designing of entire pieces. In the fifteen years from 1725 onwards, we find cabinets and bookcases which suggest buildings in timber rather than examples of cabinetmaker work and design, nor are chairs free from this architectural suggestion.

The easy method of describing this rapid evolution in furniture fashions would be to select examples and illustrate them in chronological order, but to do this must convey the idea that there was an orderly progression, without over-lapping. I adopted this system in my first book, "English Furniture of the Eighteenth Century," and I have regretted it since, yet in a work of the size of that book I am unable to suggest another method.

One point cannot be over-emphasised; that is, that the latest detail in any piece establishes its date, no matter how early the other features may be. There is another caution to the student, which may be no more than hinted at here; that is, to remember that forgeries of this early mahogany furniture abound, especially in the pieces of the Lion Period, and while these may be the work of skilled craftsmen, (practised deceivers would be the better description, perhaps) they are, as a rule, ignorantly designed, with a jumble of details which were never used at any one period, combined with others which were never used at all. Once the mistake is made of accepting these pieces as genuine examples of their time, we begin to erect false theories on inaccurate premises. These theories have the unhappy knack of persisting for many years. The "faker" is older than the expert; and that is why nearly all the earlier books on English furniture (my own among the number) are nearly worthless as far as accurate data is concerned. In this connection, the temptation is irresistible to point out that the untechnical expert in antique furniture is a contradiction in terms. This is not to say that a maker of furniture is necessarily an expert, but it is certain that from his ranks the experts of the future must be drawn. The knowledge of woods (the reference here is not to the differences between oak, walnut, mahogany or other woods, but to the varieties of each, the countries of origin, the date when imported and such-like minutiæ) of constructional details, of tools which were, and which were not, used at certain periods, the instantaneous appreciation of the kind of saw which has been used to cut a plank or a fret, all knowledge which is indispensable to the expert, must be acquired in the workshop. It is assimilated there, sub-consciously, in the daily routine, and it is impossible, in later years, to state when and where particular information was gathered. To attempt to gain this knowledge outside the workshop is hopeless; it is akin to learning surgery outside the walls of the hospital and operating theatre, from the pages of a book, for instance, or attempting to pick up a language without either book or instructor. It is just in these minute points where the greatest gulf yawns between amateur and expert, which no "flair" can bridge.

It must not be supposed that the brief description given in these pages exhausts all the changes which English furniture undergoes in the years from 1720 to 1750. One meets with perfectly genuine examples quite frequently which introduce new details, or others in which the different features are all well known but combined in a novel way. In addition, several pieces are to be found which are new in purpose as well as in design. The walnut dining table is practically unknown and was, probably, never made. The walnut side table is very rare, and the pedestal—or flat-top writing table had not superseded the bureau or escritoire before about 1735. In fact, the slant-top bureau was still made, right up to the close of the eighteenth century, if not to a still later date. The sideboard (using the term in the modern sense as indicating a piece of furniture with cupboards or drawers) belongs neither to the walnut nor to the early mahogany years. The bergère chair, one with open padded arms and solid-upholstered back and seat, is essentially a mahogany piece, that is, it belongs to the mahogany years; the same may be said of the multiple-top card table. The corner cupboard or cabinet is conspicuously rare in the walnut years, and the glazing and latticing of cabinet or bookcase doors is just as exceptional. The law of progress, as outlined by Herbert Spencer in his "First Principles," a progression from the homogeneous to the heterogeneous, is true of English furniture as of every other change in the organic world. The piece of many functions gives way to the other with one or none. In this multiplication of types are found "occasional" tables and small articles, made only to fill, or "furnish" a room, not to serve any useful purpose. At the first thought, this increasing variety in furniture types might be held to indicate the growing wealth of the English people. In fact, the reason is much more basic, and infinitely more grim. From the fifteenth century, up to the middle of the nineteenth, the status of the English working classes had steadily deteriorated. It has been computed that the produce which could have been bought with the reward of seven weeks of labour in *circa* 1450 could not have been purchased with sixty-seven weeks' pay in 1820. This fine eighteenth-century furniture was the work of poorly-paid craftsmen, and labour was reckoned as of little account in computing the cost. The Earl of Mansfield does not concern himself with the price to be charged for the frames of the great pier-glasses at Kenwood, but he is most precise and particular about the cost of the silvered glass. Modern machinery has considerably lessened the prices of present-day reproductions, and it is difficult to apprehend the amount of labour which must have been necessary when every plank and board had to be sawn and planed by hand, and when machinery of any kind was something of the far-distant future, the only labour-saving device being the treadle lathe. If there be one change more marked than any other, since the close of the eighteenth century, it is that materials have gradually cheapened and the cost of labour has correspondingly increased. It is difficult to imagine the days when the price of the actual labour must have been considered as something of little account, almost as an afterthought. Little wonder, then, that so much fine furniture was made at this period, sufficient almost to re-furnish modern America. Its cost must have been almost negligible, compared with that of the present day, even with modern machinery thrown in.

In conclusion, if the reader, looking through the illustrations of this chapter, has the idea that many of the pieces have every appearance of belonging to what is generally regarded as the Chippendale Style, the main purpose of the chapter will have been served. Actually, when Thomas Chippendale came to London, in *circa* 1748, English furniture styles were in a highly-developed state, and he did little more than to collect the available trade patterns and give them artistic permanence in his book, "The Gentleman and Cabinet Maker's Director," the first edition of which was published in 1754.

CARVED MAHOGANY WRITING TABLE. THE ARCHITECT-INSPIRED FURNITURE OF *1730-5*

MAHOGANY AND PARCEL-GILT WRITING TABLE. PROPERTY OF THE DUKE OF DEVONSHIRE. THE SEMI-ARCHITECTURAL MANNER OF *1730-5*

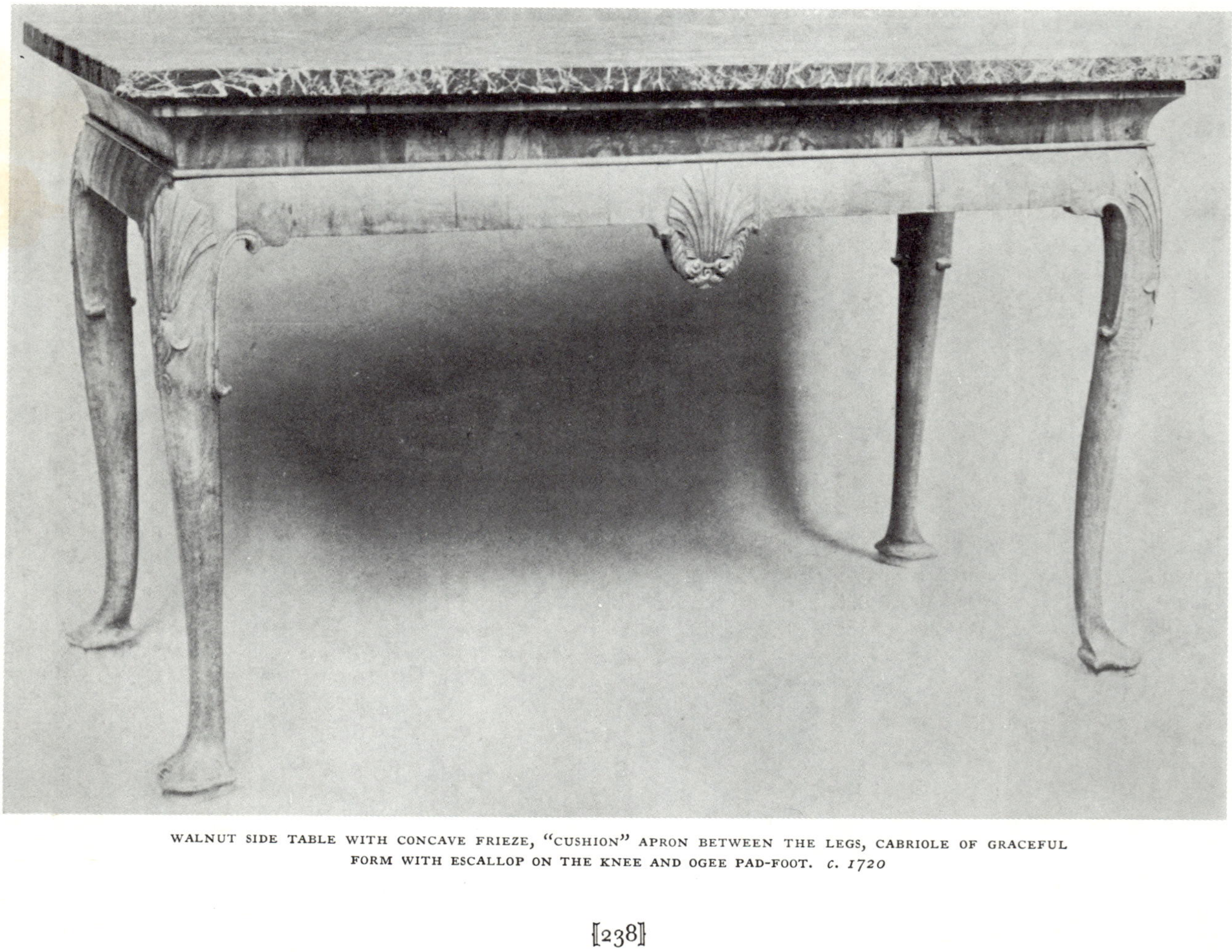

WALNUT SIDE TABLE WITH CONCAVE FRIEZE, "CUSHION" APRON BETWEEN THE LEGS, CABRIOLE OF GRACEFUL FORM WITH ESCALLOP ON THE KNEE AND OGEE PAD-FOOT. *c. 1720*

ENLARGED DETAIL OF THE LION MAHOGANY SIDE TABLE BELOW, SHOWING THE LEGS AND CENTRAL CARTOUCHE

ONE OF A PAIR OF MAHOGANY SIDE TABLES WITH MARBLE TOPS. *c. 1735.* THE LION PERIOD OF ENGLISH MAHOGANY. THIS TABLE REPRESENTS THE MOST VIRILE PERIOD OF ENGLISH FURNITURE OF THE EIGHTEENTH CENTURY. THE FRIEZE IS CROSS-BAND VENEER WITH THE CENTRAL CARTOUCHE AND ITS FOLIAGE APPLIED

Courtesy of the Kent Gallery

CARVED AND GILT ARMCHAIR. THE INFLUENCE OF THE ARCHITECT (WILLIAM KENT?) IS MORE NOTICEABLE IN THE PROPORTIONS THAN IN THE ACTUAL DESIGN. NOT A CHAIR-MAKER'S PATTERN. *c. 1730*

CARVED AND GILT SIDE TABLE OF SIMILAR TYPE TO THAT SHOWN BELOW. THE INFLUENCE OF THE ARCHITECT IS NOTICEABLE IN THE DESIGN OF THESE TABLES. *c. 1730-40*

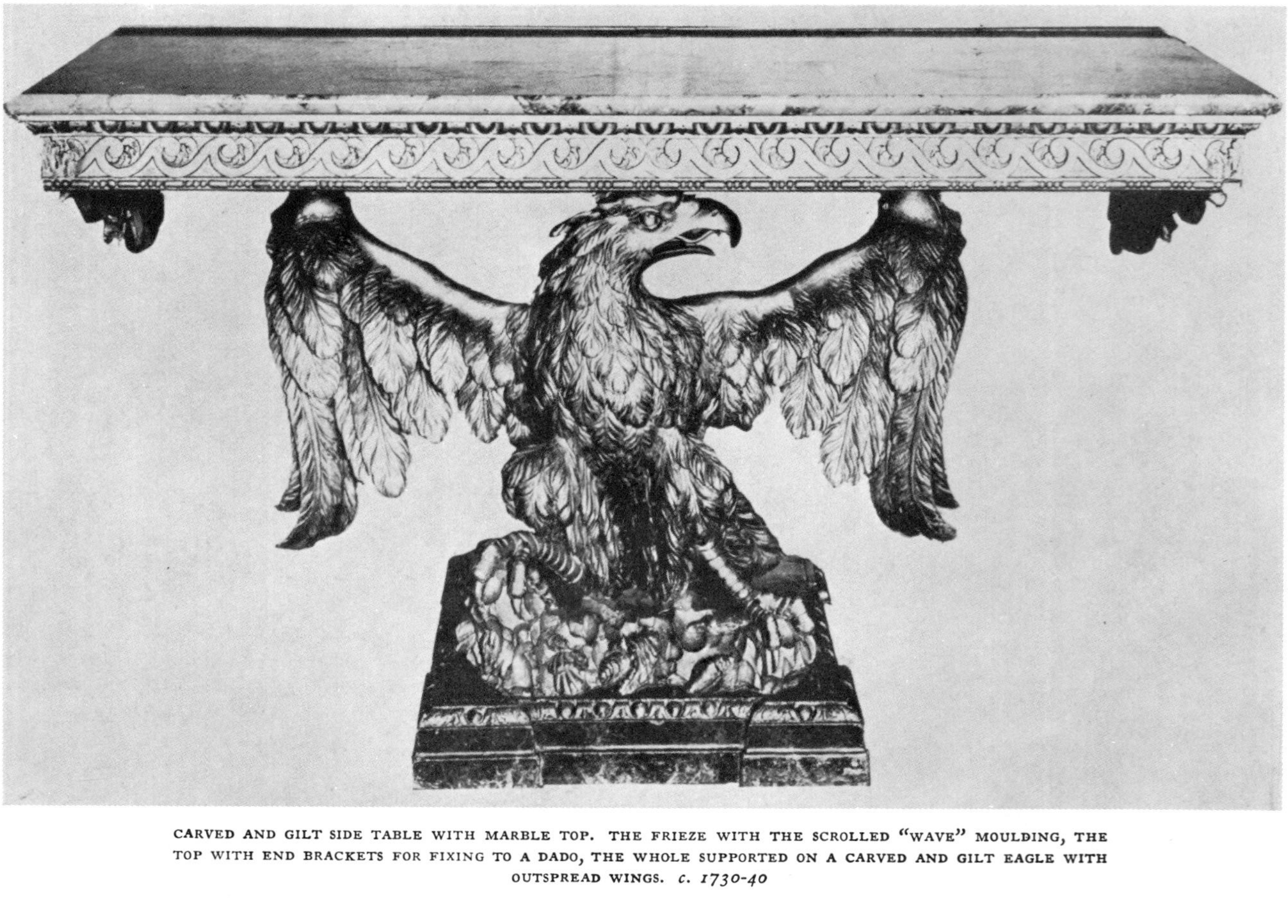

CARVED AND GILT SIDE TABLE WITH MARBLE TOP. THE FRIEZE WITH THE SCROLLED "WAVE" MOULDING, THE TOP WITH END BRACKETS FOR FIXING TO A DADO, THE WHOLE SUPPORTED ON A CARVED AND GILT EAGLE WITH OUTSPREAD WINGS. *c. 1730-40*

WALNUT TABLE. THE CABRIOLE LEGS OF THE GEORGE I PERIOD WITH THE ESCALLOP SHELL ON THE KNEE, LEAF-CARVED EAR-PIECE AND SCROLL-AND-LEAF FOOT. *c. 1720*

A RARE EXAMPLE OF A PIER TABLE WITH MARBLE TOP, CENTRAL LEG, AND SIDE BRACKETS FOR WALL FIXING. *c. 1740*

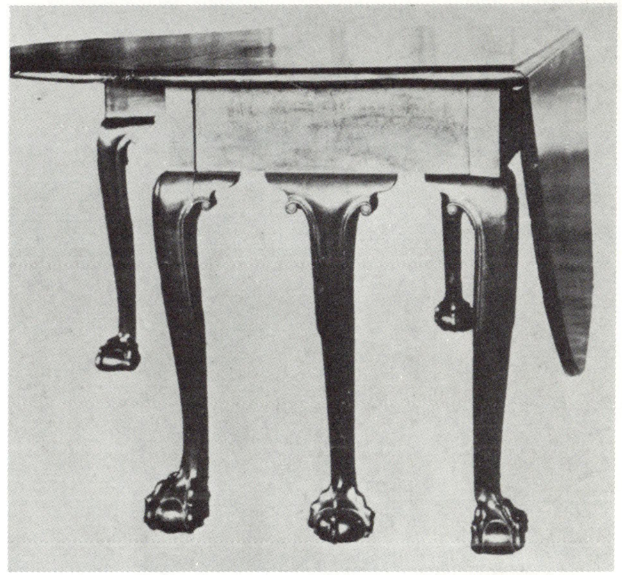

MIDDLE SECTION OF A MAHOGANY DINING TABLE. THE TOP HAS BEEN ROUNDED AND EDGE-MOULDED AT A LATER DATE. THIS TABLE HAS TWO HINGED LEGS AT EACH SIDE. *c. 1735-40*

MAHOGANY CARD TABLE WITH EARLY TYPE OF CLAW-AND-BALL, WITHOUT WEBBING; KNEES CARVED WITH ORNATE CABOCHON-AND-LEAF. *c. 1750*

CARVED AND PARCEL-GILT TABLE WITH MARBLE TOP. THE ARCHITECTURAL TYPE OF *1730*

CARVED AND GESSO GILT SIDE TABLE WITH HEADS OF RED INDIANS ON THE KNEES AND CURIOUSLY HOCKED PAW FEET. *c. 1730*

WALNUT CARD TABLE. THE TYPE FROM WHICH THE PHILADELPHIA MAHOGANY OF *1760-80* DEVELOPS. *c. 1710-15*

MAHOGANY TRIPLE-TOP CARD, TEA AND BACKGAMMON TABLE (SEE BELOW). NOTE THE UNUSUAL TREATMENT OF THE KNEE. *c. 1740*

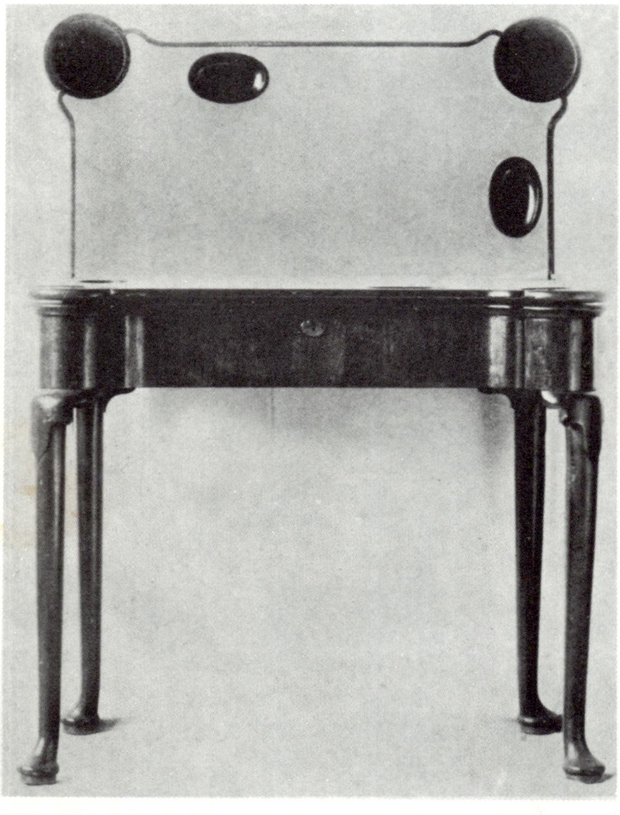

THE TABLE ABOVE AT THE RIGHT WITH THE FIRST TOP RAISED TO SHOW THE FLAT DISHINGS FOR CANDLESTICKS, AND THE MONEY SAUCERS OR "GUINEA POCKETS"

THE TABLE ABOVE WITH THE SECOND TOP RAISED TO SHOW THE CHESS BOARD AND THE INLAID DARTS FOR BACKGAMMON. WITH THIS GOES A FRAME WITH PINS WHICH DROPS INTO THE BUSHED HOLES IN THE TOP TO ACT AS A RIM WHEN THE GAME IS PLAYED

MAHOGANY CARD TABLE (OPEN AND CLOSED) *c. 1750*. THE HINGED SIDE, OR "CONCERTINA" OPENING WHERE BOTH LEGS ARE PULLED BACKWARDS, AND THE SIDES KEPT RIGID BY A SLIDE IN GROOVES INSIDE THE FRAMING

MAHOGANY CARD TABLE (OPEN AND CLOSED) *c. 1745*. UNLINED TOP AND SINGLE PULL-OUT LEG

CARVED MAHOGANY SIDE TABLE WITH CONVEX APRON. THIS STYLE OF TABLE HAS BEEN INCORRECTLY KNOWN AS "IRISH CHIPPENDALE." THERE IS NO EVIDENCE FOR THE IRISH ORIGIN, AND THE DATE IS CERTAINLY PRIOR TO THAT OF CHIPPENDALE BY MORE THAN TEN YEARS. NOTE LATER FORM OF BALL-AND-CLAW WITH WEBBING BETWEEN THE CLAWS. *1740-5*

MAHOGANY BUREAU ON CABRIOLE-LEG STAND. *c. 1750.* THE FINAL PHASE OF THE LION MAHOGANY CARRIED ALMOST INTO THE FIRST YEARS OF THE CHIPPENDALE PERIOD

CARVED MAHOGANY CENTRE TABLE WITH MARBLE TOP. THIS TYPE PROBABLY ORIGINATED FROM THE WESTERN MIDLAND AND HAS BEEN KNOWN AS "IRISH CHIPPENDALE." *c. 1740-5*

MAHOGANY CARD TABLE. THE EARLY CLUB FEET ARE RETAINED IN A TABLE OF *c. 1745*. THE SIDES PULL OUT IN CONCERTINA FORM

MAHOGANY CARD, TEA, BACKGAMMON AND WRITING TABLE—THREE TOPS. THE BOX SEEN IN THE ILLUSTRATION RISES WHEN A SPRING-CATCH IS DEPRESSED. AT THE BACK IS A HINGED FLAP WHICH ACTS AS A READING DESK. NOTE THE "BLOCKING" OF THE DRAWER FRONTS, A FEATURE MORE USUAL IN AMERICAN THAN IN ENGLISH FURNITURE. *c. 1740*

MAHOGANY DRESSING OR POWDER TABLE. *c. 1740*. THE TYPE OF THE GEORGE II MAHOGANY WHICH CARRIES ON THE TRADITION OF THE LATE WALNUT YEARS. THE LATEST DETAIL HERE IS THE SCROLLED FOOT

MAHOGANY CARD TABLE WITH EXTENDING "CONCERTINA" SIDES. A LATE SPECIMEN PRESERVING ALL THE VIGOUR OF THE EARLY WORK. NOTE THE TENDONS OF THE CLAWS CARRIED UP THE LEG. A VERY FINE EXAMPLE. *c. 1750*

MAHOGANY SIDE TABLE OF THE LION PERIOD. THE KNEES OF THE LEGS CARVED WITH A VARIATION OF THE CABOCHON-AND-LEAF. THE LION'S MASK CENTRES THE FRONT FRAMING AND THE FEET ARE PAW-AND-BALL IN PLACE OF THE MORE USUAL CLAW-AND-BALL. *c. 1735*

MIDDLE SECTION OF A DINING TABLE MADE FROM SABICU, A VERY HARD AND HEAVY WOOD IMPORTED FROM CUBA. THIS TABLE IS UNUSUAL IN HAVING TWO HINGED LEGS ON EACH SIDE, PROBABLY NECESSARY TO SUPPORT THE HEAVY FLAPS. *c. 1730*

MIDDLE SECTION OF A MAHOGANY DINING TABLE. THE USUAL PLAN WAS TO CUT THE TOPS TO OVAL OR ROUND FORM FOR USE AS CENTRE TABLES. ORIGINAL TABLES OF THIS KIND ARE IN THREE TO FIVE SECTIONS. *c. 1730*

GILT GESSO TABLE. THE ORNAMENT IS OF GYPSUM, RESIN AND GLUE, MODELLED PARTLY WITH THE BRUSH, AND FINISHED WITH THE CARVER'S TOOLS, AND OVERLAID WITH GOLD. THE TURNED-IN CORNERS TO THE TOP AND THE CONCAVE FRIEZE ARE TYPICAL OF THE *1720* PERIOD TO WHICH THIS TABLE BELONGS

MAHOGANY CARD TABLE OF THE FIRST CHIPPENDALE YEARS, *c. 1750.* HERE WE HAVE A NEW VARIATION OF THE PAW-AND-BALL FOOT

GILT CARVED AND GESSO SIDE TABLE. LIONS' HEADS ON KNEES AND LIONS' PAW FEET. THERE IS SOME SUGGESTION OF ARCHITECT-INFLUENCE IN THE DESIGN OF THIS TABLE. *c. 1735*

MAHOGANY CARVED AND PARCEL-GILT SIDE TABLE. A VARIATION OF THE LION PERIOD, WITH HEADS STRONGLY RESEMBLING THOSE OF RED INDIANS ON THE KNEES. THE LION'S HEAD IS IN CENTRE OF "APRON." *c. 1735*

CARVED MAHOGANY SIDE TABLE; IN THE CENTRE IS A CREST WITH A WINGED HART. SATYR MASKS ON THE KNEES OF THE LEGS. THE FINER DEVELOPMENT OF THE CRUDE WEST COUNTRY STYLE USUALLY INCORRECTLY KNOWN AS "IRISH CHIPPENDALE." *c. 1740*

THE TOP OF THE GESSO SIDE TABLE BELOW WITH A CARVED GADROON ON THE SURROUNDING THUMB-MOULDING

GILT SIDE TABLE AND STOOL WITH CARVED AND GESSO DECORATION. BOTH PIECES BELONG TO THE LION PERIOD. THE TOP OF THE TABLE IS SHOWN ABOVE. *c. 1735*

MAHOGANY SIDE TABLE WITH MARBLE TOP. THE DEVELOPMENT AWAY FROM THE LION PERIOD, WITH THE PAW STILL RETAINED, BUT THE GRECIAN KEY-PATTERN USED FOR THE FRIEZE. NOTE THE POWERFUL DESIGN OF THE KNEES OF THE LEGS. *c. 1740*

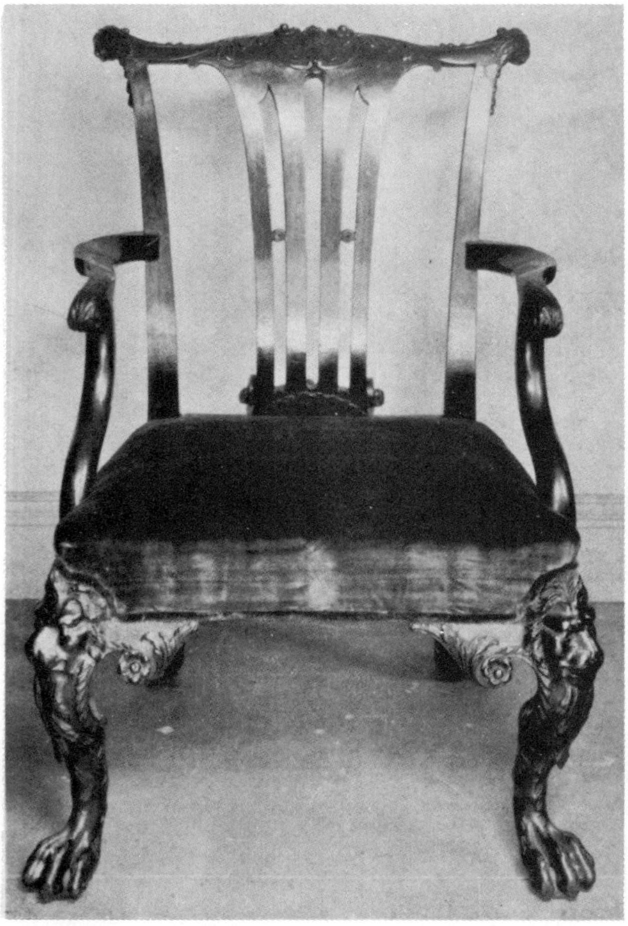

MAHOGANY ARMCHAIR. PROBABLY THE LATEST DEVELOPMENT OF THE LION PERIOD. THIS CHAIR HAS THE EARLY VERTICAL PIERCING OF THE BACK SPLAT, WITH SCROLL FINISH TO THE TOP RAIL OF THE BACK. *c. 1740*

CARVED AND GILT SIDE CHAIR OF THE LION PERIOD. *c. 1735.* THE BOLD CABRIOLE LEGS ARE MANED, HOCKED AND FINISHED IN PAW-AND-BALL FEET. OLD FORM OF THE HOOP BACK AND SEAT RAIL WITH GRECIAN KEY-PATTERN

FRONT AND BACK VIEWS OF ONE OF THE CHAIRS FROM THE SET BELOW. THE OLD FORM OF HOOP-BACK HAS BEEN RETAINED, HERE UPHOLSTERED SOLID. THE WOOD IS HARD SPANISH MAHOGANY FROM SAN DOMINGO. NOTE THE ENORMOUS PROJECTION OF THE LION MASKS AND THE PAW FEET AND THE THICK TIMBER FROM WHICH THE LEGS HAVE BEEN CUT

A REMARKABLE SET OF TWELVE SINGLE CHAIRS AND ONE SETTEE, ALL IN ORIGINAL FINE-STITCH NEEDLEPOINT. *c. 1730-5*

CARVED MAHOGANY SETTEE OF THE LION YEARS, *c. 1735.* HERE WE HAVE THE LION-MASK ON THE KNEES OF THE OUTSIDE FRONT LEGS AND ON THE TERMINALS TO THE ARMS, AND THE CABOCHON ON THE CENTRE LEG AND THE TOP RAILS OF THE BACKS. THE CARVED APRON-PIECES UNDER THE SEAT RAIL SUGGEST THE SO-CALLED IRISH CHIPPENDALE

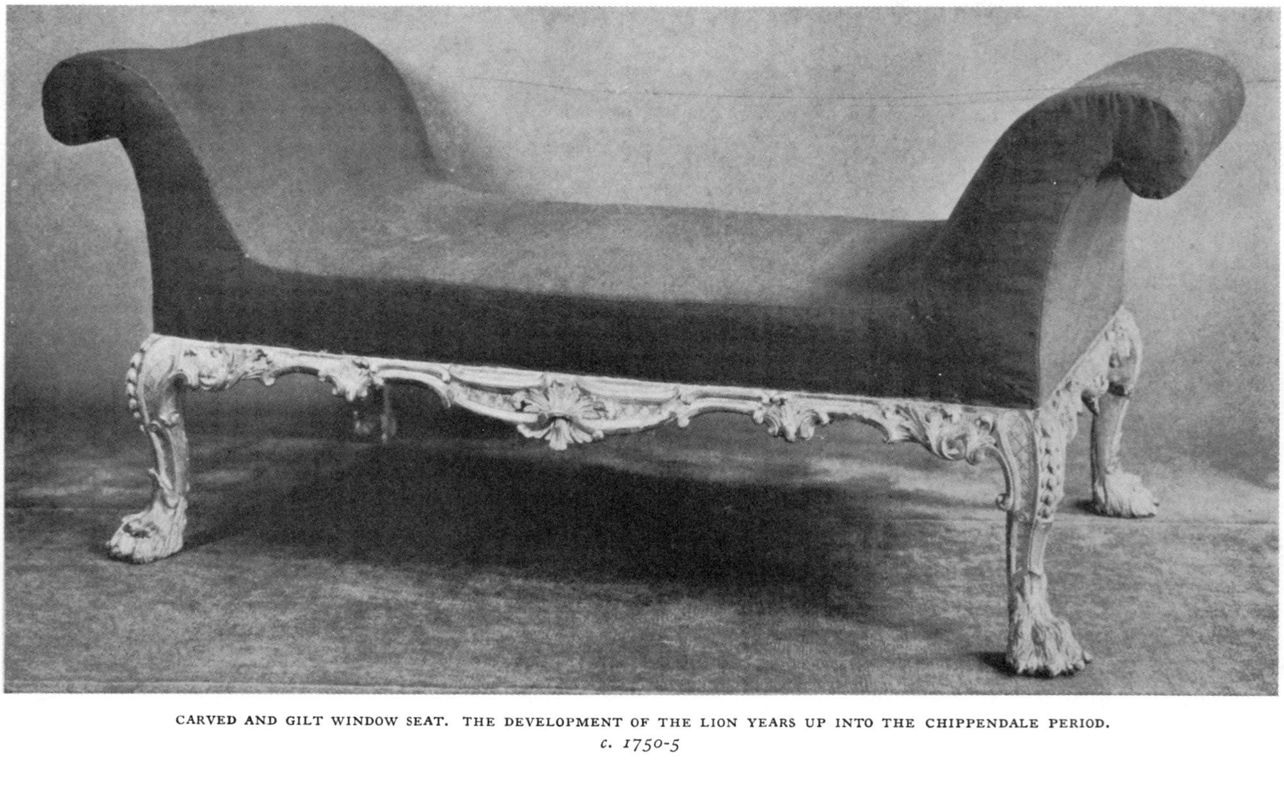

CARVED AND GILT WINDOW SEAT. THE DEVELOPMENT OF THE LION YEARS UP INTO THE CHIPPENDALE PERIOD. *c. 1750-5*

MAHOGANY ARM AND SIDE CHAIR (FRONT AND BACK VIEWS) SHOWING THE VERTICAL PIERCING OF THE BACK SPLAT, THE DEVELOPMENT FROM THE HOOP-BACK TO THE FLATTENED TOP RAIL, THE USE OF THE VOLUTE AT THE BACK AND THE MARKED OUTWARD SPLAY OF THE BACK AND LEGS. *c. 1735*

WALNUT SIDE CHAIR. THE SIMPLE VERTICAL PIERCING OF THE CENTRAL SPLAT. *c. 1725*

MAHOGANY SIDE CHAIR. ANOTHER VARIATION; THE VASE-SHAPING OF THE CENTRAL SPLAT. *c. 1745*

WALNUT ARM AND SIDE CHAIR. THE FASHION FOR THE SCROLL FINISH TO TOP RAIL, ARMS AND FEET. *c. 1740*

WALNUT SIDE CHAIR. THE SIMPLE PIERCED VASE-SPLAT. *c. 1725*

WALNUT CHAIR WITH FAN SHELL OR PALMETTE AND SHAPED OR "APRON" FRONT RAIL. *c. 1735.* NOTE SIMILARITY TO TWO CHAIRS BELOW

WALNUT CHAIR. A VARIATION ON THE PATTERN ABOVE AT RIGHT, HERE WITH STRAIGHT SIDE BALUSTERS AND SEAT RAIL. THE CRESTING PALMETTE IS HERE ELABORATED. *c. 1735-40*

MAHOGANY CHAIR. THE ELABORATED DEVELOPMENT OF THE CHAIR ABOVE AND AT THE LEFT WITH THE SCROLL USED MORE EXTENSIVELY, BUT WITH THE SAME CRESTING AS AT THE LEFT. *c. 1740*

MAHOGANY SETTEE OF RARE FORM, WITH TWO OUTER BALUSTERS AND FOUR SPLATS TO THE BACK. THE SPLATS ARE PIERCED IN IMITATION OF TAPE PATTERNS. THIS EXAMPLE, ALTHOUGH HAVING THE FLATTENED "CUPID'S BOW" TOP RAIL, IS EARLIER THAN THE CHIPPENDALE PERIOD. THE SEAT IS UNUSUALLY DEEP, NEARLY 25 INCHES. *c. 1740*

MAHOGANY SIDE CHAIR. THE DEVELOPMENT FROM THE HOOPED-BACK, WITH THE VASE-SHAPED PIERCED SPLAT. *c. 1740*

MAHOGANY SIDE CHAIR. THE STYLE JUST DEVELOPING AWAY FROM THE HOOP-BACK. CENTRAL SPLAT SHAPED IN THE FORM OF THREE BELLS, ONE PIERCED AND TWO CARVED. *c. 1745*

CARVED MAHOGANY CHAIR-BACK SETTEE. THIS IS A LATE EXAMPLE, AS INDICATED BY THE PIERCING OF THE SPLATS AND THE CARVING OF THE FRONT LEGS, BUT THE OLDER FORM OF HOOP-BACK IS RETAINED. *c. 1745*

MAHOGANY SIDE CHAIR. THE EARLIER HOOP-BACK USED IN A LATER MODEL. NOTE THE SWAG-AND-TASSEL CARVING TO THE TOP RAIL OF THE BACK, AND THE TYPICAL PIERCING OF THE CENTRAL SPLAT. *c. 1745*

MAHOGANY CHAIR WITH SWAG-AND-TASSEL CARVING AND FRONT LEGS, SIMILAR TO CHAIR AT THE LEFT, OF ABOUT SAME DATE, IN SPITE OF LATER STYLE OF TOP RAIL

MAHOGANY SIDE CHAIR. EXTREME DEVELOPMENT OF INTERLACED CENTRAL SPLAT. THE KNEES CARVED WITH OAK LEAVES AND ACORNS. HEAVY SCROLLING OF TOP RAIL. *c. 1745-50*

MAHOGANY SIDE CHAIR. THE INTERLACED BACK SPLAT OF *c. 1745*

MAHOGANY ARMCHAIR, INTERLACED FORM OF CENTRAL SPLAT. *c. 1745*

MAHOGANY ARMCHAIR WITH DRAPERY SWAGS AND TASSELLED CORDS TO THE TOP RAIL OF THE BACK, AND CENTRAL SPLAT DESIGNED IN IMITATION OF THE INTERLACING OF TAPE. *c. 1740*

WALNUT SIDE CHAIR WITH SIMPLE PIERCED SPLAT AND SCROLL FINISH TO THE TOP RAIL. *c. 1745*

MAHOGANY ARMCHAIR WITH THE PIERCED BACK SPLAT OF *c. 1750* PERIOD. THE KNEES ARE CARVED WITH THE CABOCHON-AND-LEAF. THIS STYLE OF CHAIR IS USUALLY REFERRED TO AS "CHIPPENDALE" ALTHOUGH IT HAS NONE OF THE CHARACTERISTICS OF THE "DIRECTOR" STYLE

MAHOGANY CHAIR, PARCEL GILT AND COVERED WITH NEEDLEPOINT. THIS CHAIR HAS BEEN DESIGNED TO STRADDLE ACROSS, HORSE-FASHION, WITH THE CHIN RESTING IN THE LUNETTE IN THE BACK, TO WATCH A "MAIN" OF COCK-FIGHTING. *c. 1750-5*

MAHOGANY BERGÈRE CHAIR. AN ELABORATED VARIATION OF THE CHAIR BELOW. *c. 1750*

MAHOGANY ARMCHAIR. THE APPROACH TO CHIPPENDALE TYPE WHERE CENTRAL SPLAT IS PIERCED AND HEAVILY CARVED. *c. 1750-5*

MAHOGANY BERGÈRE CHAIR. A TYPICAL EXAMPLE OF THE CABOCHON-AND-LEAF DECORATION HERE USED ON THE KNEES AND THE ARMS. *c. 1740*

MAHOGANY SIDE CHAIR OF THE LION PERIOD. THE TASSEL CARVING OF THE TOP RAIL IS FOUND ON MANY CHAIRS AT THIS DATE. *c. 1735*

MAHOGANY BERGÈRE CHAIR WITH LION MASKS ON THE KNEES AND ALSO AS A FINISH TO THE ARMS. *c. 1735-40*

MAHOGANY BERGÈRE AND SIDE CHAIR. THE FULL DEVELOPMENT OF THE CABOCHON-AND-LEAF, THE CRESTING UP OF THE FRONT LEGS OVER THE SEAT FRAME, AND THE FRET APPLIED OVER THE UPHOLSTERY AND THE PAW FEET ARE ALL DETAILS OF *c. 1740*

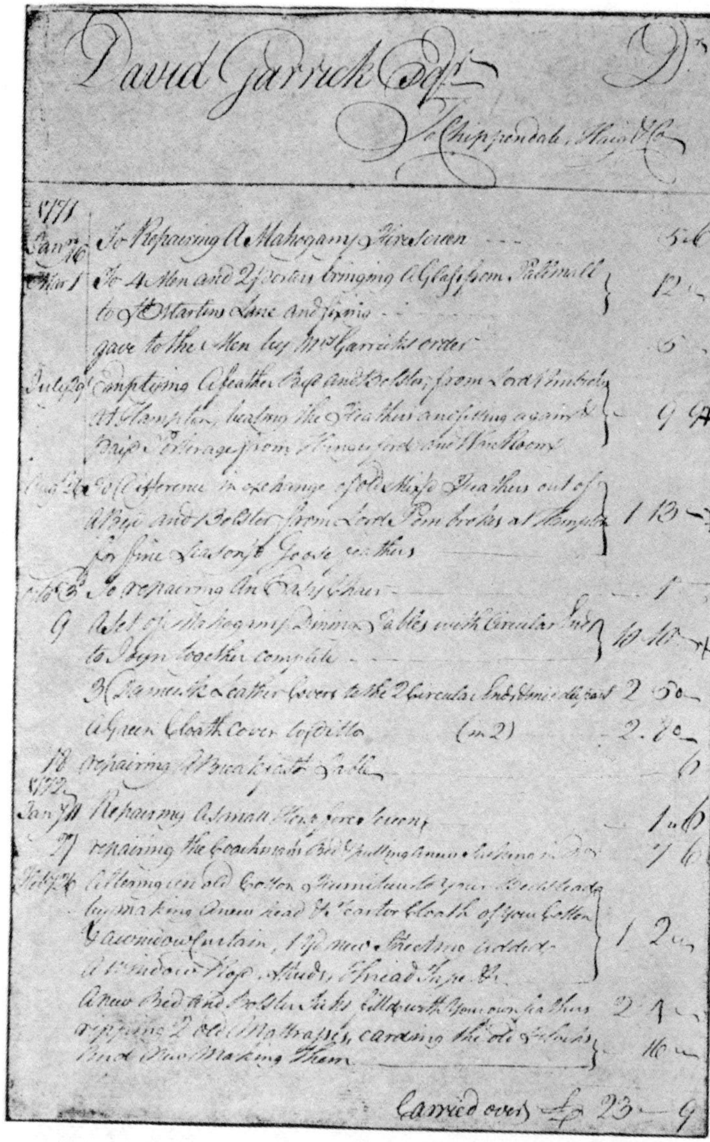

FAC-SIMILE OF FIRST PAGE OF ACCOUNTS OF CHIPPENDALE, HAIG & CO. FOR THE FURNISHING OF DAVID GARRICK'S HOUSE IN THE ADELPHI

David Garrick Esq. Dr.

To Chippendale, Haig & Co.

			£	s	d
*1771					
Jan	16	To Repairing a Mahogany Firescreen		5	6
Mar	1	To 4 Men and 2 porters bringing a Glass from Pallmall to St. Martins Lane and fixing		12	—
		gave to the Men by Mrs. Garricks order		5	—
July	29	Emptying a feather Bed and Bolster, from Lord Pembrokes at Hampton, beating the Feathers and fitting again & paid Porterage from Hungerford and Ware Room		9	9
Aug	26	To difference in exchange of old Mixd Feathers out of a Bed and Bolster from Lord Pembrokes at Hampton for fine season'd Goose feathers	1	13	—
Oct	3	To repairing an Easy Chair		1	—
	9	A set of Mahogany Dining Tables with Circular Ends to Joyn together complete	10	10	—
		3 Damask Leather Covers to the 2 Circular Ends & middle part	2	5	—
		A Green Cloath cover to ditto (in 2)	2	8	—
	18	repairing a Breakfast Table			6
1772					
Jan	11	Repairing a small Horse fire Screen		1	6
	27	Repairing the Coachman's Bed and putting a new Sacking in Do		7	6
Feb	26	Altering an old Cotton Furniture to your Bedstead by making a new head & Teastor Cloath of your Cotton & a window Curtain, 1 yd new Sheeting added A window Rod studs, Thread Tape etc	1	2	—
		A new Bed and Bolster Ticks† filld with your own feathers	2	4	—
		ripping 2 old Mattrasses, carding the old Flocks and new making them		16	—
		Carried over	£23	—	9

* Allowance should of course be made for the difference in the value of currency in the eighteenth century.

† Case.

A PAGE FROM THE ACCOUNT BOOKS OF CHIPPENDALE, HAIG & CO.

CHAPTER XV

Thomas Chippendale and the "Director"

TO STATE THE LEADING FACTS in the life of Thomas Chippendale, so far as they concern this enquiry, it is not necessary to enter into any minute details. He was born at Otley, a Yorkshire village, some time during the early part of 1718. He was baptised June 8th of that year, as the registers show. He was the son of John Chippendale, a joiner, his mother being Mary, the daughter of Thomas Drake, an Otley mason. The Chippendales had married three years before, and the mother did not die until ten years after Thomas was born; so he was, in all probability, not the only child.

How far the early Yorkshire years, and his father's connections, subsequently served Thomas Chippendale in securing for him the patronage of Sir Rowland Winn of Nostell Priory or that of Edwin Lascelles of Gawthorp (afterwards Harewood House) no precise information is available. His work in both houses was done under the superintendence and to the designs of Robert Adam, whose influence may have been, and probably was, more certain than any locally-acquired wealthy patronage.

Thomas Chippendale married Catherine Redshaw at St. George's Chapel, Hyde Park, May 19th, 1748, being then in his thirtieth year. The following December he commenced business on his own account, in Conduit Street, Long Acre (his first shop in London after his arrival from Otley) removing to St. Martin's Lane, not far away, in 1753. There is some reason to suppose that Chippendale was financed in his business venture, since in 1754 he published "The Gentleman and Cabinet Maker's Director," an expensive folio book of 160 plates, engraved on copper and sold at £2:8:0; a large price in those days. This assistance may have been in the form of a pre-paid subscription, but some influence must have been necessary to obtain such sponsors as the Duke of Beaufort, the Earl of Chesterfield, Lords Feversham, Guildford and Guernsey, the Duke of Hamilton, the Duke of Norfolk and the Earl of Northumberland (to the last-named nobleman the book is dedicated).

The "Director" must have been a financial success, as a second edition was called for the following year, and a third, (enlarged) in 1762.

Some idea may be formed of the size of Chippendale's establishment at this date, from the account, in the Gentleman's Magazine of April 1755, of a fire which broke out in his workshop, in which the chests of twenty-two workmen were burnt. He must have been in a large way of business at this date, as tool-chests would imply cabinetmakers only, and would take no account of carvers, polishers or finishers, upholsterers, clerks and other people incidental to such a factory.

In 1766 Chippendale advertises a sale of furniture, owing to the death of his partner, James Rannie. In 1771 he takes his bookkeeper, Thomas Haig, into partnership, and the bills of the firm are headed "Chippendale & Haig," until the death of the former in 1779. Two years before that date he had married again, his second wife being Elizabeth Davis of Fulham. He was buried in the old churchyard of St. Martins-in-the-Fields, probably the ground on which the present National Gallery is built.

In 1771 and 1772 he furnished the house of David Garrick, the famous actor-manager, in the Adelphi,§ and between 1766 and 1770 he made a considerable amount of furniture of Sir Rowland Winn at Nostell, and in 1770–72 was working at Lansdowne House for the Earl of Shelburne. Much of the Chippendale furniture at Harewood (none of which is in the "Director" style, be it remembered) dates from 1771 to 1775, and in the brief years of his second marriage he was engaged at Sandon Hall, Staffordshire, on work for Nathaniel Ryder.

Apart from Chippendale's actual work at the various houses referred to above, and at Kenwood, Mersham Hatch and elsewhere, (which is practically all in the manner of Robert Adam) we know the Chippendale Style, if such a style may be said to exist at all, only from the designs in the "Director." If the man, as a designer, is to be judged, it must be by this book. The first question which arises is: Are these designs those of a practical cabinetmaker, such as we know Chippendale to have been? The second query is: Are the pieces illustrated in a definite style and one peculiar to Chippendale, and may he, therefore, claim any credit for originality? The answer to both questions must be in the negative.

As far back as 1909 I had formed the idea that Thomas Chippendale did not make the designs from which the "Director" plates were engraved, but I had the difficulty, at that time, of being unable to get behind the personality of the engraver. Those acquainted with copper-plate engraving of that period will appreciate how radical are the departures from the original, in nearly every instance. In their engraved state, very few of the "Director" designs could be realised in wood without serious modification, but that did not warrant the statement that the original sketches might not have been the work of a practical cabinetmaker, rendered impractical only by undue license on the part of the engraver.

I had the opportunity, in 1925, of examining the original drawings from which these "Director" plates were engraved, and my suspicions of sixteen years before were confirmed. These sketches were not the work of one man, the hands of six, at least, being evident in them. The account of how these original drawings came into the

§This furniture, and the bills, are now in the Victoria and Albert Museum in London.

possession of the Metropolitan Museum of Art in New York, reads almost like a romance. At a sale at Ruxley Lodge, Claygate, Surrey, in October, 1919, two leather-covered scrap books, containing two hundred and seven sketches, in pencil, wash, and Chinese white, were sold. They had the book-plate of Baron Foley of Kidderminster in each, and must have come from his library. The two books were bought for a nominal sum, quite unrecognised, and from London they reached New York, and were bought by the Metropolitan Museum in 1920. It was only then that the discovery was made that one hundred and seventy of these sketches were the original drawings from which the "Director" plates were engraved, only a few being missing. Of these, the Victoria and Albert Museum possesses fifteen; but even then the number is not complete. It is possible that the missing drawings may never have existed as far as Chippendale was concerned, the plates, or the proofs, being bought outright from other persons at the time. In the third edition, especially, some have this appearance, bearing not the remotest connection to what we know as the Chippendale Style.

I formed the idea, in 1909, that the "Director" plates were never specially engraved for that book, and, even in the face of the later evidence, I see no reason to change my opinion. The sketches, or the greater number of them, are admittedly not from the hand of Thomas Chippendale himself, and he must have employed designers from outside, and to a considerable extent, as the drawings date from within a year or two of each other, that is, if he ever specially ordered these sketches at all. Chippendale could hardly have had six or more draughtsmen at one time, in his own place of business. We are asked to believe that Chippendale had all these sketches made to his definite order, and that he commissioned the engraving of new copper plates from them, the cost of which must have been formidable. Had the plates been unique, had the "Director" inaugurated an entirely new style, the venture might have been worth the expense, no matter how great the risk, but we know that there is nothing new in the "Director" manner; it is not a style at all, only a jumble of several. As an advertisement for Chippendale's factory, therefore, the "Director" must have been a failure. The "System of Household Taste" of Ince & Mayhew (1763), although one year later than the third edition of the "Director," contains designs of mirror frames which cannot be differentiated from those of Chippendale, and the "System" must have taken years to prepare. Lock & Copeland's "Ornaments" (1752), Edwards & Darly's "Chinese Designs" (1754), T. Johnson's "Designs for Picture Frames" (1758), his "New Designs" (1761), all show that there is nothing intrinsically original in the "Director" Style, any more than there is in the catalogue of a present-day retail furnishing store. Knowing this, recognising that he was using patterns which were the common property of his trade at the time, I cannot believe that Chippendale would have faced all the expenses of original designs, engraved plates, printing, paper and binding. Had he done all this, he would have taken the greatest care to see that all his designs were thoroughly practical and could have been made as they were drawn. Had Chippendale obtained an order for many of the pieces which he illustrates, he would have been compelled so greatly to modify his patterns (as every maker did who reproduced any of the "Director" pieces) that it would have been tantamount to an open confession that the designs were the work of other people. Yet, in his preface, Chippendale definitely claims the credit for their authorship. It is significant, also, that on the preface to the first edition, he cites certain criticism, which must have been made before the book was issued!

From the indisputable fact that pieces were made from the "Director" designs (or subsequently to the publication of that book, which is not quite the same thing) nearly always with drastic modifications necessitated by practical considerations, and, coupled with this, that some of these pieces were made to the order of persons who figure in the list of the "Director" subscribers, the curious theory has been advanced that this is a proof of such pieces having been made by Thomas Chippendale. It might be argued, and with much greater reason, that this evidence may be construed the other way. If we examine the "Director" designs illustrated here, and compare them with the articles which were actually made from them, one can hardly believe that Chippendale would have modified his own patterns to this extent; it would have been too marked a confession, either of want of practical knowledge, or of "ghosting" in the designing. Let us imagine a patron such as Paul Methuen of Corsham possessing the "Director" and being desirous of having one of the pieces illustrated there. What would have been more natural than for him to place his order with a good cabinet-maker in his own county of Wiltshire, in which case, the workman would be certain to point out the impossibility of making the piece as drawn, and would insist on altering the design? Good makers abounded in the country districts of England during the eighteenth century, London-trained, possibly, but who would return to their native village or town to seek the patronage of the neighbouring great houses. I have found furniture, magnificent examples of craftsmanship and design, in Norfolk, Yorkshire, Lancashire and Cheshire, which I have been able to establish as being of local origin. Gillow of Lancaster, for example, was a name second to none at that period, and but for the fact that he did not publish a "Director" or a "System" might have been bracketted with Chippendale in the history of English furniture of the middle-eighteenth century.

The evidence against the attribution to Chippendale of these "Director" pieces would not have been so overwhelming had Chippendale ever been known to have copied the patterns in his own book. We know that this was his intention and hope when he published the first edition in 1754, but, eight years later, he can point to only one chair, of which he says that a set has been made "which gave entire satisfaction." To the day of his death he was employed making furniture to the designs of Robert and James Adam, and it is certain that Chippendale never succeeded in popularising the style which bears his name. There was nothing novel in it, nothing which would have compelled anyone to employ Chippendale, instead of another maker. There is every evidence to show that, while the book may have been a publishing success, as a trade venture or as an attempt to found a new style, the "Director" was a failure. There is furniture existing, and to a considerable amount, for which Chippendale invoices exist, or where inventory records establish Chippendale authorship. Why is it that among all this evidence no single piece of "Director" Chippendale is to be found? The answer is simple; Chippendale could never persuade his patrons, as far as we know them today, to order one of the pieces from his book. They preferred to entrust the designing to Robert Adam, and Chippendale, who was certainly a good business man, put his business ahead of his artistic ideals; and the "Director," as far as he was concerned, was allowed to sink into oblivion. The style could never have been popular, and that is why so much of what posterity has dubbed "Chippendale" and so very few of the genuine "Director" pieces exist at the present day. I have seen, possibly, six pieces of the latter.

MAHOGANY DOUBLE CHEST. THE DESIGN OF THE BRACKET-PLINTH IS OF A KIND TO BE FOUND IN MANY OF THE PRE-CHIPPENDALE PIECES OF *c. 1740*, YET WAS ADAPTED, WITH SLIGHT MODIFICATIONS, IN SOME OF THE "DIRECTOR" DESIGNS

MAHOGANY DOUBLE CHEST WITH SECRETAIRE, CLOSED AND OPEN. THE CENTRAL ORNAMENT TO THE PEDIMENT IS OF DECIDED "DIRECTOR" CHIPPENDALE CHARACTER, YET IS VERY SIMILAR TO THE AKROTERIA OF MANY OF THE PHILADELPHIA HIGHBOYS OF *1770*

COMMODE IN THE FRENCH TASTE, WITH BRASS MOULDINGS. THE VENEER IS "HAREWOOD" (SYCAMORE STAINED WITH OXIDE OF IRON) BANDED WITH ROSEWOOD AND INLAID WITH MARQUETERIE. THIS IS THE TYPE OF SOME OF THE FURNITURE MADE BY CHIPPENDALE FOR HAREWOOD HOUSE, AND FOR WHICH THE ORIGINAL BILLS EXIST. *c. 1770*

A CHIPPENDALE "RIBBAND-BACK" CHAIR, ADAPTED FROM THE THIRD DESIGN ON PLATE *16* OF THE FIRST (*1754*) EDITION OF THE "GENTLEMAN AND CABINETMAKER'S DIRECTOR." EVEN IN ITS MODIFIED STATE, IT IS NOT A CONSTRUCTIONALLY-SOUND CHAIR AS THE SPLAT IS VERY FRAGILE

ONE OF TWO SIMILAR COMMODES FROM RAINHAM HALL. THERE ARE EVIDENCES, IN BOTH DESIGN AND WORKMANSHIP TO SHOW THAT THIS IS THE FIRST OF THE TWO. THE CARVING, ALSO, IS THOROUGHLY ENGLISH IN CUTTING

MAHOGANY COMMODE FROM RAINHAM HALL, NORFOLK, THE SEAT OF THE MARQUIS OF TOWNSHEND, BASED ON THE DESIGN, PLATE *44*, IN THE FIRST EDITION OF THE "DIRECTOR" (*1754*) AND DATED *1753* (SEE NEXT PAGE). THIS COMMODE, AND ANOTHER (ALSO SHOWN HERE), FIGURE IN THE *1756* INVENTORY OF RAINHAM, AND HAVE BEEN SAID TO HAVE COME FROM BALLS PARK. THEY MAY BE ACTUAL CHIPPENDALE WORK (FOR WHICH NO EVIDENCE EXISTS) BUT MAY ALSO BE PRIOR TO *1754* OR *1753* (THE DATE ON THE "DIRECTOR" PLATE). IF THIS BE THE FACT IT IS CURIOUS THAT THE "DIRECTOR" PLATE IS JUST AS IMPRACTICAL AS MANY OF THE OTHERS IN THAT BOOK

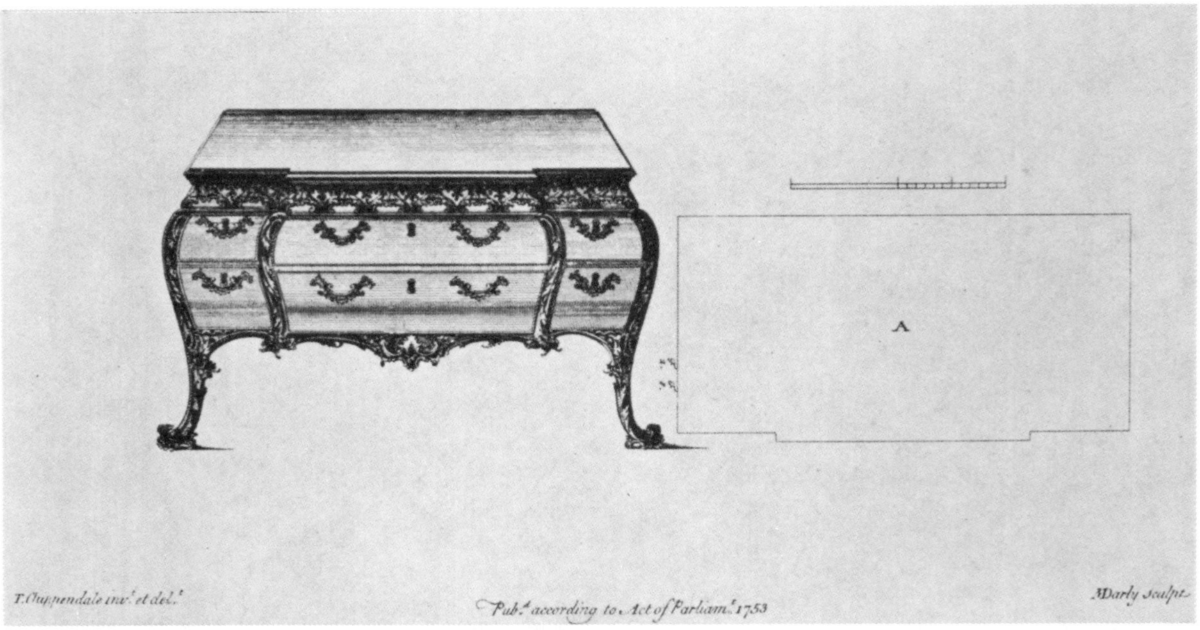

THE "DIRECTOR" PLATE OF THE "FRENCH COMMODE TABLE" ON WHICH THE TWO COMMODES, ILLUSTRATED HERE, WERE BASED. THE DIFFERENCE BETWEEN THE ACTUAL DESIGN AND THE TWO RENDERINGS BY A PRACTICAL CABINETMAKER, MAY BE STUDIED WITH ADVANTAGE

DETAIL OF THE RAINHAM COMMODE ILLUSTRATED ON THE PREVIOUS PAGE. THE CARVING SUGGESTS THE HAND OF A FRENCHMAN; THIS CHARACTER IS ABSENT IN THE OTHER COMMODE

A MAHOGANY WARDROBE, MADE AFTER THE LEFT-HAND SIDE OF THE DESIGN ON PLATE *104* IN THE *1754* EDITION OF THE "DIRECTOR," WITH MODIFICATIONS. SEE PLATE BELOW

THE "DIRECTOR" DESIGN ON WHICH THE WARDROBE, ILLUSTRATED ABOVE, WAS BASED, DATED *1753*

SIDEBOARD TABLE, "DIRECTOR" PLATE *36* (*1753*), A COMPLETE DESIGN MADE BY A PRACTICAL CRAFTSMAN. THE SIZES MARKED, *5* FT. *6* IN. LONG BY *3* FT. *0* IN. DEEP BY *2* FT. *9* IN. HIGH ARE NOT THE STANDARD WHICH WAS USUALLY ADOPTED. WITH A LENGTH OF *5* FT. *6* IN., THE DEPTH WOULD BE *2* FT. *6* IN. AND THE HEIGHT *3* FT. *3* IN., WITH A SIDE TABLE

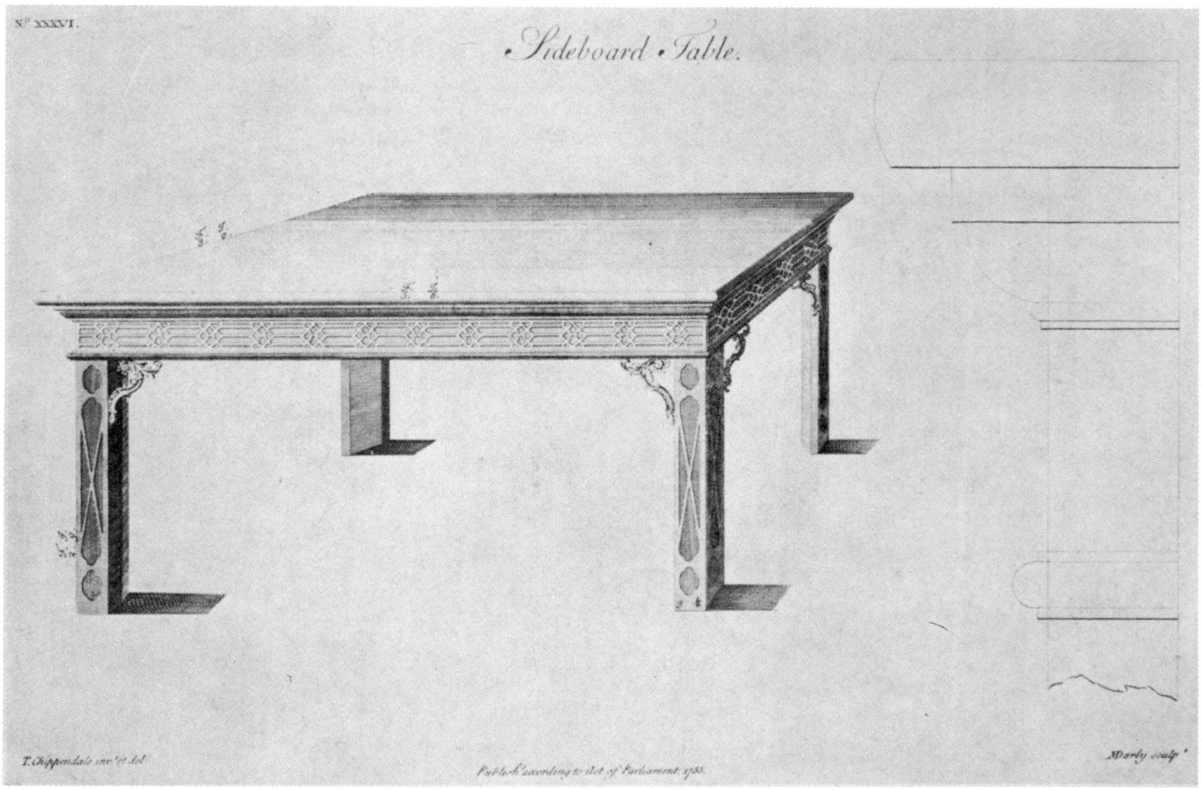

SIDEBOARD TABLE, "DIRECTOR" PLATE *35* (*1753*), A PRACTICAL DESIGN, BUT OF A CHARACTER SO SIMPLE THAT IT MUST HAVE BEEN COMMON TO THE TRADE OF CHIPPENDALE'S TIME

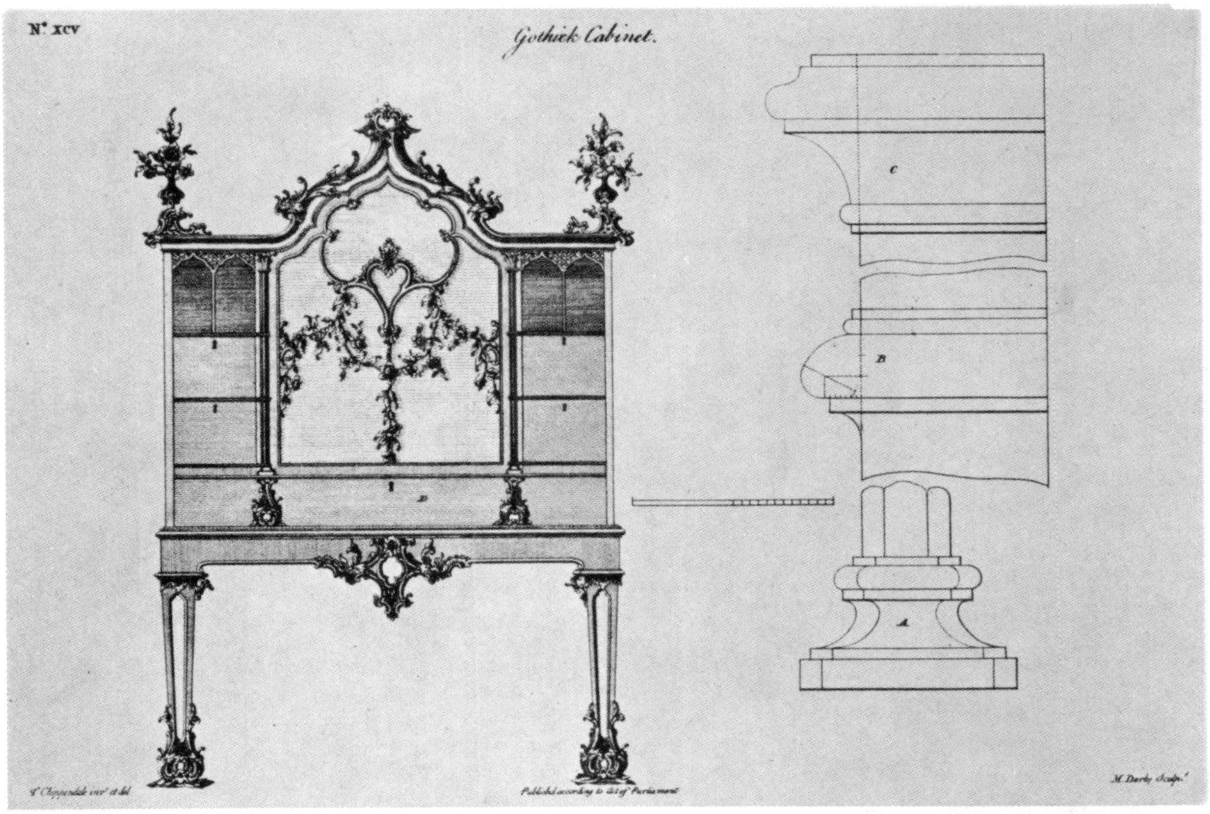

A "GOTHIC CABINET" FROM THE "DIRECTOR," AN EXAMPLE OF AN IMPRACTICAL DESIGN AS REPRESENTED BY AN ENGRAVER. A CURIOUS FACT IS THAT THE DETAILS AT THE SIDE ARE THOROUGHLY PRACTICAL, BUT DO NOT CORRESPOND WITH THE DESIGN

SIDEBOARD TABLE, "DIRECTOR" PLATE *40* (*1753*), A TYPICAL EXAMPLE OF A TABLE (EACH HALF A DIFFERENT DESIGN) WHICH COULD NOT HAVE BEEN MADE WITHOUT SERIOUS MODIFICATION

THE ORIGINAL CHIPPENDALE DRAWINGS. A PLATE FROM THE THIRD (*1762*) EDITION OF THE "DIRECTOR." THE STYLE IS PURELY ROCOCO FRENCH AND WHOLLY IMPRACTICAL

THE ORIGINAL CHIPPENDALE DRAWINGS, NOW IN THE METROPOLITAN MUSEUM, NEW YORK. A PRACTICAL DESIGN WHICH HAS THE APPEARANCE OF HAVING BEEN MADE FROM A FINISHED PIECE OF FURNITURE, PROBABLY AS A RECORD. THE STYLE (IF THE DESIGN POSSESSES ANY) IS ONE COMMON TO ANY OF THE CABINETMAKERS OF THIS PERIOD

MAHOGANY BOOKCASE OF PRE-CHIPPENDALE TYPE, PROBABLY INSPIRED BY THE DESIGNS OF BATTY AND THOMAS LANGLEY, WHO PUBLISHED DESIGNS OF FURNITURE IN *1740*

CHAPTER XVI

The Chippendale Style

THE CHIPPENDALE STYLE is a generic term which has very little to do with Thomas Chippendale, and still less with the "Director." It includes not only the work of his contemporaries but much which was made before his time, or, to be exact, prior to the publication of the first edition of "The Gentleman and Cabinet Maker's Director," in 1754.

I have attempted to segregate much of this earlier work, (often collectively dubbed as "Chippendale") in previous chapters, since, if no line of demarcation be drawn, the whole of the mahogany furniture from 1725 onwards must also be included under the same name. This would result in chaos and would be grossly inaccurate, as well. The problem is difficult enough as it is, even if the actual contemporary work be included—as it must be—for not only did Chippendale adopt many of the current patterns of his time, but also a considerable amount of furniture was made which bears no relation to the "Director" manner, and which bridges the two styles of the Chippendale and of the Hepplewhite Schools.

It has been pointed out, in the previous chapter, that there is little that is original in the "Director" designs. If there be such a thing as a "Director" Style at all then the same name must be applied to the patterns in other books, such as the "System of Household Taste" of Ince & Mayhew, where the same design-inspiration is strikingly evident. Actually, much of this 1750–80 furniture entirely ignores all these design books. One may vainly search these "Directors," "Systems" and all the other design books of this period to find a single representation of the ball-and-claw foot, which is such a feature of what is usually known as the Chippendale Style. The term itself, therefore, indicates a school rather than a man, and one might go further and say that it excepts the man almost entirely.

The Chippendale style is not simple; it is compounded of many manners, integrally different. Some attempt must, in consequence, be made to resolve it into its component parts. In a broad sense only, it may be divided into five classes:§ the cabriole, the tripod, the straight-leg and fretted, the Chinese and the Gothic. Further sub-divisions might be attempted but the above are sufficient to establish some kind of order.

§One might name a sixth: the so-called "French Taste," but this merges into the cabriole so imperceptibly that it is difficult to segregate it as a separate sub-division. Several examples of this "French" manner are illustrated here.

The Chippendale cabriole develops directly from the early mahogany years, and differs only in some small degree. The ball-and-claw is still retained, but in a somewhat depraved manner, with little or nothing of its earlier vigour. The paw foot is rarer, if it is not entirely obsolete after 1750; the same may be said of the club foot. The scrolled or leaf-carved finish is the most usual, known at this time as the French foot. It was borrowed from the Louis XV, with little or no modification.

Belonging to the cabriole style, and, in a way a part of it, is the tripod furniture, which may be described as originating with the Chippendale School. It is more than a fashion; it is an invention, as it is a property of the tripod that it will stand firmly on an uneven floor. On this principle the older grand pianos had three legs only, and it is doubtful whether the modern "trestle-leg" be an improvement on the original form.

The tripod was used by the Chippendale School for small tables, vase-, lamp-, and candle-stands, and for pole- and banner-screens. At a later date, nearly at the close of the century, we find the tripod on "tea-poys" (boxes made to contain two kinds of tea, green and black, and also sugar, all costly commodities at this date). Shortly after 1800 we have the tripod on dining tables of the "pillar-and-claw" variety. It might be supposed that the unique property of the tripod, of standing evenly on any floor, would have caused it to be retained for dining tables more than for any other piece of furniture, yet it gives way to the four-fold support very quickly, and tripod, pillar-and-claw tables are much more rare than one would imagine.

The banner- and pole-screens belong more to the category of ornamental than to that of useful furniture. These pieces are instances of how types multiply at the expense of utility; the change from the homogeneous to the heterogeneous. Nevertheless, many of the tripod bases of these screens and small tables are examples of fine designing and beautiful workmanship. Many have been invested with a later useful character by cutting the screen pole away and fitting to them the small trays of the same period; a gain in utility at the expense of integrity.

The tops of the tripod-tables of this date are flat and plain, or bordered in direct imitation of the silver-trays of the period. Thus we have the "pie-crust," the gadroon and the scalloped edges and the spindle gallery. All these were originally silver patterns. The border of fret-work is a true woodwork style; here the silversmith borrows from the cabinetmaker. With the small oblong "silver-tables" the fret gallery is the most usual. Unfortunately, these galleries, especially those in which the fret is cut from one thickness of wood, without lamination, are very fragile and are rarely found in perfect state at the present day. With the lamination of three or five veneers—with the grain alternately vertical and horizontal—even the most delicate fret acquires extraordinary strength. This method was known in the Chippendale period but was not always practised. Because nearly all of these tables which have survived to the present day have laminated frets, one might be tempted to make the deduction that lamination was the rule rather than the exception. The obvious reasoning is that only those with these built-up frets have survived; I have seen too many in which the galleries have disappeared entirely, or have been replaced at a later date, not to be certain that lamination was exceptional.

Small bureaux on stool-bases conclude the list of this cabriole furniture, of which chairs are the most representative pieces. Wall pieces on short cabriole legs are very exceptional in this Chippendale style, although they are to be found in the later walnut and the early mahogany years. The name of "Cabriole Style" is certainly more appropriate and exact than that of "Chippendale" for this furniture.

The square-section leg (to be precise, the section is more often almost triangular, the inside edge being broadly chamfered, as shown on one of the "Director" plates of a Side Board Table illustrated in the preceding chapter) belongs also to the Chippendale School, and is almost confined to it. Hepplewhite used the taper in preference, and without the inside chamfer. Finishing on the floor with a small moulded block, but more often without it, this square-leg style demands exact proportions to be successful from the dual points of view of strength and of appearance. Sometimes, in the case of tables, more rarely with chairs, the outer faces of the legs are ornamented with applied frets, cut in a single veneer thickness and glued down. The proper way is, of course, to cut these frets from the solid, but this was rarely, if ever, done at this period. The applied fret is earlier than the Chippendale years, but is rare before 1740.

If we adopt the general name of "Fretted" to indicate this sub-division of the Chippendale Style, then both the Gothic and the Chinese must be included, as both rely, almost exclusively, on fret-work for their decoration. The latter was the result of the rage for "Chinoiserie," inaugurated, perhaps, by Sir William Chambers, who, in 1757, published "Designs for Chinese Buildings." It is more probable that Edwards & Darly, with their "Chinese Designs," of 1753, may have had the greater effect in moulding popular taste. Matthias Darly was one of those men of genius whose lot it was to act as the "ghost" for others. He was the engraver of many of the "Director" plates, and the whole of those in the Ince & Mayhew "System." If we could only know exactly, the credit not only for the Chinese fashion, but also for the whole of what we know as the "Director" Style of Chippendale, might be given to Darly.

The rage for this Chinese taste was general and every designer pandered to it, not only in England but also in France. The French Rococo is based on Chinese decorative forms.

The Gothic of the mid-eighteenth century is, perhaps, the most misnamed of all these styles, the connection between the "Gothick" of the Chippendale School and the national style of England from the thirteenth to the sixteenth centuries being remote, indeed. In *circa* 1760, any piercing in the form of a pointed arch was hailed as "Gothick," and the style—if such it may be called—must have had a considerable vogue at the time. Batty Langley was the chief apostle of this Gothic manner. It was greatly admired by some, and just as strongly condemned by others. Of the latter, Horace Walpole was not the least—or the most modest. The man who could design Strawberry Hill would be capable of any criticism.

There is one feature of the true Gothic which was adopted for some of the most original and the most successful of the pieces of Chippendale, namely, the cluster-column used for the legs of tables, and, very rarely, for chairs. One of these cluster-leg designs from the "Director" is given here, together with an actual table in the same style. Although both have the appearance of great fragility, this form of built-up leg is, in reality, stronger than one fashioned from the solid timber of equal girth. I have seen tables of astonishing delicacy, which were in reality strong. The example illustrated here is one which has persisted from *circa* 1760, yet has never been either restored or mended. Of course, the fragility of its appearance would be some safeguard against rough usage.

This cluster-column is borrowed directly from the Early English Gothic of the thirteenth century, but the constructional idea of building up, possible with wood but impossible with stone, is an actual innovation of the Chippendale School.

Among the most charming, and, at the same time, the most original pieces of this Chippendale fretted style, are the small hanging-cabinets, made either for small books or for pieces of china. Several designs of these "Girandoles" are given in the "Director," none of which is of a practical character. The examples which are to be found "in the wood" differ, very widely, from these "Director" patterns, as one would expect. Not the least of their merits, as a rule, is that they are inexpensive to make, although costly to buy; one pays for rarity only. Several of these pieces are illustrated here. Again, the idea may have originated during the early mahogany years, as one example here has every appearance of dating from before 1750. To the Chippendale School belongs the credit, however, for the open-fret sides and the pierced galleries to the shelves. It is only the mere suggestion of the hanging-cabinet which is adopted. The same idea was used for candle-lanterns, which were often made in balancing pairs, such as the two illustrated in this chapter.

The suggestion may be ventured here that the most successful productions of this Chippendale School are in this fretted manner; the plain square leg on tables or chairs, these fretted hanging-cabinets, and the plainer wall furniture. The general proportions are admirable, as a rule, but in collecting, as in many other hobbies, *chacun à son goût*.

MAHOGANY ARM AND SIDE CHAIRS, FROM A REMARKABLE SET CONSISTING OF SIX ARM AND SIX SIDE CHAIRS, MADE TO ALTERNATE AROUND THE DINING ROOM. THE COVERINGS ARE OF FINE NEEDLE-POINT AND DIFFER, BOTH IN DESIGN AND COLOURING, WITH EACH CHAIR. *c. 1755*

MAHOGANY ARMCHAIR. THE PIERCED CHINESE MANNER OF THE CHIPPENDALE SCHOOL. *c. 1750*

MAHOGANY SIDE CHAIR COVERED WITH FINE PETIT-POINT NEEDLEWORK. THE SQUARE LEG CHINESE MANNER OF THE CHIPPENDALE SCHOOL. *c. 1750-5*

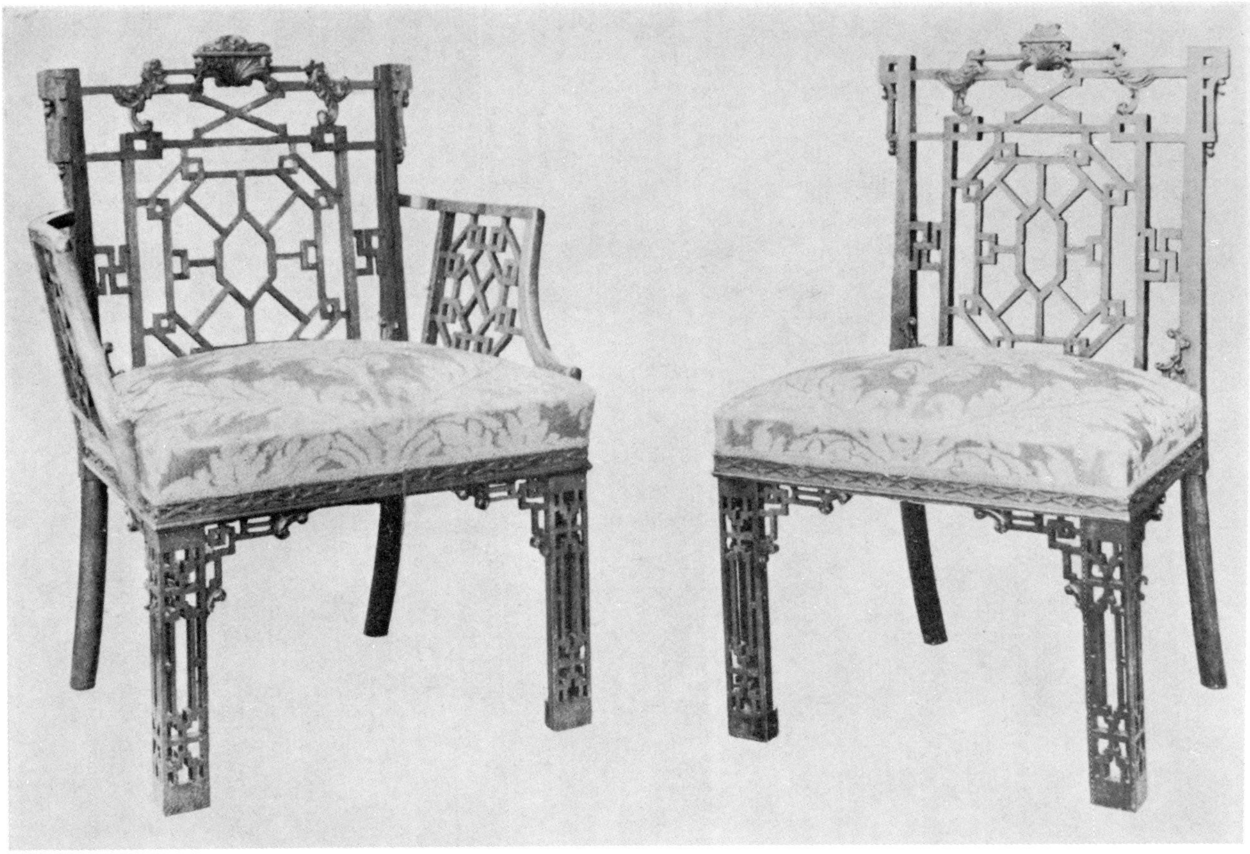

MAHOGANY ARM AND SIDE CHAIRS IN THE "CHINESE TASTE." AN ACTUAL "DIRECTOR" PATTERN. THE FRETWORK OF THE BACKS AND ARMS IS ALL BUILT UP, OR LAMINATED. *c. 1755*

MAHOGANY SIDE CHAIR. THE SIMPLE CHIPPENDALE GOTHIC MANNER. *c. 1750*

MAHOGANY SIDE CHAIR. ELABORATELY INTERLACED SPLAT. *c. 1750*

MAHOGANY ARMCHAIR. EARLY CHIPPENDALE, WITH THE FIGURE *8* INTERLACED SPLAT OF *c. 1740* RETAINED. *c. 1755*

MAHOGANY LADDER-BACK ARMCHAIR. CHIPPENDALE SCHOOL OF *c. 1755-60*

MAHOGANY LADDER-BACK ARMCHAIR. ROUNDING OF TOP RAIL OF BACK AT CORNERS, AND SLIGHT TAPER OF LEGS INDICATE BRIDGING OF CHIPPENDALE AND HEPPLEWHITE MANNERS. *c. 1780*

MAHOGANY LADDER-BACK SIDE CHAIR OF THE CHIPPENDALE SCHOOL. *c. 1760*

MAHOGANY SIDE CHAIR. A VERY RARE EXAMPLE OF THE CHIPPENDALE FRETTED MANNER OF *c. 1760*

MAHOGANY SIDE CHAIR. THE SIMPLE BUT REFINED MANNER OF THE CHIPPENDALE STYLE OF *c. 1750*

MAHOGANY HALL CHAIR WITH WOOD "SADDLE" SEAT. A VERY RARE EXAMPLE. *c. 1760*

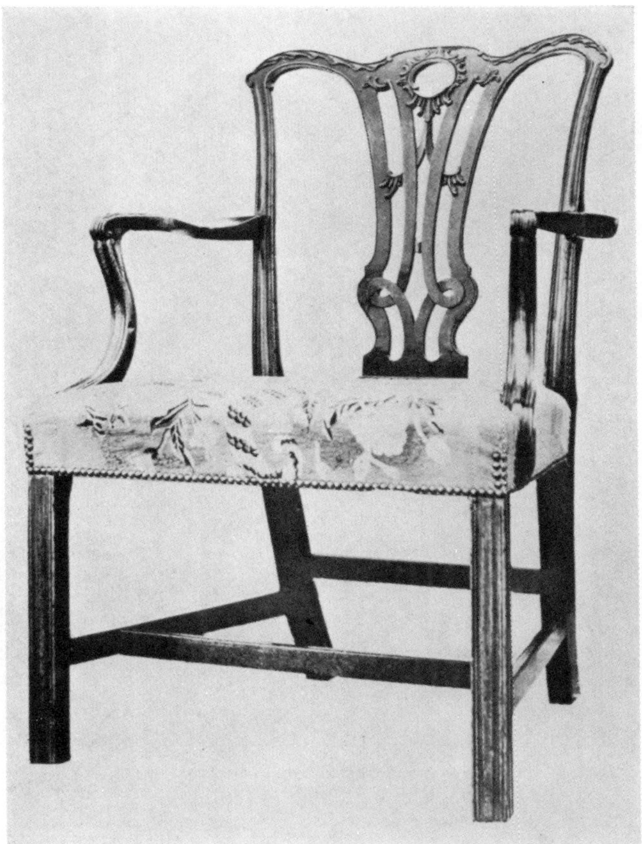

MAHOGANY ARMCHAIR. TYPICAL SQUARE-LEG CHIPPENDALE OF THE FINEST QUALITY. *c. 1755*

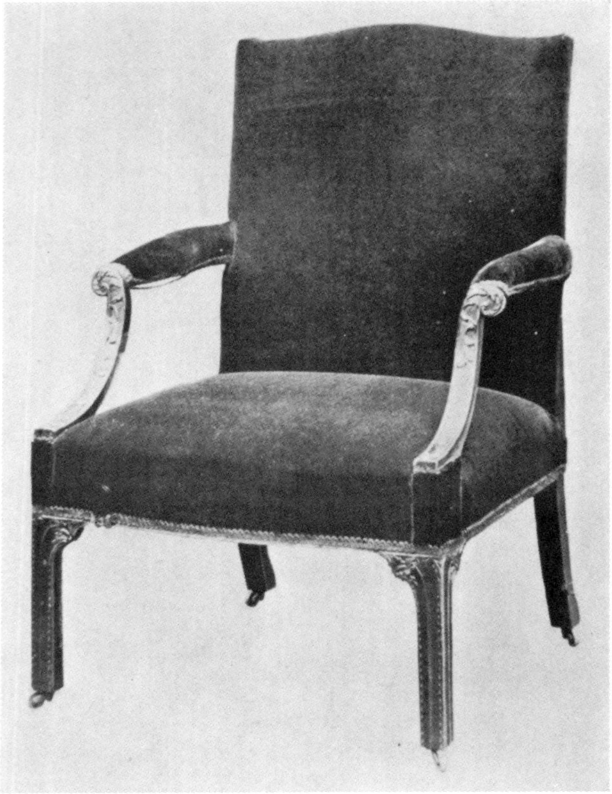

MAHOGANY BERGÈRE CHAIR. THE ABSENCE OF UNDER-RAILING TO THE LEGS IS UNUSUAL. *c. 1755*

MAHOGANY BERGÈRE CHAIR. THE SQUARE-LEG VERSION OF THE FRENCH MANNER OF THE **CHIPPENDALE SCHOOL.** NOTE THE FASHION OF THE ARM SUPPORTS AND THE SEAT RAIL. *c. 1760*

MAHOGANY BERGÈRE AND SIDE CHAIRS, WITH STOOL. ADAPTED TO BE PLACED TOGETHER TO FORM A CHAISE LONGUE. FROM A LARGE SET AT RAINHAM HALL, NORFOLK. *c. 1755*

MAHOGANY SIDE CHAIR. THE SIMPLE SQUARE-LEG CHIPPENDALE. *c. 1755*

MAHOGANY BERGÈRE CHAIR WITH FRETS ON LEGS AND ARMS. SIMPLE BUT FINELY DESIGNED. *c. 1755*

MAHOGANY ARMCHAIRS. SIMPLE SQUARE LEGS WITH UNDER-RAILING. COVERED WITH BLACK HIDE, TRIMMED WITH CLOSE BRASS NAILING. *c. 1750*

MAHOGANY BERGÈRE CHAIR OF THE EARLY CHIPPENDALE SCHOOL, *c. 1750.* MANY OF THE FEATURES OF THE EARLY MAHOGANY YEARS HAVE BEEN RETAINED IN THIS MODEL

MAHOGANY FRETTED BERGÈRE CHAIR. A LATE EXAMPLE OF THE CHIPPENDALE MANNER. *c. 1770.* NOTE THE PERSISTENCE OF THE OLDER STRETCHER RAILING TO THE LEGS

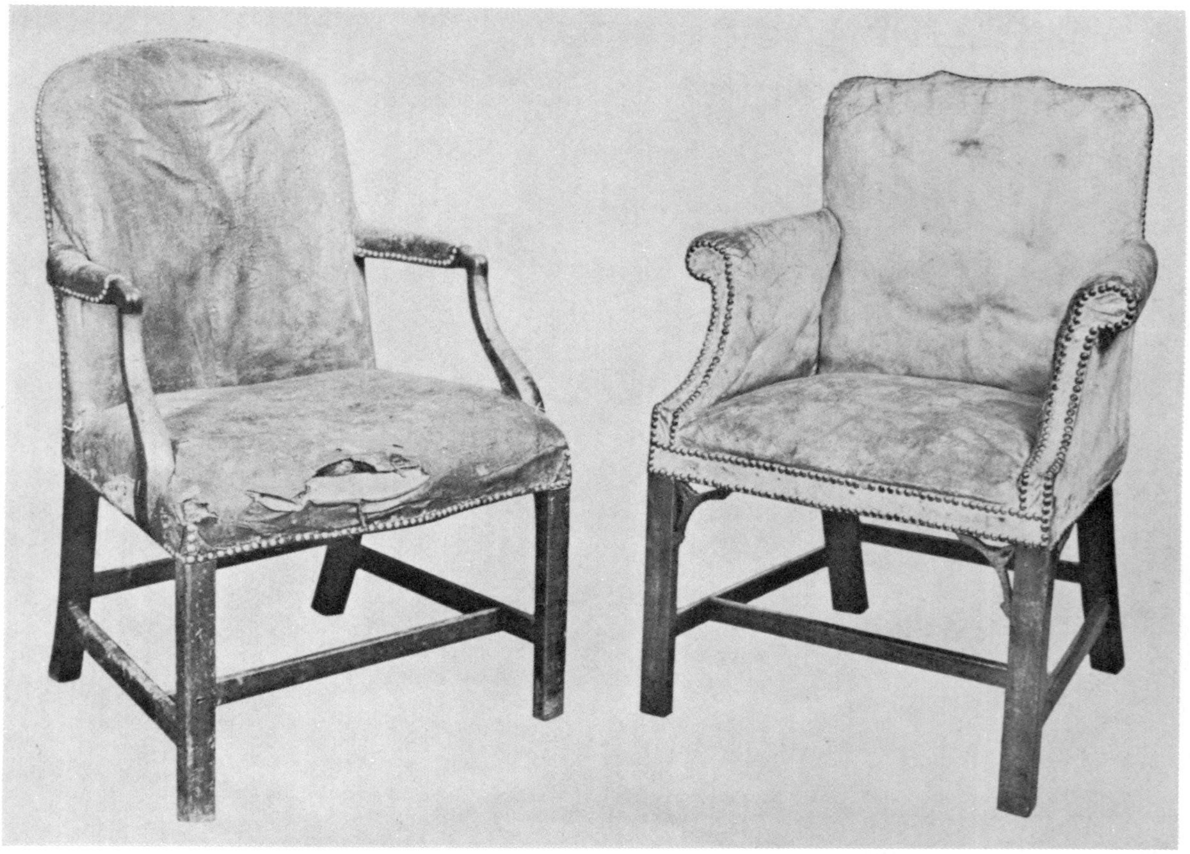

SIMPLE MAHOGANY ARM OR BERGÈRE CHAIRS. CHIPPENDALE SCHOOL OF *c. 1755*

MAHOGANY SIDE CHAIR. A PROVINCIAL MODEL WHICH BELONGS TO THE CHIPPENDALE STYLE, BUT ONLY IN A REMOTE DEGREE. *c. 1760*

MAHOGANY SIDE CHAIR. THE REVIVAL OF THE OLDER HOOP-BACK IN THE CHIPPENDALE PERIOD. NOTE THE CARVING OF THE TOP RAIL AND COMPARE WITH THE CHAIR BELOW. *c. 1760*

MAHOGANY ARMCHAIR. THE RESTRAINED EXPRESSION OF THE GOTHIC MANNER. *c. 1755*

ANOTHER VERSION OF THE CHAIR ABOVE WITH THE INTERLACED SPLAT OF THE EARLY MAHOGANY YEARS. *c. 1760*

MAHOGANY "RIBBAND-BACK" SETTEE OF RARE AND ELABORATE FORM. *c. 1760*

MAHOGANY ARM AND SIDE CHAIRS. THE "GOTHICK" MANNER OF THE CHIPPENDALE SCHOOL. *c. 1755*

MAHOGANY PRE-CHIPPENDALE ARMCHAIR SHOWING THE SOURCE FROM WHICH THE STYLE EVOLVED. *c. 1745*

MAHOGANY SIDE CHAIR. TYPICAL MODEL IN THE STYLE OF THE CHIPPENDALE SCHOOL BUT WHICH HAS LITTLE OR NO CONNECTION WITH THE "DIRECTOR" MANNER. *c. 1750*

MAHOGANY ARMCHAIR (ONE OF SIX). THE SEAT COVERING OF THESE CHAIRS IS HISTORICAL, BEING PORTIONS OF THE EMBROIDERED CLOAK WORN BY CHARLES I ON THE DAY OF HIS EXECUTION. THE CHAIRS HAVE BEEN SPECIALLY DESIGNED, HAVING THE MONOGRAM C. R. INTERLACED IN THE CENTRAL SPLAT OF THE BACK. DATE OF CLOAK *1645*; OF CHAIR *c. 1755*

MAHOGANY STUFF-OVER SIDE CHAIR IN THE FRENCH MANNER OF THE CHIPPENDALE SCHOOL. NOTE THE RARE FEATURE OF THE BACK LEGS, WHICH ARE ALSO OF CABRIOLE FORM

ROSEWOOD THREE-CHAIR-BACK SETTEE OF THE EARLY CHIPPENDALE PERIOD. *c. 1750*. THE USE OF SOLID ROSEWOOD IS VERY EXCEPTIONAL

MAHOGANY ARM AND SIDE CHAIRS OF TRUE CHIPPENDALE STYLE. THE LEAF-CARVED, SCROLLED FOOT IS IN THE "DIRECTOR" MANNER OF *1754*

MAHOGANY SETTEE OF THE EARLY CHIPPENDALE PERIOD, SHOWING THE EARLIER CABOCHON-AND-LEAF INTRODUCED INTO THE FRENCH MANNER OF THE CHIPPENDALE SCHOOL. *c. 1750*

MAHOGANY ARM AND SIDE CHAIRS IN THE FRENCH MANNER OF THE CHIPPENDALE SCHOOL. SEATS AND BACKS ARE COVERED WITH FINE NEEDLE-POINT IN IMITATION OF FRENCH TAPESTRY. *c. 1760*

MAHOGANY ARM AND SIDE CHAIRS IN THE FRENCH MANNER OF THE CHIPPENDALE SCHOOL. *c. 1760*

MAHOGANY FRETTED SIDE TABLE OF THE CHIPPENDALE SCHOOL SHOWING THE DOUBLE CHAMFER OF THE SQUARE LEG ON THE OUTER AND INNER EDGES. *c. 1760*

OCTAGONAL WINE COOLER OF THE CHIPPENDALE PERIOD. DATING FROM *1755* TO *1775*. AT A LATER DATE THEY GIVE WAY EITHER TO THE CELLARETTE IN THE SIDEBOARD, OR TO THE SARCOPHAGUS KEPT UNDER THE SIDEBOARD IN THE CENTRE

MAHOGANY CLUSTER-LEG TABLE WITH THE ORIGINAL FRETTED GALLERY MISSING. *c. 1755*

MAHOGANY FRETTED "SILVER" TABLE OF THE CHIPPENDALE PERIOD. A PERFECT EXAMPLE WHICH HAS NEVER BEEN REPAIRED NOR RESTORED. AN INSTANCE OF REAL STRENGTH IN AN, APPARENTLY, DELICATE TABLE. *c. 1755*

MAHOGANY FRETTED "SILVER" TABLE OF THE CHIPPENDALE PERIOD WITH CLUSTER-COLUMN LEGS AND FRETTED STRETCHER. *c. 1755*

MAHOGANY FRETTED "SILVER" TABLE. *c. 1755*

MAHOGANY FRETTED COFFEE TABLE. CHIPPENDALE PERIOD. *c. 1760*

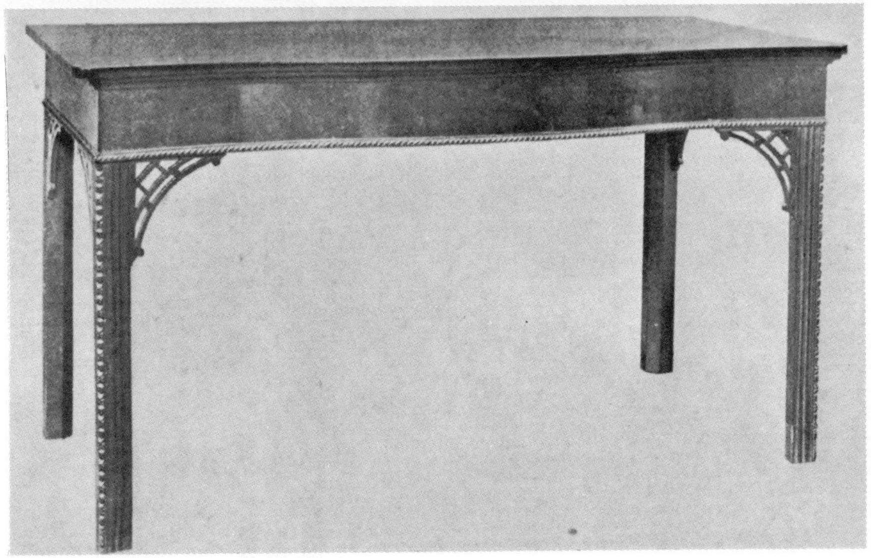

MAHOGANY TABLE OF THE CHIPPENDALE SCHOOL. THE STRAIGHT LEGS ARE MOULDED, CHAMFERED ON THE INSIDE EDGE, WITH FRETTED BRACKETS AT THE CORNERS. A REPRESENTATIVE TYPE OF *1755*

MAHOGANY CABRIOLE TABLE IN THE GOTHIC MANNER OF THE CHIPPENDALE SCHOOL. THE PERSISTENCE OF THE PAW FOOT IS VERY EXCEPTIONAL. *c. 1750*

MAHOGANY CABRIOLE SIDE TABLE OF THE CHIPPENDALE SCHOOL. VERY RARE IN THE LATE USE OF THE FORMER PIED-DE-BICHE OF THE LAST YEARS OF THE SEVENTEENTH CENTURY. *c. 1750*

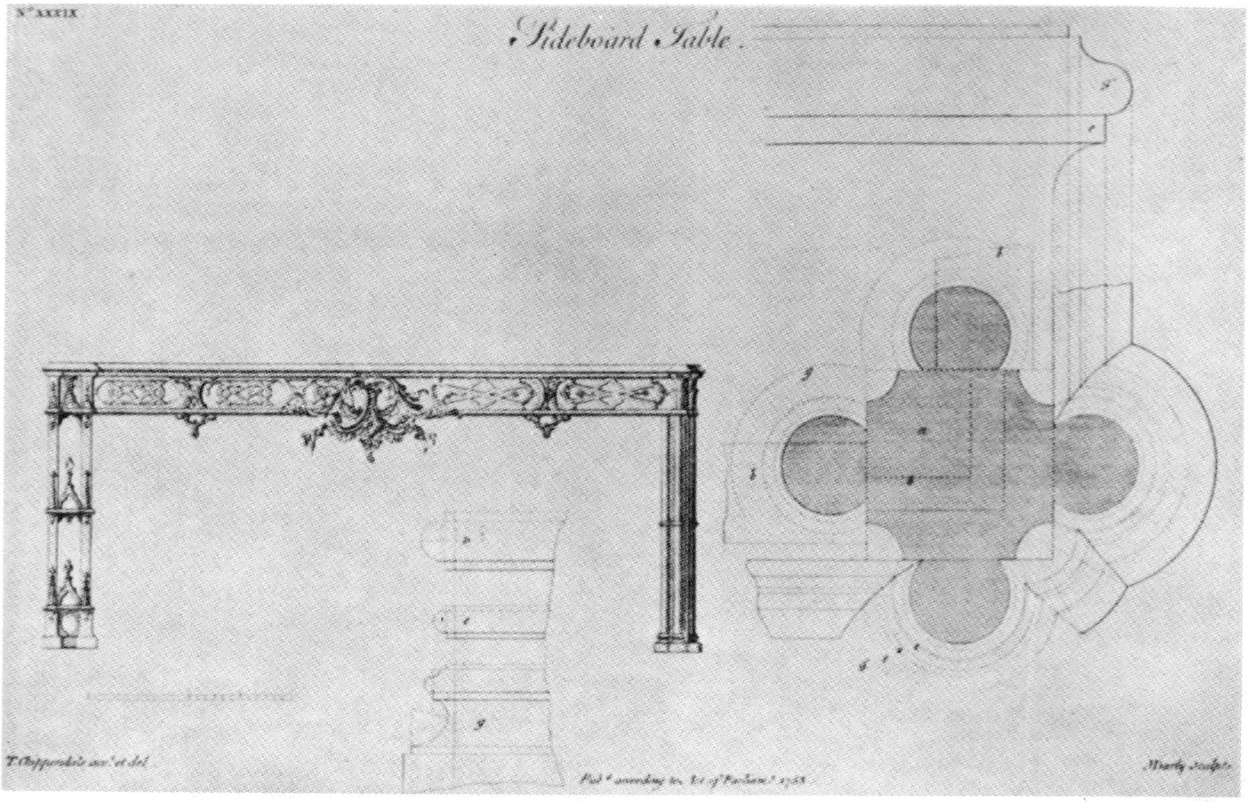

SIDEBOARD TABLE, "DIRECTOR" PLATE *39* (*1753*). THIS IS THE TRUE CHIPPENDALE SIDEBOARD, AND IS AMONG THE MORE PRACTICAL OF THE "DIRECTOR" DESIGNS, YET TABLES OF THIS KIND ARE EXCEEDINGLY RARE. IT IS ALSO AN EXAMPLE OF THE CLUSTER-COLUMN LEG (SHOWN IN PLAN AT THE SIDE) WHICH HAS THE APPEARANCE OF GREAT DELICACY, YET IS REALLY STRONGER THAN A LEG OF THE SAME GIRTH MADE FROM SOLID TIMBER INSTEAD OF BEING BUILT UP

MAHOGANY SIDE TABLE OF THE CHIPPENDALE PERIOD. EXCEPTIONAL IN HAVING TAPERED LEGS AND MOULDED BLOCK FEET. AN EXAMPLE WHICH BRIDGES THE CHIPPENDALE AND THE HEPPLEWHITE STYLES. *c. 1755*

MAHOGANY HANGING CHINA CASE OF *1740* SHOWING THE ARCHITECTURAL INFLUENCE OF THAT TIME

MAHOGANY HANGING CANDLE LANTERNS IN THE CHINESE MANNER OF THE CHIPPENDALE SCHOOL. *c. 1760*

LACQUERED HANGING CHINA CASE WITH FRAMED BACK FORMED OF CHINESE PANELS. PROBABLY MADE BY THOMAS CHIPPENDALE FOR RAINHAM HALL, NORFOLK. *c. 1755*

MAHOGANY HANGING BOOK-SHELVES WITH FRETTED SIDES. *c. 1755*

MAHOGANY HANGING BOOK-SHELF. *c. 1780*

MAHOGANY FRETTED HANGING BOOK-SHELVES IN THE GOTHIC MANNER OF THE CHIPPENDALE SCHOOL. *c. 1750*

MAHOGANY FRET-SIDED HANGING BOOK-SHELVES. *c. 1750-60*

MAHOGANY FRETTED HANGING BOOK-SHELF OR CHINA CASE. *c. 1760*

MAHOGANY CHEST OF DRAWERS WITHOUT CARVING OR ORNAMENTATION OF ANY KIND. CHIPPENDALE PERIOD. *c. 1750*

MAHOGANY CHEST OF DRAWERS. CHIPPENDALE PERIOD. *c. 1750-60.* REEDED ANGLES AND GADROON-CARVED TOP MOULDING

MAHOGANY CHEST OF DRAWERS. CHIPPENDALE PERIOD. *c. 1760.* SPLAYED ANGLES, ORNAMENTED WITH APPLIED FRETS

MAHOGANY CHEST OF DRAWERS. CHIPPENDALE PERIOD. *c. 1760.* SERPENTINE FRONT, AND TOP SHAPED ONLY AT SIDES. SPLAY CORNERS WITH APPLIED FRETS. THE COMMODE IN EMBRYO

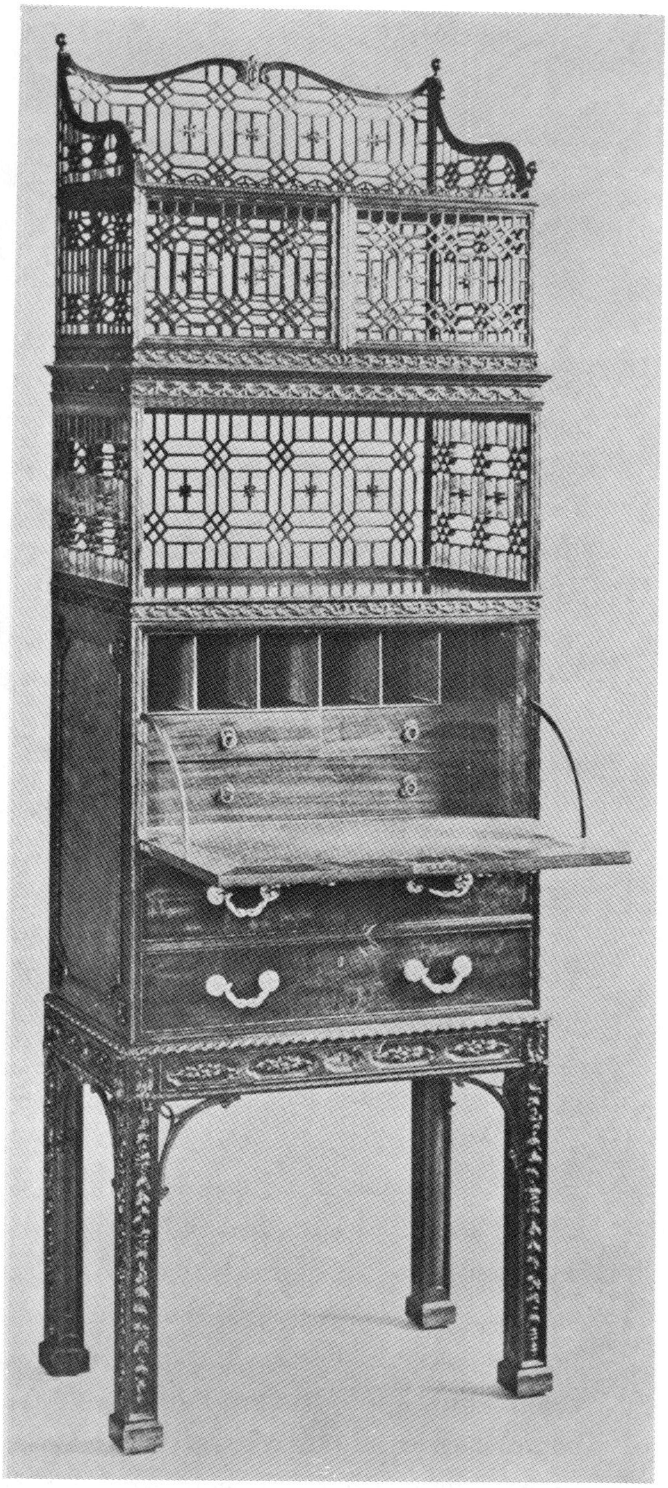

TWO VIEWS OF A REMARKABLE MAHOGANY UPRIGHT SECRETAIRE CABINET (OPEN AND CLOSED) THE WORKMANSHIP IS OF THE HIGHEST ORDER AND THE CARVING IS ALMOST MICROSCOPIC IN ITS DELICACY. IN THE FRIEZE OF EACH STAGE IS A SHALLOW DRAWER. *c. 1750*

CHAPTER XVII

Robert and James Adam

IN A SURVEY of English furniture the place of the Brothers Adam—the "Adelphi" of a famous London lottery—falls naturally between an account of the work of the Chippendale and of the Hepplewhite Schools. Robert Adam certainly employed the former, and probably the latter, and the Adam Style in furniture directly influenced that of Hepplewhite. Perhaps there was a reacting influence, at the same time, at least as far as furniture was concerned, as the designs of Robert and James Adam, undoubtedly, became more rational during the years of their practice.

Of the four brothers—John, Robert, James and William—it is the second who was the dominant factor in the London practice, and when we speak of "Adam" it is to the style of Robert that we really refer. To divorce the furniture of Adam from his decoration, or his building, is almost impossible, all the more so as there is the same affinity, or rather want of comprehension of the possibilities and disabilities of material, in them all. Herein lies the inherent weakness of the Adam Style. The outside façades of the houses on the Adelphi Terrace, for example, (the Adelphi was the famous speculation of all the four brothers) have the same anthemion decoration (and in stucco) that one finds also on the ceilings, on the mantels, and also on the furniture inside. Robert Adam was never true to his materials; he positively loved shams. The "marble" columns in the house of the Society of Arts in the Adelphi (in John Street) are painted and "marbled"; the "carving" on the mantels is composition, and the work of the brothers abounds in similar deceptions. When Adam ornament is overdone (as it is, too often) the effect is like the attempt of a confectioner rather than of an architect. This fault may have originated, at the outset, from ignorance of the nature of materials or from lack of tradition, but two factors demanded that they should be perpetuated, the first being the financial interest which Adam acquired in the Liardet stucco (how appropriate is the name of the inventor!); the second, that a manner becomes a style only by reiteration, and a fashion condemns the stylist to the one mannerism, forevermore. Robert Adam, therefore (who was the ruling spirit of the "Adelphi" in all its ventures) was an abler architect than he was a decorator, and as either he was more original than as a designer of furniture.

To give an account of Adam furniture and decoration involves some mention of the brothers and their work, especially in architectural fields. The four brothers were the sons of William Adam of Maryburgh, (now Blair Adam) near Kinross, in Scotland. Adam senior is known chiefly as the author of "Vitruvius Scoticus," an imitation of Campbell's "Vitruvius Britannicus" (1715–25). Robert, the second son, with whom we are here chiefly concerned, was born in 1728. To his father's large practice he doubtless owed his sudden leap to fame, after he returned from his continental tour in 1758. It may be as well to give the dates of the brothers here, for easy reference; John, 1721–92; Robert, 1728–92; James, 1730–94; and William, 1738–1822. Of the four, the eldest does not appear to have taken any active part in the London business; the youngest was the bookkeeper, and afterwards perpetuated the name of Robert by collecting the original sketches and drawings which are now in the Soane Museum in Lincoln's Inn Fields. James was the principal draughtsman, and in this he excelled, being both neat and painstaking, as the preserved drawings show. As a designer, he was markedly inferior to Robert, judging from the evidence of some of the houses in Portland Place, for which he was responsible.

Some mention of the Soane collection of the original Adam drawings must be made here, if only to give some idea of the immense practice which Robert and James Adam had, in London and throughout England, Ireland and Scotland. They are incomplete, as one would expect, considering that so many of the original sketches must have passed into clients' hands, been lost or mislaid. On the other hand, of the entire number, comprising nearly nine thousand, contained in fifty-three large folios, many are mere suggestions which were either abandoned or superseded. The entire collection was purchased by Sir John Soane in 1833, from the trustees of Robert Adam's estate, for £200, and they are now permanently housed in Soane's old house in Lincoln's Inn Fields, and available to all students. To William Adam we owe the labour of collecting these sketches from various clients, although a number were independently sold in 1821, apart from those in the Soane collection.

To give anything like a complete list of the Adam clients would, in itself, absorb far more space than is here available. Those who are interested in the study of the brothers and their works may be referred to the two monumental volumes of Arthur T. Bolton, the present Curator of the Soane Museum. Even within the narrow zone of thirty miles 'round London, there are records of work for William Aislabie at South Lodge, Hendon; David Garrick's Villa at Hampton, (Garrick occupied one of the houses on the Adelphi Terrace, next door to that of Robert Adam; the furniture for this house was made by Thomas Chippendale, both furniture and invoices being now preserved in the Victoria and Albert Museum in London); that of the Earl of Ashburnham at Teddington, Hatchlands Park, near Guildford, for Admiral Boscawen; Luton Park, Bedfordshire; for the Earl of Bute (patron of the Adam Brothers, and the Minister who did so much to pass the Act legalising the Adelphi Lottery) Osterley

Park, Middlesex, for Robert Child, the banker; Copped Hall, Epping, for John Conyers; Claremont, Surrey, for Sir John (afterwards, Lord) Delaval; West Wycombe Park, Bucks, for Lord Le Despencer; Moor Park, Hertfordshire, for Sir Lawrence Dundas; Richmond Park, for H. M. King George III; Kenwood, at Hampstead, for the Earl of Mansfield, Lord Chief Justice of England and Premier Earl of Scotland; Syon House, Middlesex, for the Duke of Northumberland; Bulstrode, Stowe House, and Shardeloes, all in Buckinghamshire; the first for the Duke of Portland, the second for Earl Temple, and the third for William Drake, a descendant of Sir Francis of Armada fame.

In London itself, to mention only a few, we have Shelburne (now Lansdowne) House, in Berkeley Square, for the Earl of Shelburne; Apsley House in Piccadilly, for Earl Bathurst; No. 20 Portman Square, for the Countess of Home; No. 10 Hertford Street, Mayfair, for General Burgoyne, who surrendered at Saratoga in 1777; No. 16 Cavendish Square, for the Earl of Hopetoun; No. 17 Hill Street, Mayfair, for Sir Abraham Hume; No. 20 St. James' Square, for Sir Watkin Williams Wynn; and last of all, the private speculation of the brothers, the houses in the Adelphi, comprising John, Robert, James, William and Adam Streets, and the Adelphi Terrace, the latter being the best expression of the Adam style.

Of the life of Robert Adam, the briefest mention must suffice. He commenced his Grand Tour in 1754 and he did not return to England until 1758. Practically the whole of this time he was busy surveying, sketching, measuring and studying the works of ancient architecture in Italy and elsewhere. The result, in part, of his extensive labours was the large folio volume, "The Ruins of the Palace of the Emperor Diocletian at Spalato in Venetian Dalmatia," with engravings by Piranesi and Bartolozzi, published in 1758.

Apart from their enormous architectural practice, which was large enough to have absorbed all their time and energies, the brothers entered into a scheme to reclaim and re-build that part of the Strand, on the south side, down to the Thames, known as the "Adelphi," from its association with the Brothers Adam. Apart from the actual building, the cost of the foundations and vaultings, to level the district with the Strand, proved so enormous that the speculation soon outran the Adams' resources. The brothers succeeded in influencing the Earl of Bute—then in power—to procure a Bill in their favour, legalising what was known as the Adelphi Lottery. Some idea of the magnitude of the Adams' commitments may be gathered from the fact that the lottery, in 1773, involved a sum of £218,500 in 4,370 tickets at £50 each, of which 108 were prizes, and Robert Adam claimed that the success of the lottery would no more than recoup the brothers for their outlay. Certain other properties of the brothers, in the neighbourhood of Portland Place, were included among the prizes. There is every reason for supposing that the lottery was a financial success, that the Adam finances were relieved, and, at the same time, that their taste for speculation was curbed. Their lease of the Adelphi property, from the Duke of St. Albans, was for only 99 years, and Bazalgette's Embankment—which has since so enormously improved the property in preventing the inundations of the Thames—was a project of the future at that time.

Robert appears to have been inclined to certain speculations. He bought the patent of the Liardet stucco—the invention of a Swiss—and the acquisition of the secret undoubtedly had a marked effect on the development of the style of the brothers. With Robert Adam's real genius for detail, planning, massing and spacing, his financial interest in this stucco was rather a disaster than a gain. It impelled him to introduce this stucco everywhere in his works.

From the Adelphi, in addition to the architectural and decorative sketches, came many designs for furniture, some very amateurish in conception, others of a practical character which suggest the editing hand of the cabinetmaker. There are no records as to the makers to whom these sketches were entrusted for realisation in wood. We know that Chippendale worked for the brothers, but only from preserved invoices in the hands of the Adelphi clients, such as Sir Rowland Winn at Nostell Priory. Of other makers—of which there must have been many—we know little or nothing. Yet the marked effect of the Adam style on that of the school of Hepplewhite suggests that Hepplewhite himself must have been employed by Adam. To treat of Hepplewhite and his style here would be to anticipate the next chapter, but it may be said that, had the Adam style not existed, the "Cabinet Maker and Upholsterer's Guide" of Hepplewhite would have been a very different production to what it is. Unfortunately, of George Hepplewhite of Cripplegate we know little or nothing. His design book is a posthumous production, published by his widow, two years after his death. Many, if not all, of the designs must have been prepared during Hepplewhite's lifetime, as their engraving would be a long process.

On the other hand, if we examine the Adam furniture designs in chronological order, it will be found that there is manifested, in the gradual technical evolution, as well as in the development of the Adam Style itself, a notable influence from outside. This practical improvement may well have come from Hepplewhite and his school; it is not of a kind which would have originated from Thomas Chippendale, obsessed, as he was, with his own "Director" manner. The early Adam designs are often wildly impossible, and with little or no artistic merit. They are original, in the sense that no cabinetmaker would have been guilty of designing them, which is dubious praise, indeed. Robert Adam had one cardinal fault; he had, as has already been remarked, very little sense of material. Thus, in his sketches, he treats stone, brick, stucco, lead, (for the tracery of fanlights) composition, wood, silver or fabrics as if their properties were alike. To use the same design for a ceiling or a carpet (as at Osterley Park) was, to him, a matter of course. It is only with the later Adam furniture that the sense of restraint and suitability of material becomes apparent. That these qualities are due to the rationalising influence of the cabinetmakers who worked for the Adelphi, there can be little question. Nor is this effect noticeable only in the later sketches; one has only to compare the designs with the work as actually executed, to see how serious were the modifications in the former as they passed through the workshop.

Robert Adam possessed the unquestionable advantage that he could afford to disregard expense, in the case of his wealthy clients. Take, for instance, the famous side board suite at Harewood, made by Chippendale, to Adam's designs. One can imagine how the idea would have been cheapened and mutilated, had Chippendale dealt directly with Edwin Lascelles. Apart from the design itself, the workmanship is of the finest and most costly quality, the ormolu mountings in particular being superb.

I came to the conclusion, nearly twenty years ago, that the debt which Adam and Hepplewhite owed to each other was nearly equal, and I then coined the name of "Adam-Hepplewhite" to describe a style which belongs properly to both. I have seen no reason to change my opinion since, although the Adam style forms only a part of that of Hepplewhite. This, however, belongs to the next chapter, in which it is proposed to examine and describe the work of the Hepplewhite School. The illustrations to this chapter will serve to illustrate the Adam Style better than any textual description.

Before closing this chapter, mention must be made of the important "Works in Architecture of Robert and James Adam," a large folio, of which the first part appeared in 1773 and continued, at intervals, until 1778. An additional volume was published by William Adam in 1812. The original sketches are not in the Soane Museum, being sold separately in 1821.

MAHOGANY BOOKCASE DESIGNED BY ROBERT ADAM FOR THE LIBRARY, *20* ST. JAMES' SQUARE. AN EXAMPLE OF ADAM'S REFINED AND RATIONAL STYLE

SIDE TABLE, PAINTED AND PARCEL GILT. A DESIGN IN THE STYLE OF ADAM

THE TOP OF THE CARVED AND GILT ADAM SIDE TABLE SHOWN BELOW. INLAID WITH SUBJECTS, IN SLIGHT RELIEF, IN COLOURED COMPOSITIONS. THE CENTRE PANEL IS "THE DANCING HOURS," WELL KNOWN IN FLAXMAN-WEDGWOOD MEDALLIONS

ONE OF A PAIR OF MAHOGANY SIDE TABLES WITH VENEERED BRESCIA MARBLE TOPS. DESIGNED BY ROBERT

SIDE TABLE VENEERED WITH VARIOUS WOODS, INLAID WITH MARQUETERIE, AND MOUNTED WITH ORMOLU. PROBABLY DESIGNED BY ADAM AND MADE BY SEDDON

PEDESTAL AND URN MATCHING SIDE TABLE SHOWN IN CENTRE

MAHOGANY SIDEBOARD PEDESTAL AND URN. ADAM'S DESIGNING AT ITS BEST

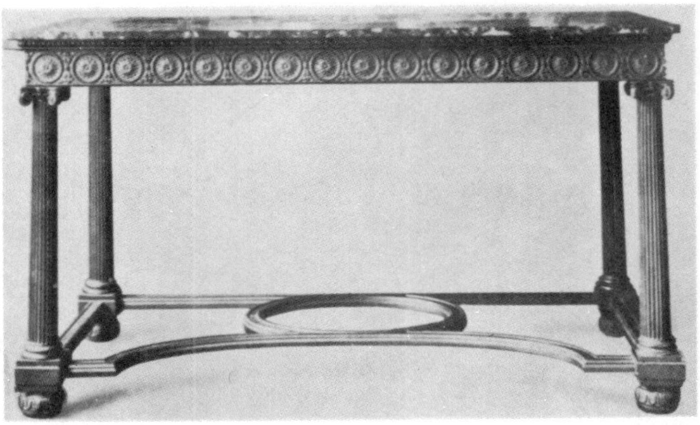

ADAM STYLE MAHOGANY SIDEBOARD-PEDESTALS AND URNS, AND CARVED AND GILT SIDE TABLE IN ADAM'S CLASSICAL MANNER

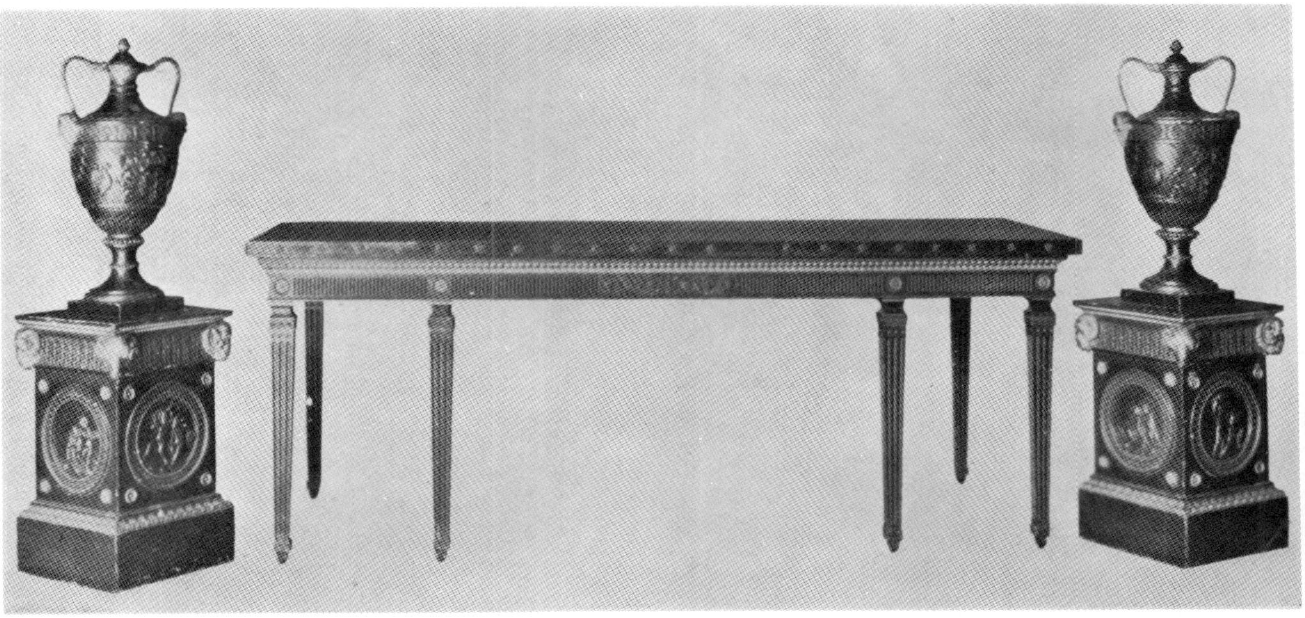

SIDE TABLE. PEDESTALS AND URNS, IN WOOD, PAINTED AND PARCEL GILT. DESIGNED BY ROBERT ADAM FOR *20* ST. JAMES' SQUARE

MAHOGANY CHAIR IN THE STYLE OF ADAM. TYPICAL ADAM CHAIRS (AS DISTINCT FROM HEPPLEWHITE) ARE VERY RARE

MAHOGANY CHAIR. A CURIOUS PATTERN DESIGNED BY ADAM SHOWING HIS LACK OF KNOWLEDGE OF CHAIR CONSTRUCTION

HEPPLEWHITE ARMCHAIR, SHOWING STRONG ADAM INFLUENCE

TYPICAL ADAM MAHOGANY CHAIR

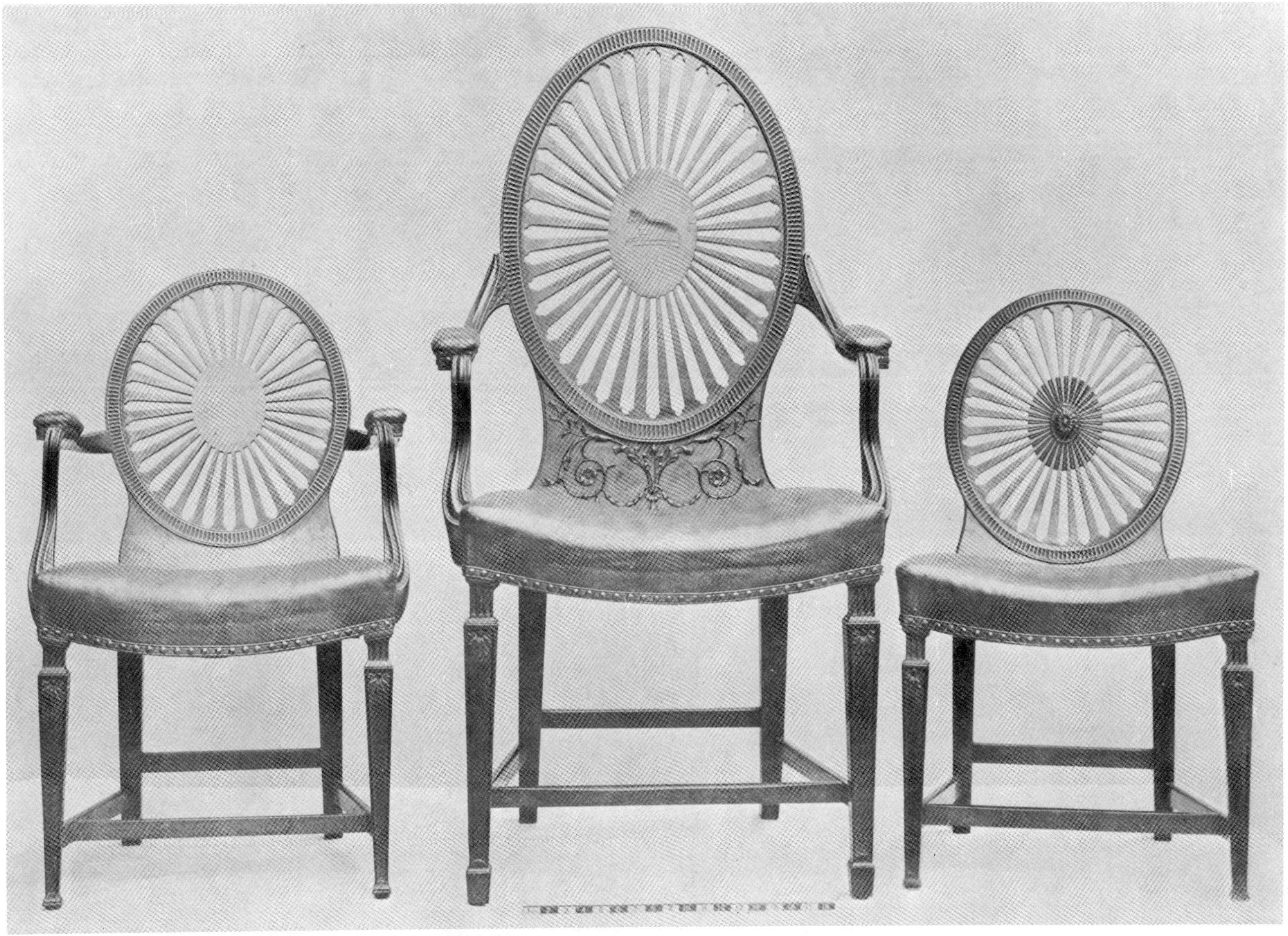

MASTER'S, WARDEN'S AND LIVERY CHAIRS, DESIGNED BY THE "ADELPHI" FOR THE DRAPER'S COMPANY OF THE CITY OF LONDON. IN THE OVALS OF EACH ARMCHAIR BACK IS THE LAMB, THE BADGE OF THE COMPANY

CARVED, SANDED AND GILT CONSOLE TABLE WITH INLAID SATINWOOD TOP. STYLE OF ROBERT ADAM

MAHOGANY WHEEL-BACK CHAIR. SCHOOL OF ADAM

SEMI-CIRCULAR COMMODE AND ONE OF A PAIR OF CONSOLE TABLES TO MATCH. VENEERED WITH SATINWOOD, BANDED WITH TULIP, INLAID FANS AND PAINTED WITH GARLANDS OF FLOWERS. THE STYLE OF ADAM IN CONJUNCTION WITH CIPRIANI

FOUR PAINTED AND GILT SIDE TABLES WITH DECORATED TOPS IN THE STYLE OF ADAM, DESIGNED IN CONJUNCTION WITH ANGELICA KAUFFMANN AND ANTONIO ZUCCHI

WHITE MARBLE MANTEL INLAID WITH COLOURED COMPOSITION. SAID TO HAVE BEEN THE SECRET INVENTION OF AN ITALIAN NAMED BOSSI, DOMICILED IN DUBLIN. HE WAS EXTENSIVELY EMPLOYED BY THE "ADELPHI"

MARBLE MANTEL IN THE STYLE OF ADAM

"SECOND DESIGN OF A CHIMNEY PIECE FOR THE GALLERY AT HAREWOOD." "ADELPHI," *22ND JUNE, 1776.*
FROM THE ORIGINAL DRAWING IN THE SOANE MUSEUM

"CHIMNEY PIECE FOR THE GREAT DRAWING ROOM AT BOLTON HOUSE." "ADELPHI," *31ST JULY, 1777.*
FROM THE ORIGINAL DRAWING IN THE SOANE MUSEUM

"CHIMNEY PIECE FOR THE SALON AT NOSTEL (NOSTELL PRIORY)," *1772*. FROM THE ORIGINAL DRAWING IN THE SOANE MUSEUM

"CHIMNEY PIECE FOR THE GREAT ROOM AT BOWOOD," *1762*. FROM THE ORIGINAL DRAWING IN THE SOANE MUSEUM

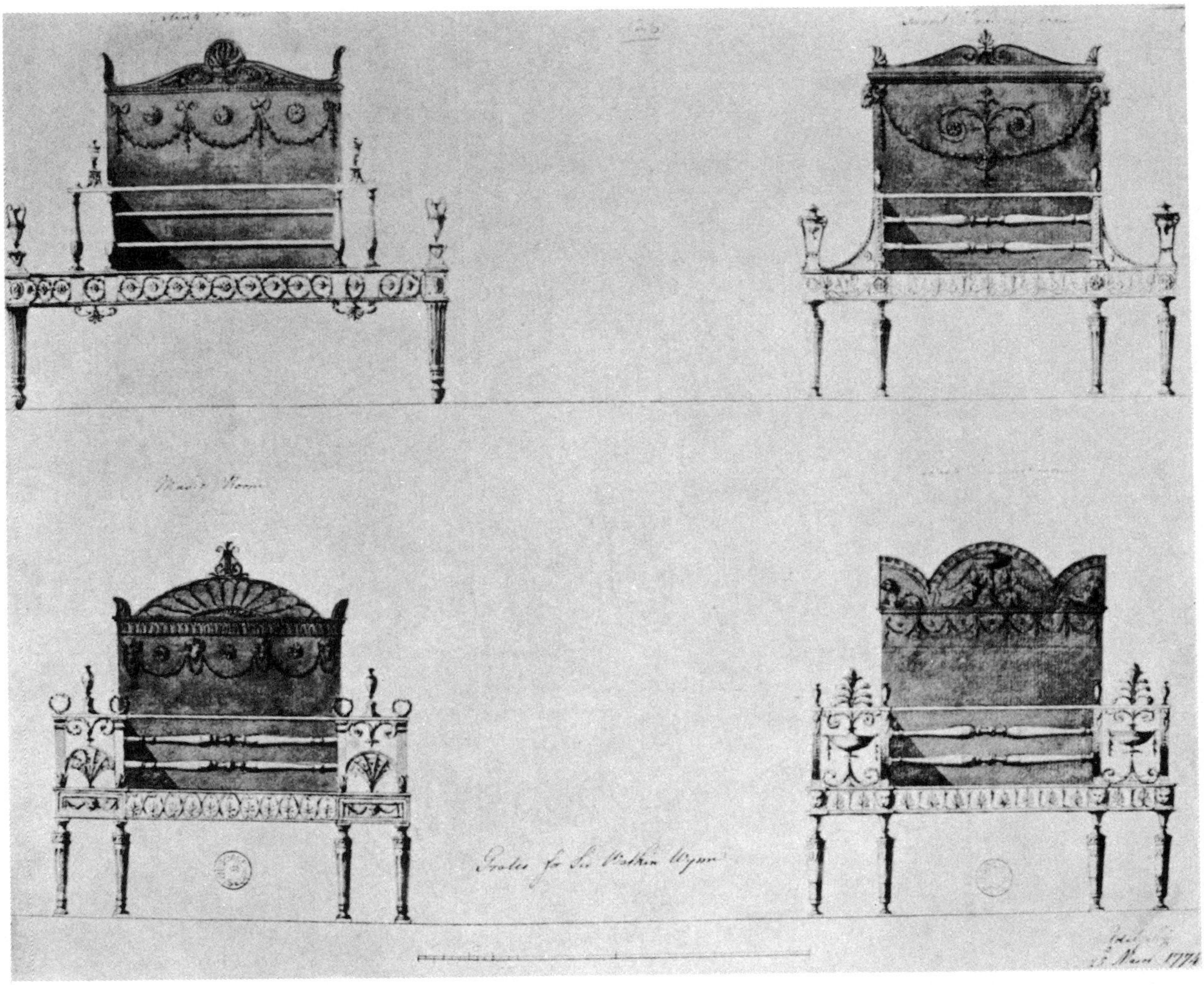

"GRATES FOR SIR WATKIN WYNN." "ADELPHI," 25TH MARCH, *1774*. FROM THE ORIGINAL DRAWING IN THE SOANE MUSEUM

"GRATE FOR ROBERT CHILD, ESQ." "ADELPHI," 22ND APRIL, *1773*. FROM THE ORIGINAL SKETCH IN THE SOANE MUSEUM

"DESIGN FOR A GRATE AND FENDER FOR THE RIGHT HONOURABLE THE EARL OF COVENTRY." "ROBERT ADAM, ARCHITECT, *1765*." FROM THE ORIGINAL DRAWING IN THE SOANE MUSEUM

"GLASS AND TABLE FRAME FOR THE BREAKFASTING ROOM AT OSTERLY." "ADELPHI," 24TH APRIL, *1777*. FROM THE ORIGINAL DRAWING IN THE SOANE MUSEUM

"GLASS AND COMMODE FOR GEORGE KEATE, ESQ." "ADELPHI," *1778*. FROM THE ORIGINAL DRAWING IN THE SOANE MUSEUM

"Chimney piece for the drawing room at Northumberland House." "Adelphi," *1773*. From the original drawing in the Soane Museum

"Chimney piece for the second drawing room at Lord Stanley's in Grosvenor Square." "Adelphi," 28th February, *1774*. From the original drawing in the Soane Museum

"DESIGN OF A CHIMNEY PIECE FOR THE DRESSING ROOM AT THE EARL OF HARRINGTON'S." FROM THE ORIGINAL DRAWING IN THE SOANE MUSEUM. THIS SKETCH ILLUSTRATES THE WANT OF APPRECIATION OF THE POSSIBILITIES AND THE LIMITATIONS OF MATERIALS. NOTE THE ORNAMENT OF THE GLASS ABOVE

"CHIMNEY GLASS IN FRONT DRAWING ROOM AT ROBERT CHILD, ESQ.'S IN BERKLEY SQUARE." FROM THE ORIGINAL DRAWING IN THE SOANE MUSEUM

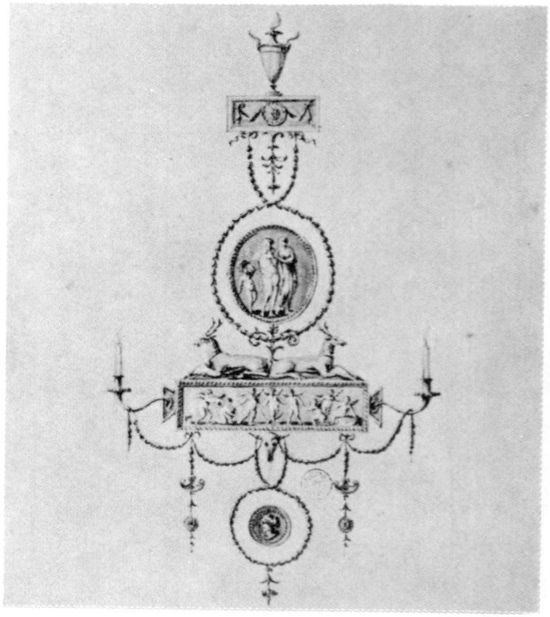

"GIRANDOL FOR LADY BATHURST'S DRESSING ROOM." "ADELPHI," *31ST JANUARY, 1778.* WITHOUT THE SHAM OF WIRED COMPOSITION, THIS DESIGN IS IMPOSSIBLE OF EXECUTION. FROM THE ORIGINAL DRAWING IN THE SOANE MUSEUM

CHAPTER XVIII

The Style of the Hepplewhite School

It is convenient, in practice, to name a furniture style after the man who first publishes a book of designs in the particular manner; but that is not to say he is, or was, the pioneer of that style. It is possible, if not highly probable, that the styles of Chippendale and Hepplewhite may have originated with other cabinetmakers, whose names posterity has failed to record. In the case of Chippendale, as we have already seen, his claim as creator of the "Director" designs is dubious, to say the least, which is suggested from internal evidences in the book itself. With Hepplewhite's "Cabinet Maker and Upholsterer's Guide" we are very differently circumstanced, as the designs in that book are those of a practical cabinet- or chairmaker. He *could* have been the originator of all the designs in the "Guide," whereas the "Director" patterns are often so impractical that no cabinetmaker would have designed them; so that we are compelled to suggest "ghosting."

Of George Hepplewhite, of Redcross Street in the ward of Cripplegate, in the City of London, we really know very little. The earliest reliable information which we have is that afforded by the "Guide," which was issued by the firm of "A. Hepplewhite & Co.," the initial being that of the widow, Alice. The husband, having died intestate, the usual bond was entered into in the sum of £800, signed by "Aleas Heppelwhite" (afterwards altered to "Alice," and the mis-spelling of the name may be due to the same cause), Robert Philp, clockmaker, of John Street, Clerkenwell, and Charles Wheeler, stocking maker, of Gee Street in the parish of St. Luke, addressed to "John, by Divine Providence, Lord Archbishop of Canterbury, etc., etc." At that date wills were proved in the surrogate's court of Canterbury. The bond is marked "under £600," which refers, obviously, to the amount of the estate as sworn to probate.

George Hepplewhite died in 1786, and the first edition of the "Guide" was not published until two years after. A second edition was called for in 1789, and a third in 1794. The book was issued by I. & J. Taylor, "at the Architectural Library, No. 56 Holborn, opposite Great Turn-Stile," in London.

The designs in the "Cabinet Maker and Upholsterer's Guide" (unlike Chippendale, Hepplewhite does not make any appeal to "The Nobility and Gentry," nor are "Gentlemen" indicated in the title) differ from those in the "Director" in one important particular; they are, without exception, thoroughly practical. That they were not original creations of Hepplewhite himself, we know from the preface, in which it is frankly stated, "To Residents in London, though our drawings are all new, yet, as we designedly followed the latest and most prevailing fashion only, purposely omitting such articles, whose recommendation was mere novelty, and perhaps a violation of all established rule, the production of whim at the instance of caprice, whose appetite must ever suffer disappointment if any similar thing had been previously thought of. . . ." (It may be remarked that these prefaces do not read like the writing of a cabinet-maker, and one is tempted to assume that Grub Street was called in to aid in their compilation.)

In the "Guide," therefore, there is no claim to originality, and little doubt can exist that many of the patterns had been made before the book was published, and probably by others. In speaking of the "Hepplewhite Style," therefore, the reference must be to the work of a school rather than to that of a man or of a firm.

Unlike the style of Chippendale, as exemplified in the "Director"—which is a mere jumble—that of Hepplewhite permits of orderly classification into four main classes, as follows:

(1) That work which shows the influence of Robert Adam, which may be conveniently designated as "Adam-Hepplewhite."
(2) Models borrowed from the Louis Quinze, which may be called "Curved or cabriole Hepplewhite."
(3) Those taken from the Louis Seize, the "Turned-leg Hepplewhite."
(4) The "Taper-leg Hepplewhite," which is, perhaps, the most original and representative of the work of this school.

In the case of chairs, which are among the most original efforts of Hepplewhite and his school, further classifications may be attempted, thus:

(1) The bridge-pieces which over-lap with the Chippendale, chiefly evident in the ladder-back chairs.
(2) The serpentine top-rail, sweeping down to the outer balusters of the back in unbroken lines, only one remove from the Chippendale.
(3) The hoop-back, almost a revival of the earlier Queen Anne, or the early mahogany period.
(4) The shield-back, in its various forms.
(5) The oval-back, sometimes found in conjunction with the French cabriole.
(6) The pear-shaped, cartouche-back, nearly always borrowed from the French, with little, if any, modification.
(7) The interlacing, heart-shaped back, usually in conjunction with the tapered leg with moulded toe.
(8) Variations on two or more of the above.

To avoid the confusion which is so general in dealing with the creations of Hepplewhite and of Sheraton, it may be said that none of the above forms are, even remotely, characteristic of Sheraton, whose chair-styles are quite distinct from those of Hepplewhite.

The practical nature of all the designs in the "Guide" may be held to imply that Hepplewhite was less ambitious than Chippendale. But that is only to say, in other words, that no constructional violations, in the way of gluing carvings on the glass of latticed doors, or reinforcing pendant swags with concealed wires, were tolerated by Hepplewhite. Had Chippendale really originated what we know as his style, the same might have been said of the Chippendale manner, as both were practical cabinet-makers, but in that case, the "Director" would have been a very different book to what it is.

Dealing with the "Guide" and its claims to originality on the other hand, we must remember that Hepplewhite's book (3rd edition; 1794) and "The Cabinet Maker and Upholsterer's Drawing Book" of Thomas Sheraton, (the first parts of which appeared in 1791) actually over-lap in point of date, and if Sheraton, at least in his chair designs, did not borrow from the Hepplewhite school to any extent, the third edition of the "Guide" (in Plate 1, the chair on the right of the page; Plate 6, left; Plate 8, right; Plate 9, left; Plate 9a, both designs; Plate 10, left; and Plates 12 and 13) does help itself, considerably, from the Sheraton manner. Perhaps that is why Sheraton, in his preface, says, "notwithstanding the late date of Hepplewhite's book, if we compare some of the designs, particularly the chairs, with the newest taste, we shall find that this work has already caught the decline, and perhaps, in a little time, will suddenly die in the disorder." The passage is more spiteful than true, as the verdict of a century and a half has proved, especially as the chair-designs referred to are in the style of Sheraton, for which he claims novelty and merit.

To the school of Hepplewhite, if not to the man himself, belongs the credit for the introduction and use of the lighter woods, satinwood, "eyre" or "harewood," (which is a name given to sycamore when stained a greyish-brown with oxide of iron, usually by immersion of the veneers in rusty water) chestnut and holly, for flat veneerings, tulip, kingwood and rosewood for bandings, amboyna and thuja for inlay in panels, and variously stained woods for marqueterie, an art which was revived at this date. The patterns of this marqueterie differ very considerably from those of the walnut years, the usual devices being those of the fan, patera, scroll and swag, such as had been popularised by the Adelphi. As an alternative to inlay, we find the fashion for garlands and swags of flowers painted on a ground of satinwood, harewood or chestnut, or for a solid painted ground, generally on beech, with decoration of medallions or floral motives. The taste for this furniture of lighter proportion and tone may be said to coincide with the later period of Adam, commencing about 1770, and may have originated from the Adelphi. That it is earlier than the "Guide" is certain, as some of the actual work of Chippendale is in this manner.

Foremost among the decorative artists who were responsible for much of this painted furniture were Angelica Kauffmann (1740–1807), her husband, Antonio Zucchi, Michel Angelo Pergolesi, and Giovanni Battista Cipriani. The first three were extensively employed by the Adelphi for the decoration of walls and ceilings, in the medallion fashion which the Adam Brothers introduced and made fashionable.

In the furniture of the Hepplewhite School we have certain innovations of type. The pull-out secretaire drawer, the pull-over tambour for small writing tables and for the centre of side boards, the pouch worktable, and the side board with drawers and cupboards, all belong to this period. It is doubtful whether the composite side board, with independent pedestals and urns, should be credited to Adam or to Hepplewhite. The same may be said of the pendant wall ornaments (for want of a better description) known at the time as "Girandoles." It is notable, also, that Hepplewhite, in the "Guide," timidly introduces the washstand as an article of household furniture, but the designs which he illustrates appear to be very inadequate affairs, more in the nature of shaving or powdering stands. It was an age when cleanliness may have been next to godliness, but both were far removed from houses, and were not catered to by cabinetmakers.

Another noticeable trend was in the direction of "occasional pieces," furniture made for ornament rather than for use, or merely to fill a room. We have journeyed far since the Gothic period, when furniture was made for special purposes. The cabinetmakers of the later eighteenth century seem to have racked their brains to invent new functions as well as new designs; they even catered to the complaint incidental to a port wine drinking age, in their "gouty stools," without which no design book was complete. Hogarth popularised this article of fashionable furniture in several of his pictures, especially in the "Marriage à la Mode" series.

Hepplewhite has been selected as representative of a particular school of his time, opposed to that of Chippendale. The former introduced the lighter woods; the latter is almost entirely a mahogany style. Hepplewhite had many imitators—or he may have imitated many others—such as Crunden and Manwaring. He must have had an establishment of some size, to justify the publication of a work as expensive as the "Guide," and in three editions. Yet we possess no single, authentic record of the firm, by way of original bill or mention in any inventory. It is a pity that when William Adam was labouriously collecting the original Adelphi drawings (which must have involved considerable trouble) he did not preserve the books of entry and account of the Adam Brothers. We know that they employed Thomas Chippendale and William

France, but we get this information from bills and documents in the hands of others. It is not only Hepplewhite who is obscure; we know practically nothing of Seddon Sons & Shackleton, who had an extensive business in Aldersgate Street, of Morant in Bond Street, or of Gillow of Lancaster and London. None of the three issued a book of designs, which may account for their obscurity, but this is analogous to stating that any artist cannot become famous unless he advertises. Had Seddon, Morant or Gillow published catalogues of their wares, we might have had three other style-names to juggle with in the "antique world." Creative or executive ability would not necessarily have mattered much; posterity would have credited them with these qualities, by the simple process of attributing to them only such pieces which possessed them, if only to enhance the market value of such furniture which had escaped the ravages of time, change of fashion, or vandalism. Chippendale must have been a busy man, indeed, if he made a tithe of the furniture which has been attributed to him.

How far the "Guide" of Hepplewhite & Co. was a creation, how much of it merely gave engraved permanence to correct patterns of its time, it is not possible to say after the lapse of nearly a century and a half. Comparing it with the other design books of the same period, it stands alone for artistic merit and practical character. Similarly, the work of the Hepplewhite School is in a class apart. Only practical chair-makers know the difficulty of copying from the actual models which have survived to our day; to originate them must have been quite an additional task. Only those who have attempted to make an oval- or a shield-back chair which, at the same time, is concave on plan, (which distorts the oval or the shield) can appreciate this. In addition, the Hepplewhite School had fine traditions behind it. Proportions and details were almost instinctive. To the trade of that time the subtle differences of one-sixteenth of an inch, which are all-important to the leg of a chair or a small table, were recognised, almost sub-consciously. The models which have come down to us show this very clearly. One hardly ever meets with a badly designed Hepplewhite chair; on the other hand, one hardly ever gets a really good copy.

Machinery and mass-production have done much to dispel this tradition, and the decline of the system of apprenticeship has completed the downfall of the trade. The furniture of the Hepplewhite period was really designed in the workshop, not in the studio, and therein lies all the difference in the world.

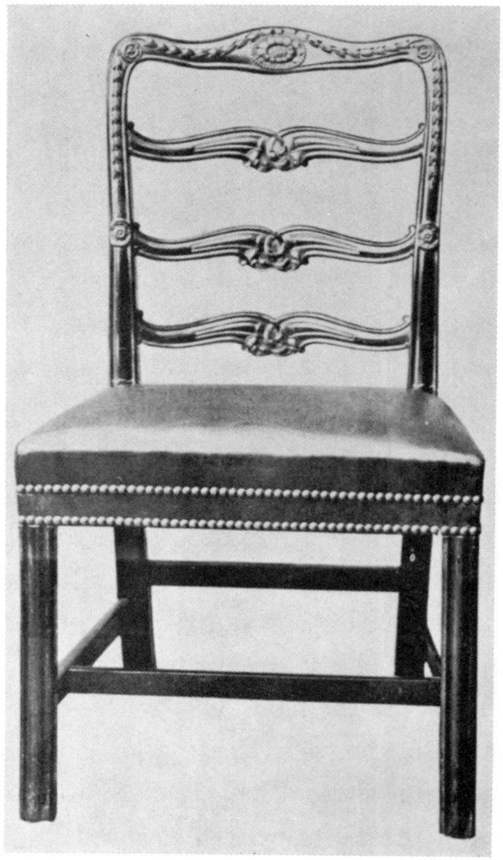

CHAIRS OF THE HEPPLEWHITE SCHOOL. TRANSITIONAL CHIPPENDALE-HEPPLEWHITE LADDER-BACK. THE TOP-RAIL MEETS THE BALUSTERS IN ONE UNBROKEN CURVE

LADDER-BACK CHAIR WITH TAPERED LEGS. THE HEPPLEWHITE SCHOOL

HEPPLEWHITE CHAIR. SERPENTINE TOP-RAIL WITH PIERCED WHEEL-SPLAT

CHAIRS OF THE HEPPLEWHITE SCHOOL. THE TRANSITIONAL CHIPPENDALE-HEPPLEWHITE LADDER-BACK

HEPPLEWHITE CHAIRS. SERPENTINE TOP-RAILS AND VERTICALLY-PIERCED SPLATS. THE REVIVAL OF THE CROSS-RAILING TO THE LEGS BEGINS WITH THE STRAIGHT-LEG CHIPPENDALE CHAIRS

HEPPLEWHITE CHAIR, OVAL BACK RICHLY CARVED. SPLAT IN THE FORM OF THE PRINCE OF WALES' FEATHERS KNOTTED WITH A RIBBON. A RARE MODEL

HEPPLEWHITE CHAIR, OVAL BACK WITH ANTHEMION PATTERN FIRST INTRODUCED BY ADAM BROTHERS. TURNED AND FLUTED FRONT LEGS WITH WATER-LEAF CAPITALS

HEPPLEWHITE CHAIR, OVAL BACK KNOWN AS THE WHEEL-AND-FAN BACK. SLENDER, TAPERED LEGS WITH X-SHAPED CROSS-RAILING. THIS TYPE NEARLY ALWAYS PAINTED AND DECORATED WITH GARLANDS OF FLOWERS

HEPPLEWHITE CHAIR, OVAL BACK. MODIFICATION OF THE ANTHEMION PATTERN IN THE BACK. FLUTED AND TAPERED FRONT LEGS

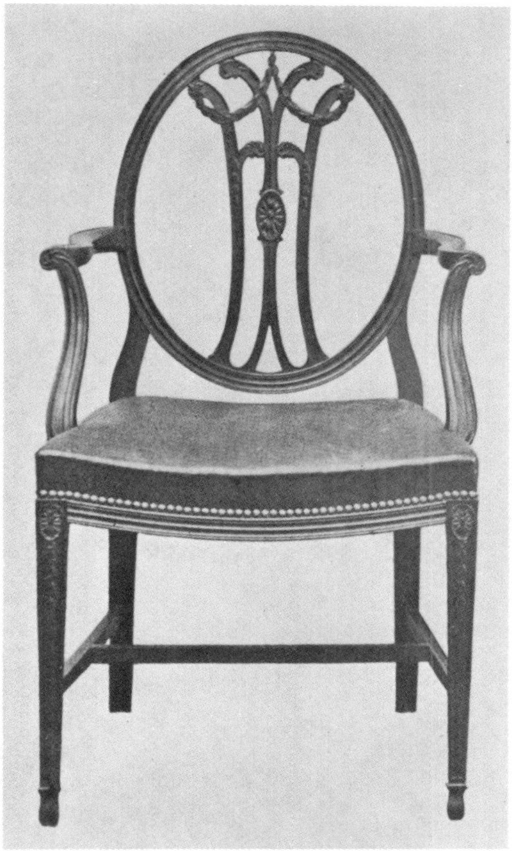

HEPPLEWHITE CHAIR. OVAL BACK WITH PIERCED CENTRAL SPLAT

CHAIR WITH OVAL BACK, UPHOLSTERED SOLID. ADAM-HEPPLEWHITE STYLE

HEPPLEWHITE CHAIR. OVAL BACK; LEGS AND FRAMING INSPIRED FROM THE FRENCH LOUIS XVI. NOTE THE OUTWARD AND BACKWARD SPLAY OF THE BACK LEGS WHICH ARE TURNED AND FLUTED

HEPPLEWHITE CHAIR. OVAL BACK, ADAM ARMS AND FRONT LEGS. THIS CHAIR SHOWS THE DEVELOPMENT FROM THE OVAL-SHAPED BACK TO THE CARTOUCHE

HEPPLEWHITE CHAIR. ALMOST A LITERAL COPY FROM THE LOUIS XVI

OVAL BACK; THE CABRIOLE OR LOUIS XV MANNER OF THE HEPPLEWHITE SCHOOL. A FINE AND GRACEFUL CHAIR

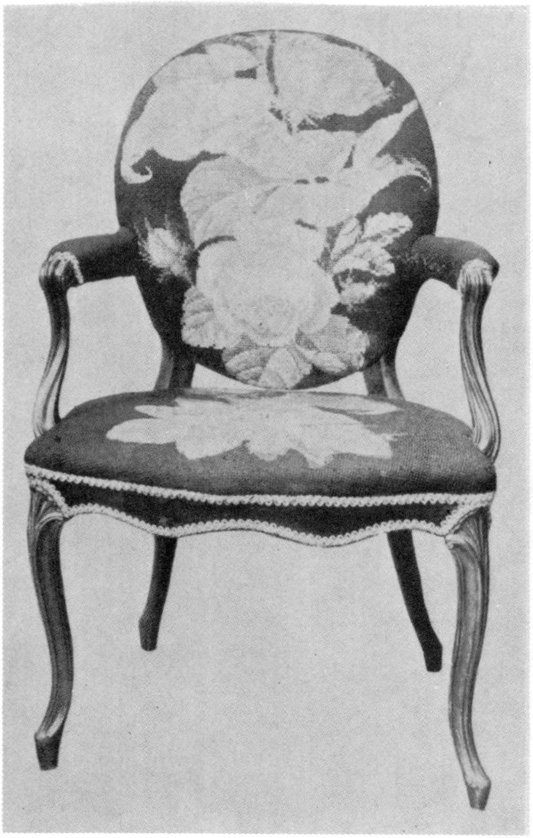

HEPPLEWHITE CHAIR. OVAL BACK, UPHOLSTERED SOLID WITHOUT VISIBLE FRAMING. THE FRENCH CABRIOLE MANNER

HEPPLEWHITE CHAIR. A VARIATION OF THE CHAIR SHOWN AT THE LEFT WITH ENGLISH TYPE OF ARM

HEPPLEWHITE CHAIR. SHIELD-BACK WITH SOLID UPHOLSTERY IN A MOULDED FRAMING. FRENCH TYPE SEAT-RAIL AND FRONT LEGS

HEPPLEWHITE CHAIR. THE LOUIS XVI MANNER, WITH THE HOOP-BACK, HERE UPHOLSTERED SOLID

HEPPLEWHITE SETTEE. THE FRENCH MANNER OF THE CHAIR SHOWN ABOVE AT THE LEFT

HEPPLEWHITE CHAIR. THE PEAR-SHAPED CARTOUCHE BACK HERE WITH THREE PIERCED SPLATS

HEPPLEWHITE CHAIR. ALMOST A LOUIS XV COPY; USUALLY IN BEECH, PAINTED OR GILDED

HEPPLEWHITE CHAIR. THE HOOP-BACK CARVED WITH WHEAT-EARS, VERTICALLY-PIERCED CENTRAL SPLAT; TAPERED LEGS WITHOUT TOES, CARVED WITH THE ADAM HUSKS

HEPPLEWHITE CHAIR. THE HOOP-BACK, WITH CONCAVE OR "SADDLE" SEAT, AND VERTICALLY-PIERCED CENTRAL SPLAT; TAPERED FRONT LEGS WITH BLOCK TOES

HEPPLEWHITE CHAIRS. FURTHER VARIATIONS OF THE HOOP-BACK

HEPPLEWHITE CHAIRS. THE USUAL FORM OF THE SHIELD-BACK WITH WHEAT-EAR CARVING

HEPPLEWHITE CHAIR. UNUSUAL SHIELD-BACK WITH TROPHY-SPLAT

HEPPLEWHITE CHAIR. SHIELD-BACK WITH LYRE-SPLAT

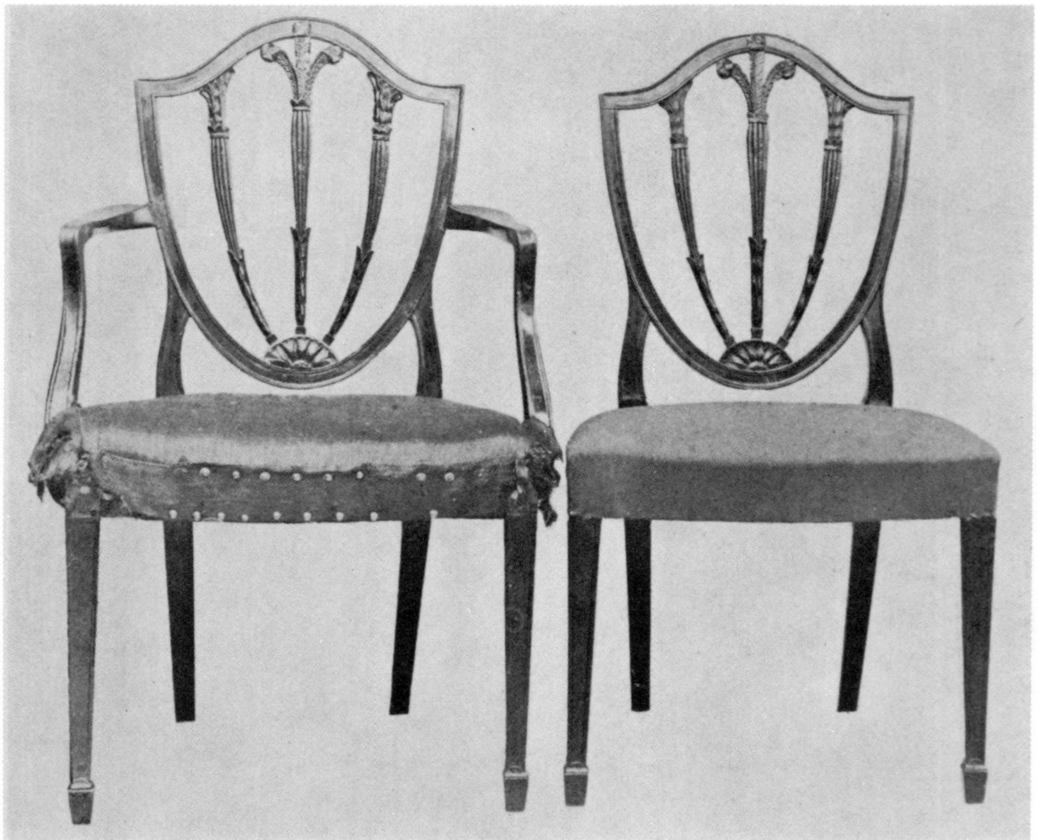

HEPPLEWHITE CHAIRS. SHIELD-BACKS WITH TRIPLE-BALUSTER SPLATS AND PRINCE OF WALES' FEATHERS IN CENTER

HEPPLEWHITE CHAIR. SHIELD-BACK WITH FIVE-BALUSTER SPLAT; WATER-LEAF CARVING

HEPPLEWHITE CHAIR. SHIELD-BACK WITH UNUSUAL FORM OF BIFURCATED BALUSTERS

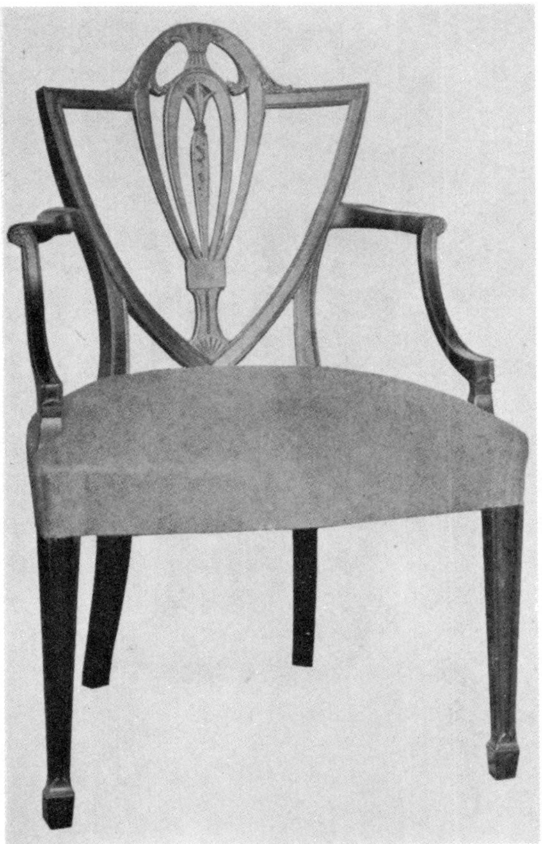

HEPPLEWHITE CHAIR. AN UNUSUAL FORM OF THE SHIELD-BACK

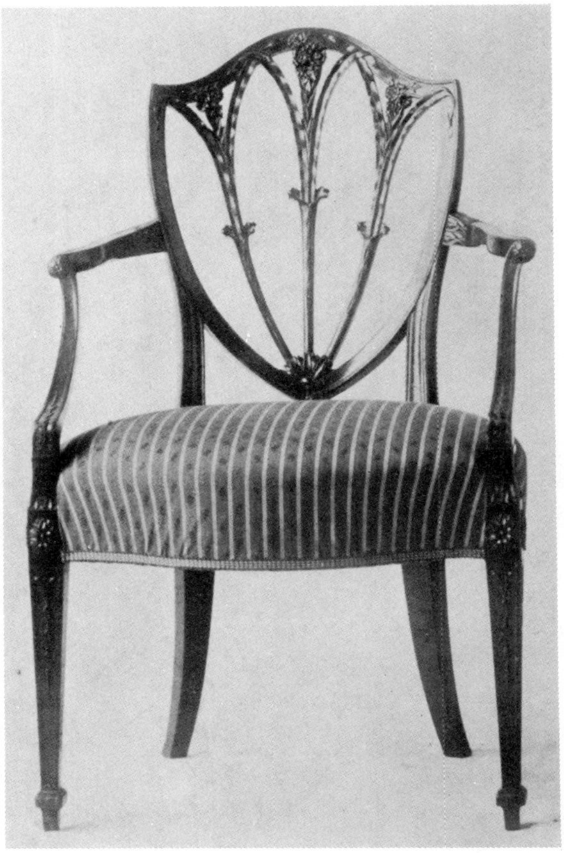

HEPPLEWHITE CHAIR. SHIELD-BACK WITH TRIPLE BIFURCATED BALUSTERS CARVED WITH WATER-LEAVES AND GARLANDS OF ROSES. FINE EXAMPLE OF THE SHIELD-BACK; CONCAVE ON PLAN

HEPPLEWHITE CHAIRS. SHIELD-BACK OF ADAM TYPE; FRONT LEGS TAPERED AND SPLAYED

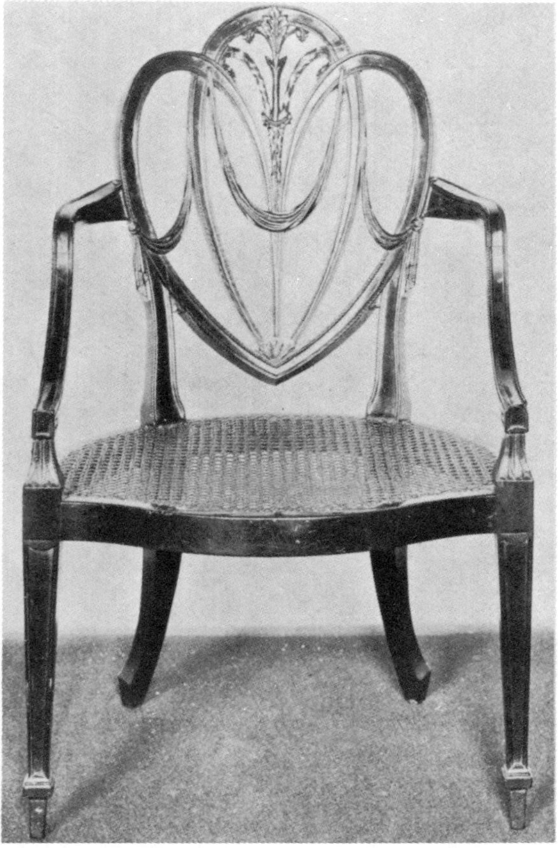

HEPPLEWHITE CHAIR. THE INTERLACING HEART-SHAPED BACK CARVED WITH WATER-LEAVES AND DRAPERY SWAGS

HEPPLEWHITE CHAIR. UNUSUAL FORM OF SHIELD-BACK WITH TRIPLE-SPLAT, THE CENTRAL BALUSTER PIERCED INTERLACED, CARVED AND INLAID

HEPPLEWHITE SETTEE. LEGS AND ARM BALUSTERS MOULDED AND PEARLED.
TYPICAL OF THE ADAM-HEPPLEWHITE STYLE

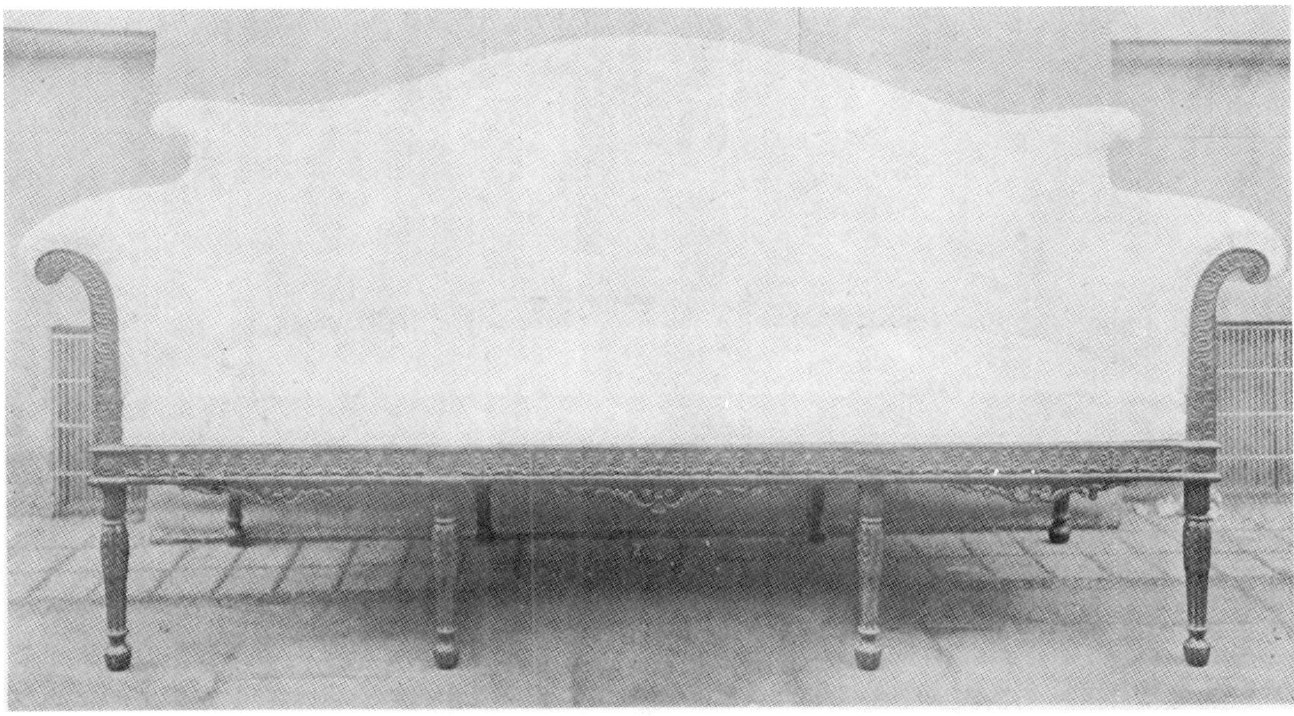

HEPPLEWHITE SETTEE. THE TRUE ADAM-HEPPLEWHITE STYLE, PROBABLY INSPIRED BY THE "ADELPHI"

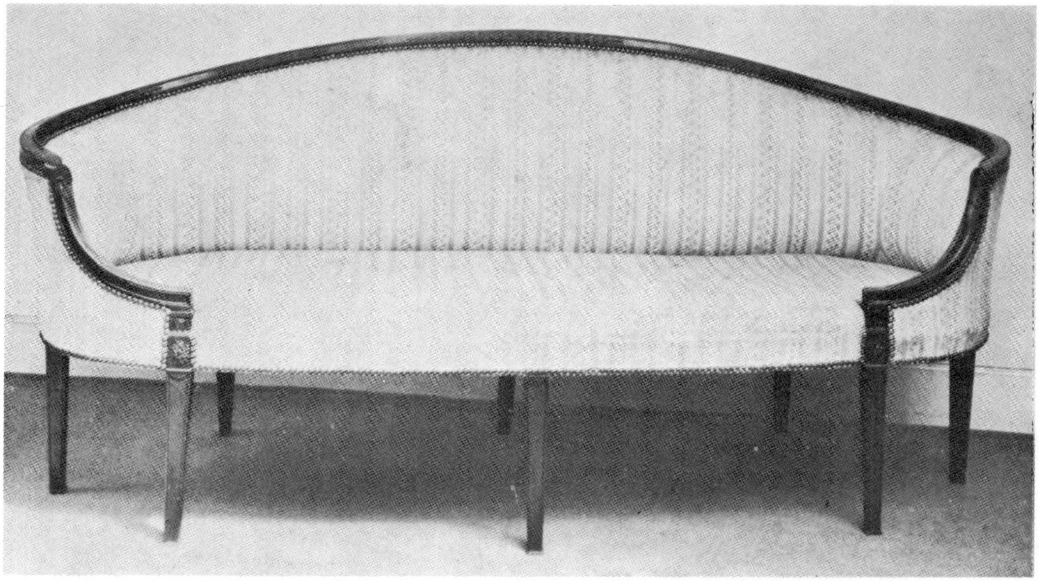

A TYPE OF SETTEE KNOWN AS A "CONFIDANTE." *c. 1795*

PAINTED OR LACQUERED SETTEE, HEPPLEWHITE-SHERATON. *c. 1790*

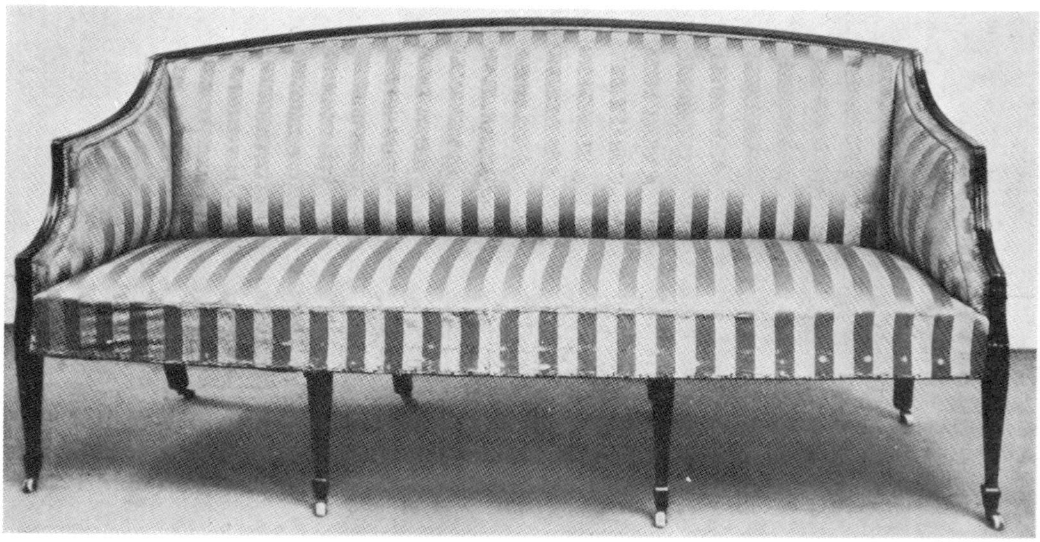

MAHOGANY SETTEE. TYPICAL SHERATON. *c. 1795*

SETTEES OF THE LAST YEARS OF THE EIGHTEENTH CENTURY. BRIDGING THE HEPPLEWHITE AND SHERATON PERIODS

HEPPLEWHITE SETTEE WITH FOUR CHAIR BACKS. FRENCH TYPE OF FRONT LEGS. VERY UNUSUAL TYPE

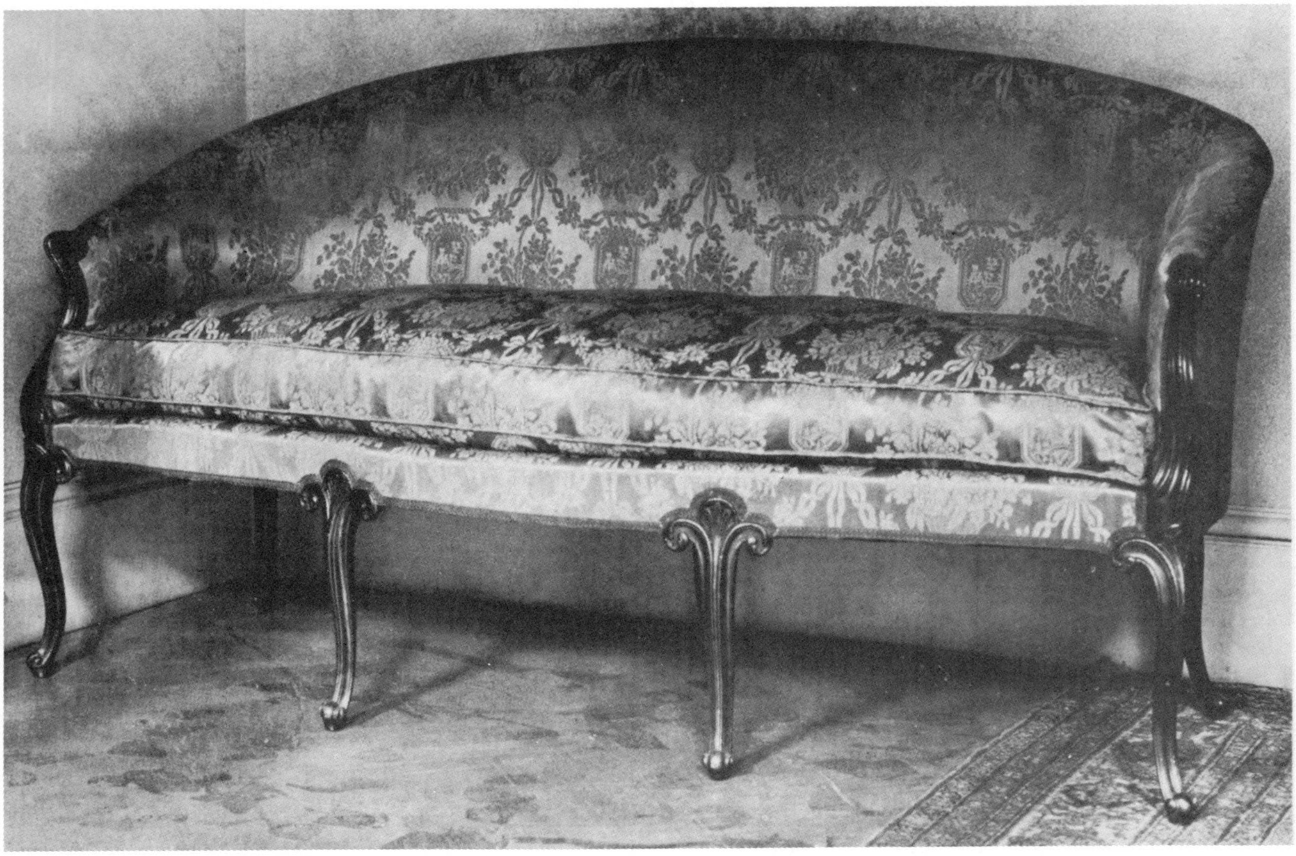

THE FRENCH, (LOUIS XV) MANNER, CABRIOLE LEGS CRESTING OVER THE SEAT FRAMING IN TREFOIL FORM; SCROLLED FEET

CHIPPENDALE AND HEPPLEWHITE OVERLAPPING IN STYLE. MAHOGANY SLANT-TOP BUREAU (OPEN AND CLOSED) VERY UNUSUAL IN HAVING A SERPENTINE FRONT. AN INGENIOUS MECHANISM SHOOTS THE BOLT OF THE LOCK WHEN THE FALL IS LOWERED, SO THAT THE FRONT MUST BE RE-LOCKED WHEN RAISED

ENLARGED VIEW OF THE PEDIMENT OF THE BUREAU CHINA CABINET BELOW

THE OVER-LAPPING OF THE CHIPPENDALE AND HEPPLEWHITE SCHOOLS. MAHOGANY BUREAU CHINA CABINET (OPEN AND CLOSED) OF SUPERB QUALITY AND DESIGN

MAHOGANY BUREAU BOOKCASE (OPEN AND CLOSED) INLAID AND BANDED.
THE GRADUAL BREAKING AWAY FROM THE CHIPPENDALE TRADITIONS

MAHOGANY BUREAU BOOKCASE, WITH SOLID UPPER DOORS. IT WILL BE NOTICED THAT THE DRAWERS HAVE BEEN VENEERED WITH PIECES FROM THE ONE LEAF, TO PRESERVE THE CONTINUITY OF THE CROTCH FIGURE

MAHOGANY BUREAU BOOKCASE. TYPICAL WORK OF THE HEPPLEWHITE-SHERATON SCHOOL

SECRETAIRE LIBRARY BOOKCASE, VENEERED WITH SATINWOOD, BANDED WITH KINGWOOD. THE TRUE HEPPLEWHITE MANNER

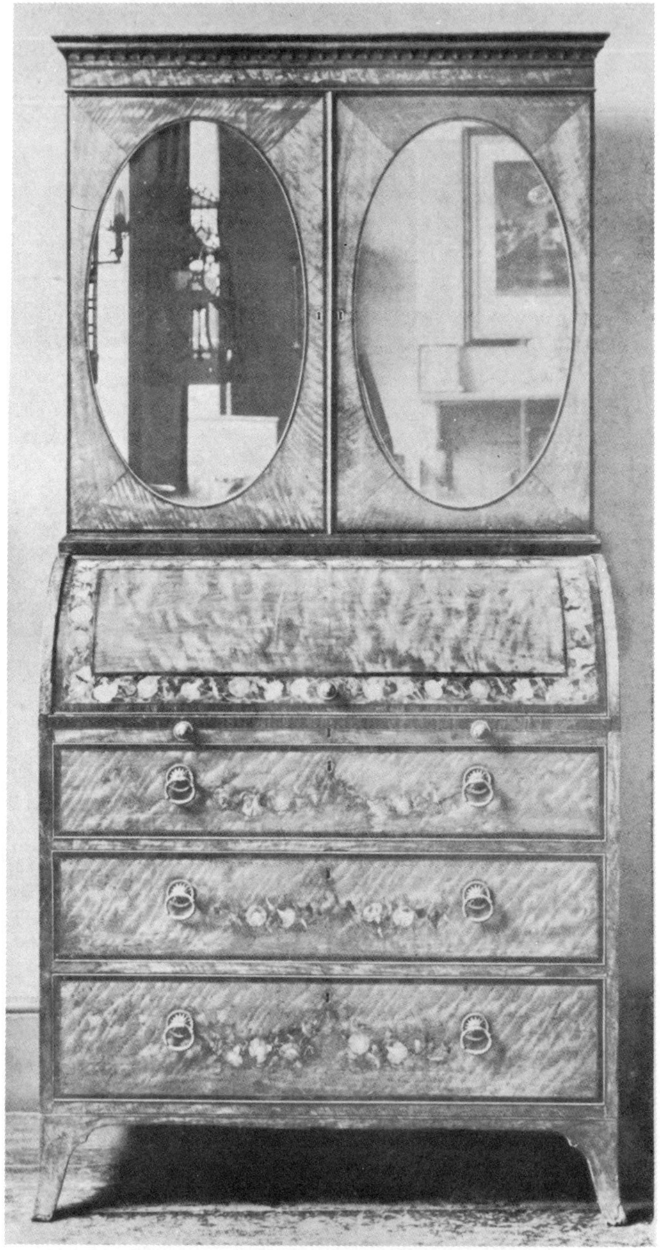

SATINWOOD CYLINDER-FRONT WRITING CABINET, PAINTED WITH BORDERS AND GARLANDS OF FLOWERS. THE STYLE OF THIS PIECE BRIDGES THE HEPPLEWHITE AND THE SHERATON

MAHOGANY BOOKCASE. COMPOSITE IN STYLE, BUT OF THE HEPPLEWHITE PERIOD. THE CARVING AND DETAILS OF THE CORNICE ARE ESPECIALLY FINE

MAHOGANY INLAID SECRETAIRE BOOKCASE. THE BRIDGING OF THE HEPPLEWHITE AND THE SHERATON

SATINWOOD LIBRARY BOOKCASE, BANDED WITH KINGWOOD AND INLAID WITH MARQUETERIE. TRUE HEPPLEWHITE

MAHOGANY LIBRARY BOOKCASE. THE ADAM-HEPPLEWHITE STYLE

MAHOGANY SECRETAIRE LIBRARY BOOKCASE. THE WORK OF THE HEPPLEWHITE SCHOOL

MAHOGANY LIBRARY TABLE. COMPOSITE OF THE CHIPPENDALE AND HEPPLEWHITE SCHOOLS. ALL THE CARVING AND WORKMANSHIP IS OF THE FINEST POSSIBLE QUALITY, AND THE WOOD IS SUPERB. THE TOP DRAWERS HAVE REBATED AND CONCEALED JOINTS, OVERLAPPING THE RAILS AND DRAWER DIVISIONS

THE END OF THE MAHOGANY WRITING TABLE AT TOP OF PAGE, SHOWING THE DETAIL, QUALITY OF THE WOOD, AND THE DROP HANDLES TO THE PULL-OUT SLIDES

MAHOGANY "RENT TABLE" ON SQUARE PEDESTAL WITH CUPBOARD, THE FRIEZE WITH SWING-OUT TRIANGULAR DRAWERS AND THE MONEY WELL, WITH SECRET LOCK, IN THE CENTER. AT ONE TIME THESE TABLES WERE FAIRLY COMMON IN THE STEWARDS' ROOMS IN LARGE COUNTRY HOUSES. THEY ARE NOW VERY RARE

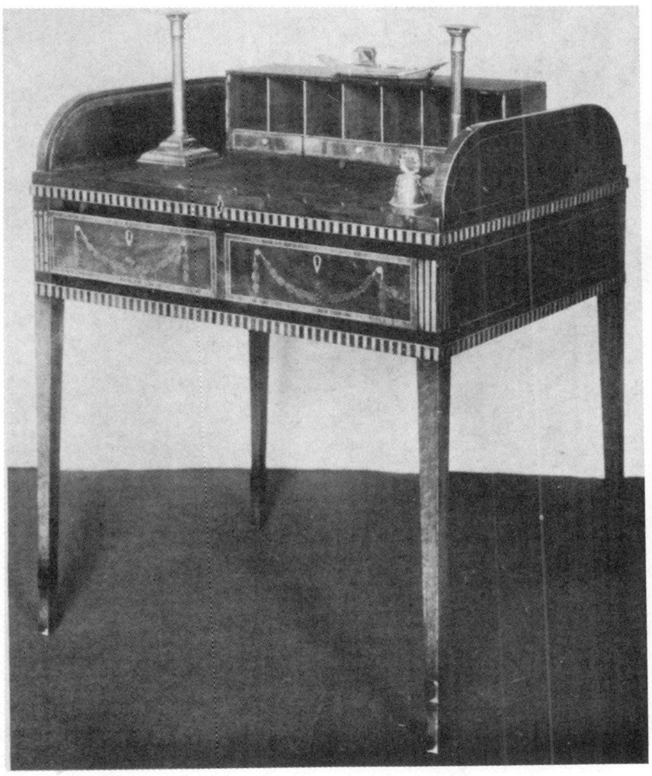

HAREWOOD "HARLEQUIN" WRITING TABLE, INLAID WITH MARQUETERIE, WITH PULL-OVER TAMBOUR TOP. THE NEST OF PIGEONHOLES RISES WHEN A SPRING IS RELEASED. TYPICAL HEPPLEWHITE

MAHOGANY TAMBOUR WRITING TABLE. TYPICAL WORK OF THE HEPPLEWHITE SCHOOL

MAHOGANY SIDEBOARD INLAID WITH FANS, FLUTES AND SCROLL MARQUETERIE.
THE DEVELOPMENT FROM THE CHIPPENDALE FORM

MAHOGANY INLAID SIDEBOARD. HEPPLEWHITE PERIOD

MAHOGANY SEMI-CIRCULAR SIDEBOARD. THE INNOVATION OF THE HEPPLEWHITE SCHOOL

MAHOGANY BOW-FRONT SIDEBOARD. HEPPLEWHITE SCHOOL

SATINWOOD PAINTED AND INLAID SEMI-CIRCULAR SIDEBOARD. HEPPLEWHITE SCHOOL. THIS EXAMPLE SHOWS THE TASTE FOR LIGHTER WOODS IN THE DINING ROOM AT THIS PERIOD

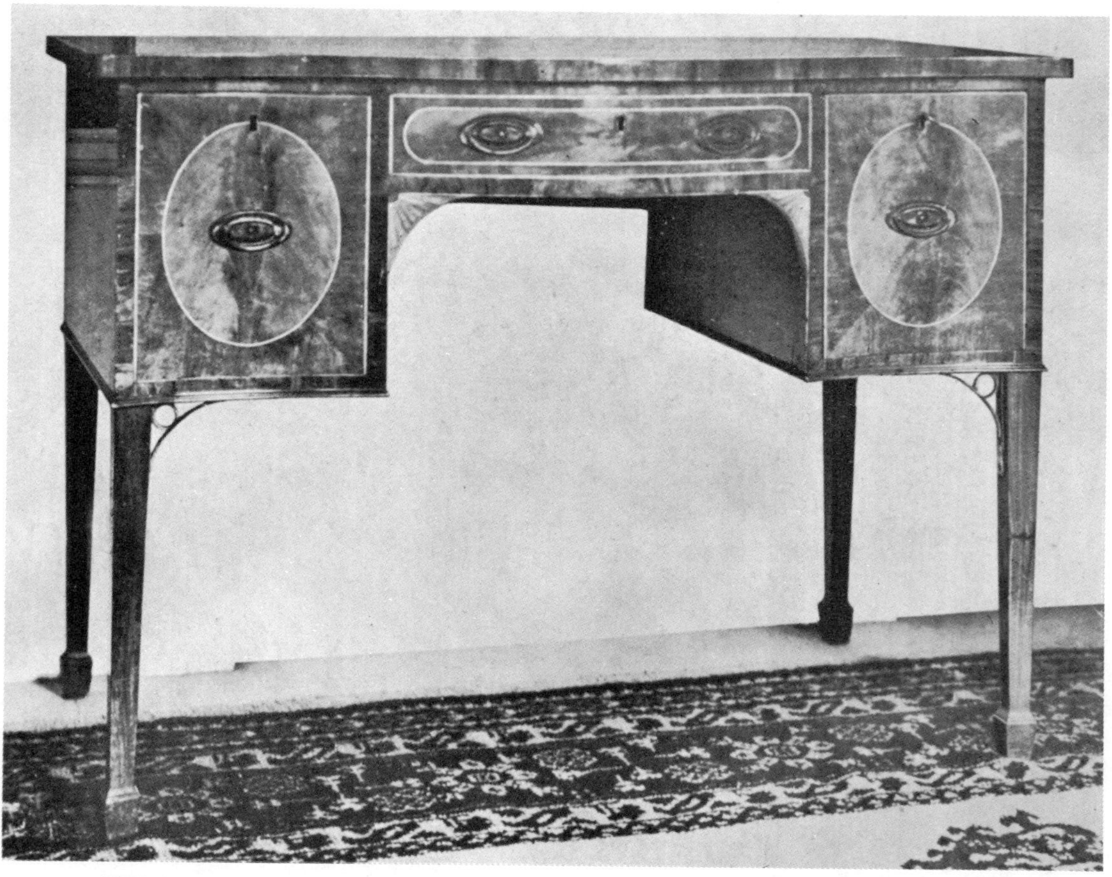

MAHOGANY INLAID SIDEBOARD, UNUSUALLY HIGH (3 FEET 3 INCHES) AND DEEP (27 INCHES). THE FRONT IS OF RESTRAINED SERPENTINE FORM. THE QUALITY THROUGHOUT IS OF THE FINEST

MAHOGANY INLAID SIDEBOARD IN TWO STAGES. THIS TYPE IS MORE USUAL IN SCOTLAND THAN IN ENGLAND

MAHOGANY SIDEBOARD BOLDLY BOW-FRONTED. TYPICAL HEPPLEWHITE

CARVED MAHOGANY SEMI-CIRCULAR SIDE TABLE. TYPICAL HEPPLEWHITE

PAINTED SIDE TABLE DECORATED WITH MEDALLIONS AND GARLANDS OF FLOWERS. HEPPLEWHITE-SHERATON SCHOOL

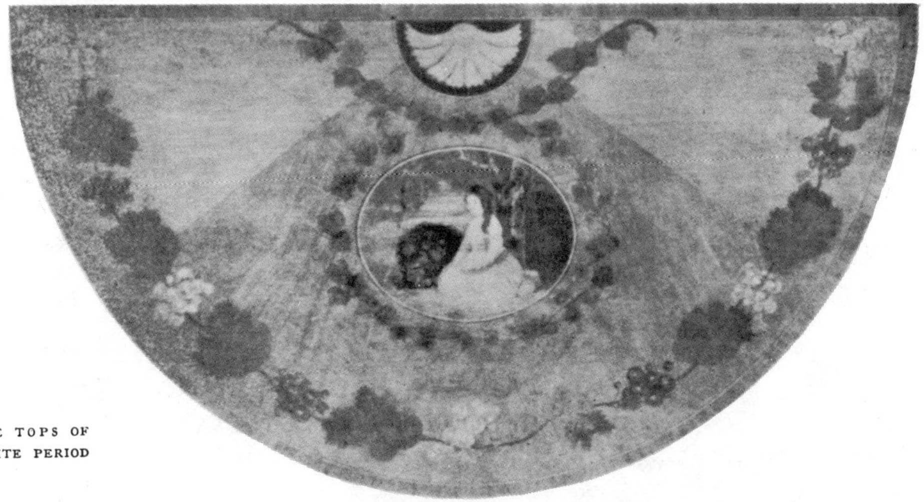

PAINTED TABLE TOPS OF THE HEPPLEWHITE PERIOD

ROSEWOOD INLAID AND PAINTED CARD TABLE. HEPPLEWHITE SCHOOL

TOP OF THE ROSEWOOD CARD TABLE AT LEFT SHOWING THE FINELY-PAINTED FLORAL BORDER

MAHOGANY SIDE TABLE, PAINTED WITH FLOWERS AND BORDERS OF PEACOCKS' FEATHERS

HAREWOOD SEMI-CIRCULAR SIDE TABLE INLAID WITH BANDINGS, STRINGING AND MARQUETERIE. HEPPLEWHITE SCHOOL

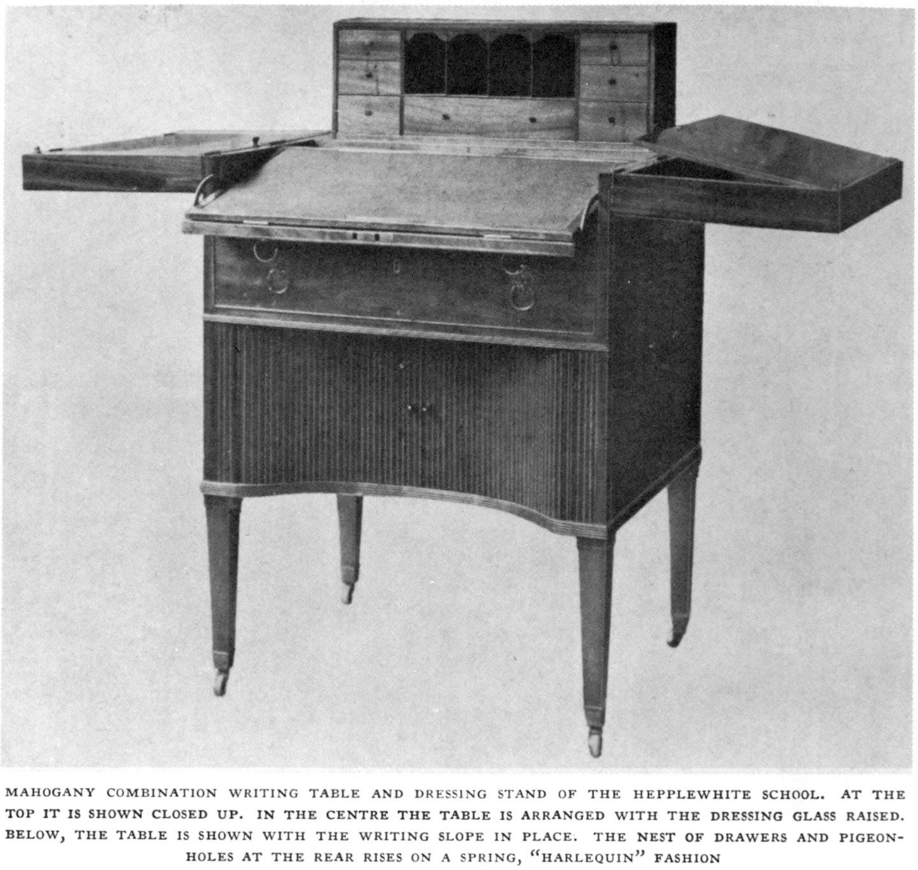

MAHOGANY COMBINATION WRITING TABLE AND DRESSING STAND OF THE HEPPLEWHITE SCHOOL. AT THE TOP IT IS SHOWN CLOSED UP. IN THE CENTRE THE TABLE IS ARRANGED WITH THE DRESSING GLASS RAISED. BELOW, THE TABLE IS SHOWN WITH THE WRITING SLOPE IN PLACE. THE NEST OF DRAWERS AND PIGEON-HOLES AT THE REAR RISES ON A SPRING, "HARLEQUIN" FASHION

ROSEWOOD INLAID WORK TABLE. HEPPLEWHITE-SHERATON SCHOOL

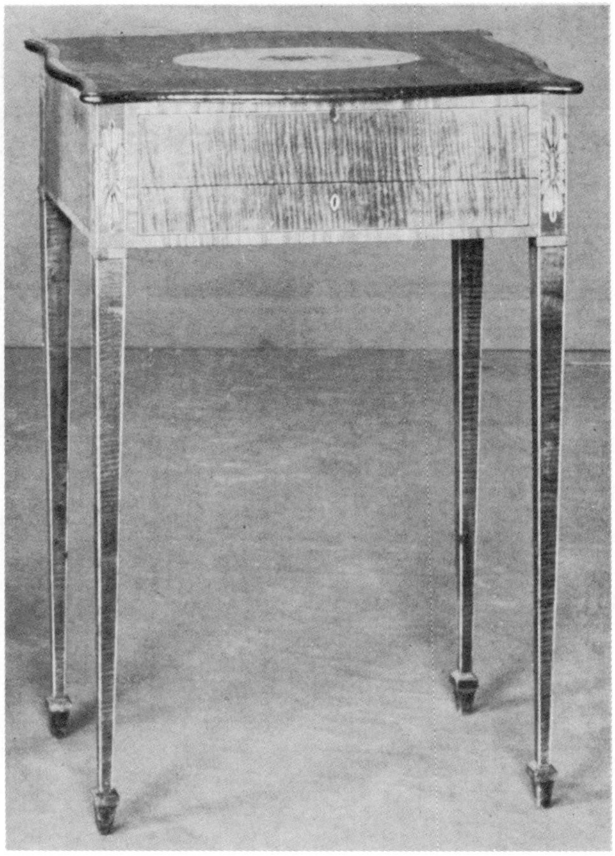

HAREWOOD INLAID DRESSING TABLE. HEPPLEWHITE

HAREWOOD INLAID OCCASIONAL TABLE. HEPPLEWHITE

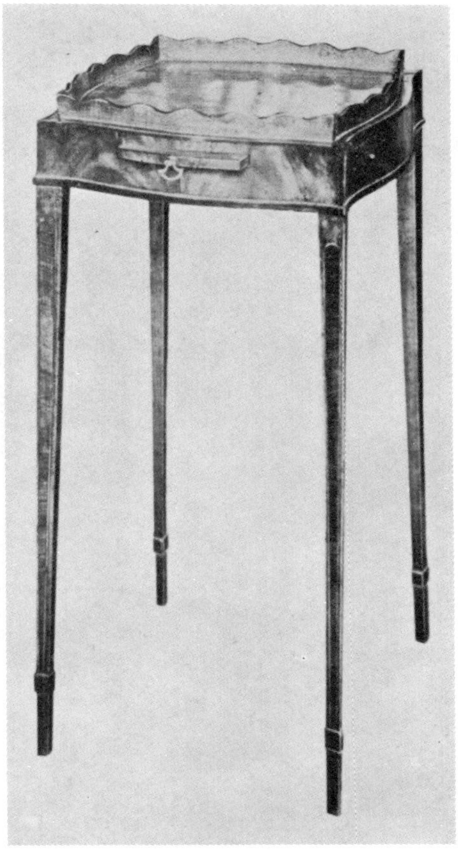

MAHOGANY URN TABLE WITH SLIDE FOR TEAPOT. HEPPLEWHITE

MAHOGANY "KIDNEY" WRITING TABLE WITH LIFTING WRITING SLOPE. HEPPLEWHITE SCHOOL

OCCASIONAL TABLE WITH SEPARATE BOOK RACK ABOVE, KNOWN AS A "SHEVERET." HEPPLEWHITE-SHERATON SCHOOL

HAREWOOD SHEVERET INLAID WITH MARQUETERIE. THE FRENCH MANNER OF THE HEPPLEWHITE SCHOOL

MAHOGANY INLAID DRESSING OR WRITING TABLE. HEPPLEWHITE

SATINWOOD INLAID CYLINDER-FRONT WRITING TABLE. HEPPLEWHITE

HAREWOOD CENTRE TABLE (WITH DETAIL OF TOP ABOVE) BANDED WITH ROSEWOOD, INLAID WITH MARQUETERIE IN A GROUND OF HOLLY, AND MOUNTED WITH ORMOLU. HEPPLEWHITE'S FRENCH MANNER

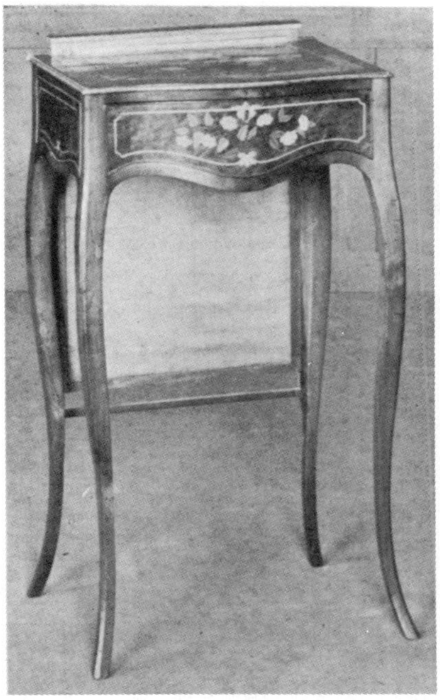

CARVED MAHOGANY CARD TABLE WITH PULL-OUT "CONCERTINA" ACTION. HEPPLEWHITE SCHOOL

HAREWOOD SCREEN TABLE INLAID WITH FLORAL MARQUETERIE. HEPPLEWHITE'S FRENCH MANNER

MAHOGANY CYLINDER-FRONT WRITING TABLE INLAID WITH OVALS OF AMBOYNA, BANDINGS OF KINGWOOD AND STRINGING OF HOLLY. THE FEET ARE MOUNTED WITH ORMOLU. THE FRENCH MANNER OF THE HEPPLEWHITE SCHOOL

TYPES OF LATE EIGHTEENTH CENTURY FOUR-POST BEDSTEADS. HEPPLEWHITE AND SHERATON PERIODS. *1785-1800*

CHAPTER XIX

The Style of the Sheraton School

THOMAS SHERATON is the last of the English cabinetmaker-designers of the eighteenth century. A native of Stockton-on-Tees, County Durham, in the North of England, he left his native town late in life, to seek fame and fortune in London. The streets of the great city may have been paved with gold but poor Sheraton found the paving blocks too heavy, or too firmly fixed, and died in obscurity and poverty.

He came in 1790, the year of the French Revolution. Chippendale had been dead eleven years and Hepplewhite four. Within two years, that patron saint of the cabinetmakers of his day, Robert Adam, was to die, and within four the vast Adelphi practice wound up. With strange events happening some twenty-five miles from the shores of England, with the country shortly to be filled with refugees bringing tales of horror and the fury of a populace, with the guillotine busy with the heads of a king and a queen, to say nothing of aristocracy, old and young, male and female, the time was hardly ripe for a new style in furniture. There were the mutterings of war in Europe, and, only seven years before, England had forever lost her American Colonies. Sheraton could not have chosen a worse period in which to make his great adventure. Had he been prepared to make fine furniture, in his own shop, had he been disposed to seek patronage, to ingratiate himself with the wealthy and the powerful, things might well have been bad enough, but Sheraton had neither capital nor workshop, and he was anything but ingratiating. The trade, if it wanted books at all in 1790, demanded new and original designs. Sheraton gave them treatises on perspective, drawing and the Five Orders, and then railed against everybody when the books remained on his hands.

Thomas Sheraton was a trained cabinetmaker, with a considerable knowledge of the artistic side of his trade, and far more than a workman's acquaintance with drawing and perspective. At the same time, he was strongly infected with the doctrines and the bigotries of the Narrow Baptists, and, even in his native town, had indulged in writing tracts. In London he continued in much the same way, dividing his efforts between the designing of furniture, the teaching of drawing (when he could find pupils, which was seldom), preaching at street corners and writing "strong" tracts, a division of labour which must have militated against his chances of success, at any time, especially when such shadows as Danton, Robespierre, Marat and, lastly, the

Little Corporal were about to darken the firmament of Europe. Whatever may be said for or against Thomas Chippendale, he was a man who gave undivided attention to his business, and the same may be said of "A. Hepplewhite & Co." and others.

In addition to the fatal drawback of divided energy added to a crabbed temperament, the period when Sheraton came to London was pregnant with events calculated to distract the attention of the "Nobility and Gentry" from furnishing their houses. Many were beginning to wonder whether they would have houses of any kind for long, and whether they might not even lose their heads in the struggle. How hopeless must have been Sheraton's idea of creating a reputation by his books and his teachings alone? To a man without charm of manner, one who had left youth behind in his native Stockton-on-Tees, with neither capital nor introductions, one seeking the patronage of a society, at all times gay and thoughtless, and now with serious misgivings, failure was inevitable.

Sheraton was born in 1750, and was, therefore, in his fortieth year when he came to London. His first book, and the one on which his reputation rests, "The Cabinet Maker and Upholsterer's Drawing Book" was first issued in parts, in London, in 1791. So there is little doubt that the first edition was in existence, if in incomplete form, before he left his native town; it must have been advanced enough to obtain subscribers in any event. In the list of these, five hundred and twenty-two names figure, and we can trace, in many of the names, the course of Sheraton's pilgrimage from Stockton-on-Tees to London. Circularising by post would have been out of the question to such a man as Sheraton in 1790. The method of country transit was by stage-coach or post-chaise, but Sheraton must have chosen a humbler means, by foot, to have procured his country subscribers. To make matters worse, Sheraton had a wife to accompany him, if not a small daughter, as in 1804, Adam Black, in his Memoirs, mentions both in his description of the Sheraton menage in London.

Of the "Drawing Book" three editions were published. The first (1791–94) contained 111 plates and text; the second, (which bears the date of 1793, and, therefore, overlaps the first one) 119 plates and text; and the third (1802) 122 plates and text. The actual additions and amendments were greater than these numbers appear to imply, as some eliminations were made from the preceding editions. Sheraton found that his public demanded original designs rather than treatises on perspective; and to the last two editions he added an "Appendix" and an "Accompaniment," at the same time curtailing some of the original matter.

While we know that Sheraton was a practical mechanic, it is certain that he was never a master man in London; and it is doubtful that he even worked as a journeyman, with the one possible exception noted in the illustrations here. Those who refer to pieces as from Sheraton's own hand are merely seeking notoriety at the expense of accuracy. It is possible that he may have taken orders for furniture to be made to his designs, and under his supervision, by others, in much the same way as Robert Adam did, but we have no reliable evidence of this. Sheraton died in October, 1806, and we know the sixteen years of his life in London fairly accurately. He was always busy with projects for ambitious publications, when not occupied with teaching or with religion and writing tracts. He issued the "Cabinet Dictionary" in 1803, after he had been converted to the English Empire Style of Thomas Hope (perhaps he was forced into the new manner by the exigencies of popular demand) and he projected "The Cabinet Maker, Upholsterer, and General Artist's Encyclopædia" in 125 folio numbers; but very little was actually accomplished at the date when he died. Miss Constance Simon in her "English Furniture Designers of the Eighteenth Century," states that three numbers were issued, up to the letters CAP.

In the preparation of this book, Sheraton had the assistance, for a short time, of one Adam Black, a bookseller's apprentice, who afterwards founded one of the most famous London publishing houses, Adam & Charles Black, in Soho Square. The simple little side board, illustrated in this chapter, is still in Soho Square, and I have always regarded this as the one probable example of Sheraton's handiwork while he was in London, made as an offering of gratitude for, perhaps, the only friend he possessed in the great, unfriendly city.

While on the subject of the design-books of the later eighteenth century, mention must be made of the "Designs of Household Furniture" of Thomas Shearer, a book of only nineteen plates, published in 1788, the same year as Hepplewhite's "Guide" and two years before Sheraton came to London. If Sheraton owed inspiration for his style to anyone, it was to Shearer and this book. It is also curious that, in his preface, Sheraton makes no mention of Shearer, yet the latter is usually credited with the compilation of the first edition (1788) of the "Cabinet Maker's (London) Book of Prices," an important work which will be noticed later on.

While the styles of Sheraton and Hepplewhite overlap, inevitably, (to say nothing of that of Shearer) yet, judging only by the standard of the "Guide" and of the "Drawing Book," it must be conceded that Sheraton was certainly the most original of the two. He may have merely collected the provincial fashions of the trade, in much the same way as Hepplewhite may have done with those of London, or he may have commenced with Shearer's book as a basis. But to the metropolis, especially on the subject of chairs, the "Drawing Book" had something new to say. It is doubtful whether Gillow of Lancaster had not said much the same thing, and at an earlier date, in the furniture produced by that firm, but Sheraton was the first to co-ordinate the style which we know by his name, and to give it artistic permanence in an illustrated book. It must not be forgotten that a part of the appeal of the new chair-style may have consisted in the fact that the square-back Sheraton chair was much less expensive to make than the shield-back of Hepplewhite. From the constructional point of view, also, the former was superior to the latter.

When we remember that the population of England, at the close of the eighteenth century, was less than one-sixth of what it is today; when we consider that the trade of the maker of furniture was in proportionately few hands, and that the age of mass-production was something of the distant future, we can easily understand how any new design-book, if possessing any merit of novelty or other appeal, would permeate the trade thoroughly. Sheraton must have had a considerable following, or his book must have had a fairly large sale to the trade, which is merely another way of stating the same thing. In any event, a considerable amount of furniture was made in the style which we know as "Sheraton," in the last decade of the eighteenth century. Even then the vogue for the English Empire was not thoroughly established until some fifteen years had gone by out of the nineteenth.

Furniture designs only begin at the drawing board; they come to real maturity at the bench, and, in considering the work of the three schools of Chippendale, Hepplewhite and Sheraton, in these pages, the judgment has been based more on the actual work which was produced than on the published designs of the three.

Sheraton's chairs are the most characteristic and the most original of all his designs, and he trenches very little of the manner of Hepplewhite. He illustrates only two patterns of the shield-back, neither of which is particularly meritorious. It is with the square-back that he is most successful. He borrows from the French, in the same way as Hepplewhite does, but from the last phase of the Louis XVI only, and he gives an unmistakable English character to his adaptations of French models. His acquaintance with current French fashions could have been acquired only at second hand. The Revolution had actually commenced in the year when Sheraton came to London; and the French king was executed two years later. At this period intercourse between England and France must have been of the slightest. It is obvious, therefore, that Sheraton could have co-ordinated only the London fashions of his time.

Sheraton's style—which is distinctive—must rest on the "Drawing Book." He adopted the English Empire in the "Cabinet Dictionary," but he can claim no credit for originality in regard to that style, which, for Sheraton's own reputation, is just as well, as it had little to recommend it. The furniture of the Sheraton School differs from that of Hepplewhite in only subtle degrees, if at all; it may be only a matter of engraved presentation. With chairs, however, we are on new ground.

In the preface to the "Drawing Book" Sheraton refers to "The Cabinet Maker's Book of Prices" (now a rare book in the earlier editions) and this volume opens a wide field of enquiry into the history of the trade. It was in current use as late as 1875, when the trade custom was still to pay by the piece instead of by the hour. Every conceivable joint, process or operation known to the furniture maker was described and priced, with all imaginable variations, and a job was given out without any preliminary estimating by the workman, priced up, in detail, afterwards from this book. A workman's cost sheet would be compiled in something like the following fashion, say, for a simple table of mahogany, on tapered legs, with castors, two drawers with handles and locks, and the top lined with leather:

A top of deal, 3 ft. x 2 ft., with three-tongued joints	00:0:0
Extra for 18 ins. width and 3 ins. depth	00:0:0
Extra for lipping with lin.; veneer	00:0:0
Extra for cross-banding veneer	00:0:0
Extra for facing edges, mahogany, tongued, etc.	00:0:0
Extra for ogee moulding to facings	00:0:0
Four legs, 2 in. x 2 in.	00:0:0
Extra for tapering on two faces	00:0:0
Extra for fitting bowl castors to each leg	00:0:0
Extra for two drawers, 1 in. fronts, $\frac{3}{8}$ in. sides	00:0:0
Extra for cock-beads to drawers	00:0:0
Extra for fitting two brass handles to each	00:0:0
Extra for fitting locks to each drawer	00:0:0
Extra for flush escutcheons to each drawer	00:0:0
Extra for lining top with leather	00:0:0
Extra for tooling and gilding	00:0:0
Extra for staining and polishing	00:0:0

Etc., Etc.

Nothing was reckoned in the above for materials; the prices were for labour only.

It must be obvious that, with such a book, no human ingenuity could prevent over-lapping, and at differing prices, with the result that the man who "knew his book" (hence the term) could make his account a few shillings more than one who had not studied it to the same extent. It was an indispensable adjunct to the knowledge of a shop foreman of that day that he should know the Price Book almost by heart.

Thomas Sheraton refers to the book only for the designs it contains. It is interesting to note that, in the edition current at his time, several of the plates are signed "Hepplewhite," the name being that of the firm, not of the man himself. Considered as the joint compilation of the trade—the names of Shearer and Hepplewhite are especially prominent—it was a masterly production, to which the best brains of the time must have contributed. It penalised the slow or inefficient workman, which was only just. Combined with the system of apprenticeship in vogue, it must have been a powerful incentive to progress in the trade. In these days of trade unions this policy has been reversed; the best have been levelled down to the worst, and there is neither reward nor other incentive to efficiency. It is not the first time that equality has been confused with uniformity.

It is curious that while Hepplewhite himself was a maker of furniture, and founded a large and influential school, the name of Sheraton has, until within quite recent years, completely over-shadowed him, although the latter made nothing in his London years, and his influence on the trade could only have been indirect. Thirty years ago everyone knew Sheraton's style (or thought he did) while the name of Hepplewhite was almost unknown. True, much that was intrinsically in Hepplewhite's manner was dubbed "Sheraton," but that does not account for the prominence of the one and the insignificance of the other. In point of date, the two are almost contemporary.

Sheraton closes the history of English furniture, at least that part which is worthy of record. The "Drawing Book" rounds off the eighteenth century, and, with the English Empire of Sheraton and Hope we approach the Dark Ages of the nineteenth century. It may be that new styles are being born in our midst today. One thing is certain; their advent will be remarked only after posterity has segregated them into definite manners and periods, by giving certain pieces undue prominence and ignoring others. With the trade of the present day, the new manners will be unnoticed in the gradual and inevitable processes of evolution. It may be that, a century hence, new names will be resurrected from the past, on the evidence of the publication of books of designs, or mere trade catalogues, original or otherwise. Unfortunately, it is possible, if not probable, that genuine creators will be ignored, and the names of one-time purveyors selected as typifying the new styles.

THE OAK LOW, OR "SUFFOLK" DRESSER. CABRIOLE LEG TYPE OF *1705-15*. (IN WALES AND LANCASHIRE, THIS TYPE WAS MADE UNTIL THE END OF THE EIGHTEENTH CENTURY). THE PROGENITOR OF THE HEPPLEWHITE AND SHERATON SIDEBOARD

SIDEBOARD TABLE, ON SATINWOOD BANDED WITH ROSEWOOD. THE SIDE TABLE PERSISTING TO *c. 1785-90*

MAHOGANY SIDE TABLE, OR "SIDEBOARD TABLE" OF THE CHIPPENDALE PERIOD. ALL "SIDEBOARDS" OF THE CHIPPENDALE YEARS ARE IN THIS FORM

SIDEBOARD TABLE, CARVED AND GILT, OF THE ADAM PERIOD, *c. 1760-70*. HERE WITH A TOP OF WOOD, BUT MORE USUALLY OF MARBLE

THE DEVELOPMENT OF THE SIDEBOARD

IF WE use the word, "Sideboard" in its literal sense, then it should be applied to the side table of the Chippendale period, which is really a board on legs. Custom, however, has dubbed the latter a side table, reserving the sideboard for the productions of the Hepplewhite and Sheraton periods, indicating a piece of furniture which possesses drawers and cupboards, made to contain silver, cutlery and napery, and with the cellarette drawer, wine also. To avoid confusion the later significance of the term is retained here.

The precursor of the sideboard—using the term in this later sense—is the low dresser of the early eighteenth century. Usually of oak, these "Suffolk" dressers, (as they are often styled, although they belong rather to the Welsh bordering counties than to East Anglia) are to be found, in Lancashire especially, of cherry, and, very rarely, of walnut. The early examples generally have turned legs and either a stretcher-underframing or a "pot-board" underneath. During the first years of the eighteenth century, the cabriole was substituted for the turned leg, as a rule. The piece is coincidental with the dresser with back, (for the display of pewter), usually, and inconsequently known as a "Welsh Dresser." Shorn of this high back, with its shelves, the low dresser is, obviously, the prototype of the Hepplewhite and the Sheraton sideboard.

The progression of type is illustrated here, from the Queen Anne to the Sheraton, with many gaps in the order of development, incidental to space limitations.

MAHOGANY SIDEBOARD. *c. 1795-1800.* ONE DRAWER IN CENTER, ONE ON LEFT WITH CUPBOARD BELOW, CELLARETTE DRAWER ON RIGHT

MAHOGANY SIDEBOARD INLAID WITH TULIP BANDING AND SAND-BURNT SHELLS AND FANS. ONE DRAWER IN CENTER, TWO ON LEFT, AND CELLARETTE ON RIGHT. *c. 1790*

MAHOGANY SIDEBOARD INLAID WITH SATINWOOD AND MARQUETERIE. CENTRAL DRAWER WITH RECESSED-FRONTED NAPERY DRAWER BELOW; AT RIGHT, DEEP CELLARETTE DRAWER WITH DOUBLE FRONT; TWO DRAWERS ON LEFT, BRASS RAIL AT BACK. *c. 1785-90*

MAHOGANY SIDE TABLE OF THE HEPPLEWHITE PERIOD. *c. 1785-90.* WITH THE EXCEPTION OF THE LEGS, ALL THE FACES ARE VENEERED

MAHOGANY INLAID SIDEBOARD OF FIVE DRAWERS WITHOUT CELLARETTE

MAHOGANY SIDEBOARD TABLE, BANDED WITH SATINWOOD AND INLAID WITH SAND-BURNT FANS OF HOLLY. THE DEVELOPMENT TOWARD THE LATER CELLARETTE SIDEBOARD

MAHOGANY INLAID SIDEBOARD. THREE DRAWERS IN FRIEZE, TWO CUPBOARDS BELOW. *c. 1790*

MAHOGANY CHAIR. *c. 1800.* LATE SHERATON WITH BROAD TOP-RAIL, DOWELLED ONTO THE BALUSTERS AND SPLAT. THE INTRICATE LATTICE-SPLAT OF THE PERIOD

MAHOGANY CHAIR, TURNED AND CARVED BALUSTERS WITH LATTICED PANEL ABOVE. SHERATON SCHOOL

BEECH PANELLED AND GILT CHAIR. TYPICAL "PARLOUR" CHAIR OF THE SHERATON SCHOOL

SHERATON ELBOW CHAIR. *c. 1800.* BEECH TURNED IN IMITATION OF BAMBOO AND DECORATED ON A GROUND OF BROWN LACQUER

SIMPLE SHERATON CHAIR WITH VERTICAL RAILING OF SPLAT AND "DIPPED" TOP-RAIL

SHERATON PAINTED AND PARCEL-GILT "PARLOUR" CHAIR. LATTICING AND RAILING OF SPLATS IS TYPICAL OF SHERATON. NOTE THE MARKED FRENCH INFLUENCE

SATINWOOD AND PAINTED "PARLOUR" CHAIR. A PATTERN FROM THE "DRAWING BOOK" OF SHERATON

SHERATON PAINTED AND PARCEL-GILT "PARLOUR" CHAIR SHOWING VERTICAL AND HORIZONTAL PIECED SPLATS ON BACK

SHERATON PAINTED AND PARCEL-GILT "PARLOUR" CHAIR. LATTICING AND RAILING OF SPLATS IS TYPICAL OF SHERATON. NOTE THE MARKED FRENCH INFLUENCE

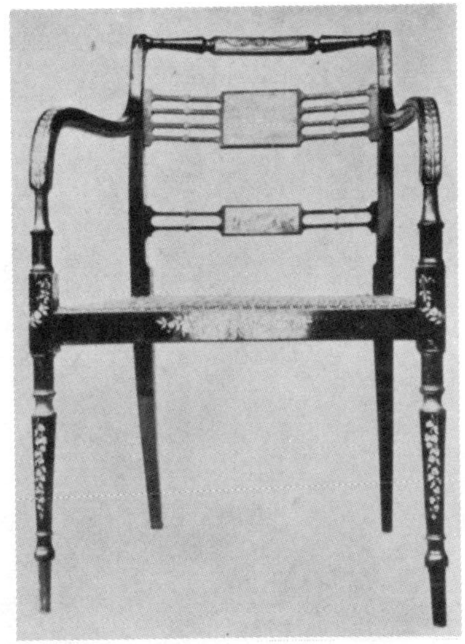

SHERATON PAINTED AND PARCEL-GILT "PARLOUR" CHAIR SHOWING HORIZONTAL PIECED SPLATS ON BACK

MAHOGANY OCTAGONAL TRIPOD TABLE WITH FOUR DRAWERS. A RARE TYPE IN THE CABRIOLE STYLE MORE USUAL IN THE LATE SHERATON **"PILLAR AND CLAW" WITH CIRCULAR BOX TOP, KNOWN AS THE "DRUM TABLE"**

THE LAST PHASES OF THE TRIPOD IN TABLES, DUMB-WAITERS AND SMALL DINING TABLES. IN THE FIRST THE USUAL **OGEE LINE** IS FOLLOWED, IN THE SECOND THIS IS INVERTED; **AND IN THE THIRD STYLE, WHICH** BELONGS TO THE LATE SHERATON PERIOD (*1795-1810*) **THE CONCAVE LEG FORM IS ADOPTED.** AT THIS TIME OCCURS THE CHANGE FROM THREE LEGS TO FOUR, THEREBY IGNORING THE PRINCIPLE OF THE TRIPOD, THAT OF STANDING FIRMLY ON AN UNEVEN FLOOR. WITH THE LATER DUMB-WAITERS, THE TOPS WERE OFTEN HINGED

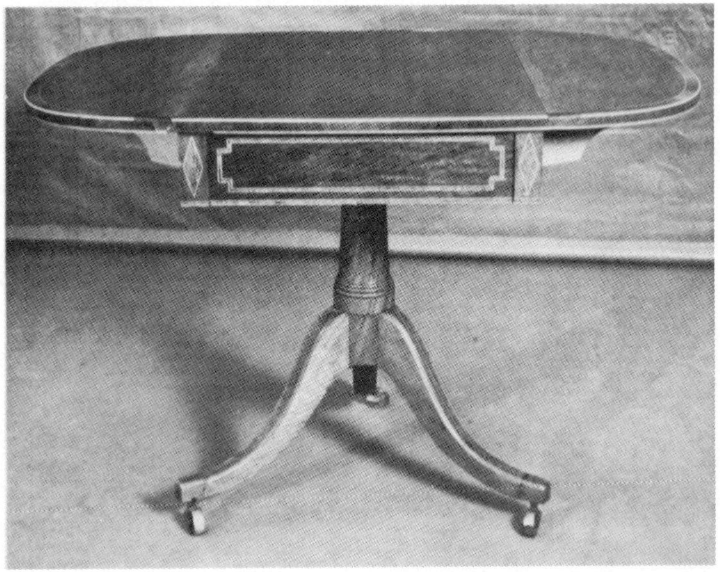

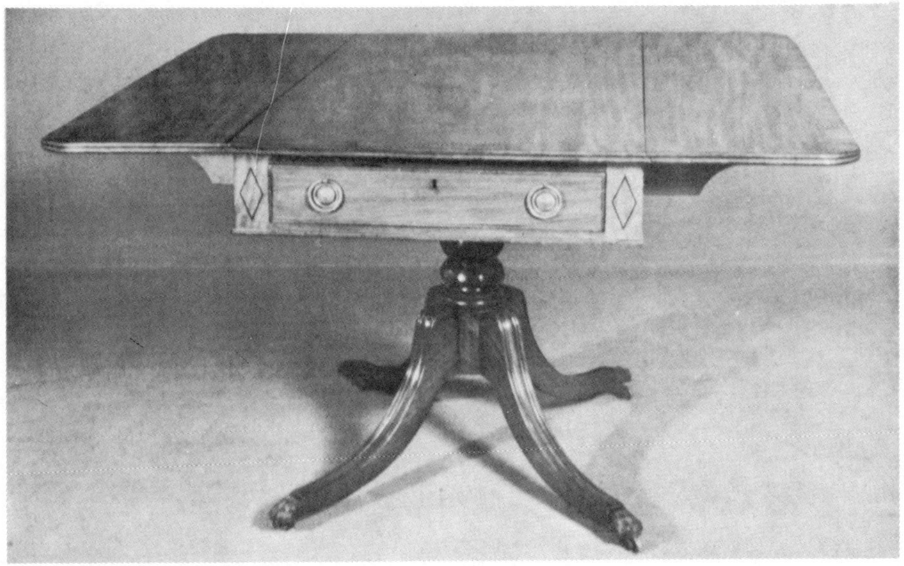

MAHOGANY CENTRAL PILLAR TABLES WITH HINGED TOPS. MADE AS "OCCASIONAL" TABLES OR FOR USE IN SMALL ROOMS FOR BREAKFAST OR FAMILY DINNERS. TO BE FOUND WITH THREE AND FOUR LEGS, NEARLY ALWAYS OF CONCAVE FORM. *1795-1820*

MAHOGANY BUREAU-BOOKCASE WITH "THIRTEEN" LATTICE IN THE UPPER DOORS. CHIPPENDALE BRIDGING HEPPLEWHITE. *c. 1780-5*

MAHOGANY BUREAU-BOOKCASE WITH "SWAN-NECK" PEDIMENT, FRET CUT, AND WITH MOULDED AKROTU. TYPE OF LATTICE OF THE SHERATON SCHOOL OF *c. 1795*

MAHOGANY BUREAU-BOOKCASE WITH THE "FIFTEEN" LATTICE PATTERN IN THE UPPER DOORS. LATE CHIPPENDALE TYPE OF *c. 1775-80*

BOOKCASES AND CABINETS

THE increasing number of these pieces in the last quarter of the eighteenth century indicates that many more books were being published than formerly, and that the English porcelains were prized and collected. Chelsea, Bow, Worcester, Swansea, Rockingham and other of the finer English factories and potteries reached their zenith at about this period, and the expensive bindings of the books of the same date show that volumes were intended to be preserved, not merely to be read and discarded. It was in these years that many of the famous libraries were founded.

SATINWOOD CABINET WITH CHINA SHELVES ABOVE. THE DOORS PANELLED IN THE MANNER OF ADAM AND PERGOLESI. THE DESIGN IS TYPICAL OF THE SHERATON SCHOOL

SERPENTINE-FRONTED DRESSING CHEST OF DRAWERS. VENEERED WITH "FIDDLE-BACK" SYCAMORE, WITH COCK-BEADS OF ROSEWOOD. THE TOP DRAWER IS ELABORATELY FITTED WITH MIRROR, PATCH AND POWDER BOXES, ETC. TYPE OF THE SHERATON SCHOOL OF *1795*

CABINET-ON-STAND OF SYCAMORE INLAID WITH AMBOYNA AND OTHER WOODS. NOTE THE INSIDE TAPER OF THE LEGS AND THE OUTWARD SPLAY, A FEATURE OF THE WORK OF BOTH THE SHERATON AND HEPPLEWHITE SCHOOLS

MAHOGANY CHINA CUPBOARD WITH CYLINDER FRONT BUREAU. TYPE OF THE SHERATON SCHOOL

MAHOGANY WARDROBE INLAID AND CROSS-BANDED WITH SATINWOOD. SHERATON PERIOD, *c. 1795*

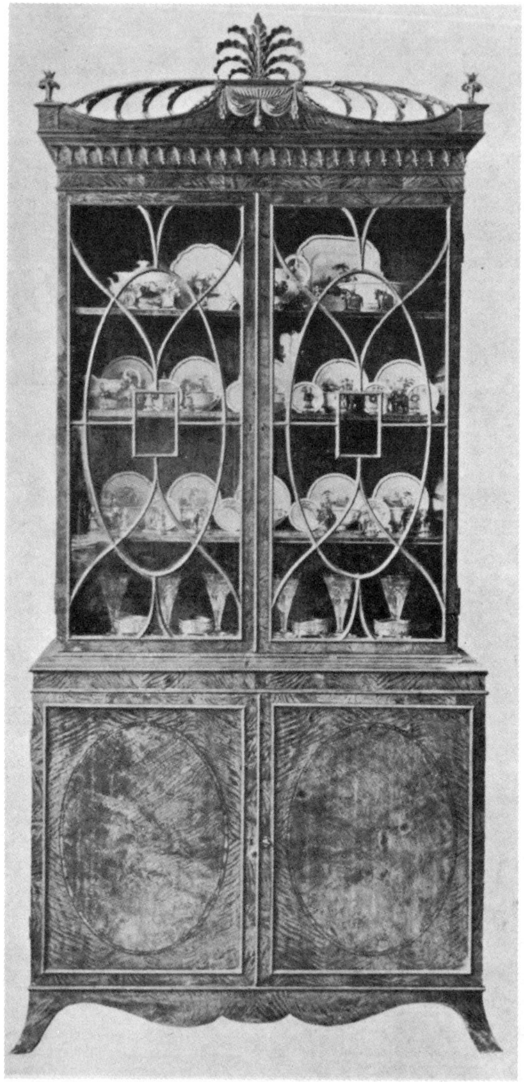

SATINWOOD BOOKCASE CABINET WITH CARVED PEDIMENT. *c. 1790-5*

SATINWOOD WARDROBE INLAID WITH ROSEWOOD AND MARQUETERIE OF FANS AND SHELLS. SHERATON STYLE

FRONT AND TOP OF A MAHOGANY INLAID SIDEBOARD, SAID TO HAVE BEEN THE PROPERTY OF ADAM BLACK, AND POSSIBLY MADE FOR HIM BY SHERATON. SEE NOTE BELOW

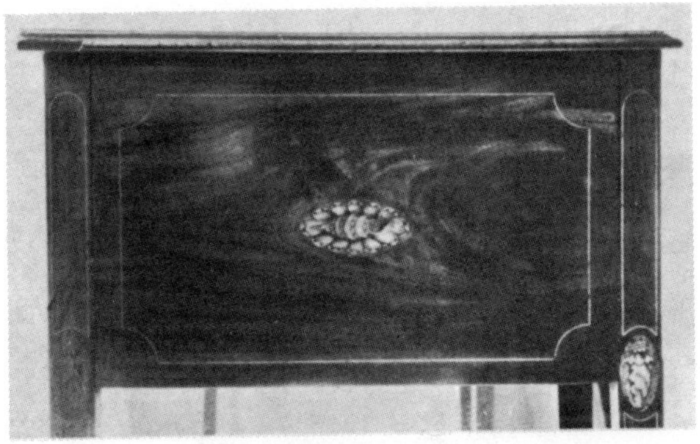

SIDE VIEW OF SIDEBOARD ABOVE

MAHOGANY INLAID SIDEBOARD. THE "THERMING" OF THE FRONT LEGS IS A SHERATON RATHER THAN A HEPPLEWHITE DETAIL

MAHOGANY INLAID SIDEBOARD OF UNUSUAL TYPE WITH DOUBLE CELLARETTE DRAWERS AT EACH SIDE BRIDGE-PIECE, HEPPLEWHITE-SHERATON

WHILE on very simple lines, both the wood and the workmanship of this sideboard are of exquisite quality. It is just the kind of piece which Sheraton might have made had he obtained a temporary "bench-room" in a London shop, with the lack of facilities which that would imply. In an age of shaping of sideboard fronts, this one is straight, and all elaborate processes of cutting or intricate veneering have been avoided. This sideboard is preserved, as Sheraton's handiwork, in the premises of Messrs. A. and C. Black, Soho Square, London.

MAHOGANY BERGÈRE CHAIR WITH EXTENSION FOOT-REST OR "GOUTY STOOL."
SHERATON, *c. 1795*

MAHOGANY SHERATON CHAIR OF AMERICAN MAKE, PROBABLY NEW YORK. *c. 1810-20*

MAHOGANY SHERATON CHAIR OF AMERICAN MAKE, PROBABLY NEW YORK. *c. 1810-20*

SATINWOOD SHERATON SETTEE OF FOUR CHAIR BACKS. THE TURNED TOP-RAIL OF THE BACKS IS TYPICAL OF SHERATON'S CHAIRS

SATINWOOD SHERATON SETTEE WITH ALTERNATING CARVED AND LATTICED PANELS IN BACK

MAHOGANY SHERATON "SOPHA" OF BERGÈRE TYPE. ARMS WITH LATTICED PANELS

MAHOGANY SHERATON SETTEE OF BERGÈRE TYPE. THE HEPPLEWHITE SETTEE NEARLY ALWAYS HAS A SHAPED BACK SWEEPING DOWN TO THE ARMS IN UNBROKEN LINES

MAHOGANY PARCEL-GILT CHAIR. SHERATON'S STYLE MERGING INTO THE ENGLISH EMPIRE. *c. 1810*

TYPES OF SQUARE-BACK, LATTICED SPLAT SHERATON CHAIRS. *c. 1795*

SATINWOOD ELBOW AND SIDE CHAIR. TYPICAL SHERATON OF *c. 1795*

SHERATON TYPE CHAIR IN BLACK AND GOLD LACQUER MADE BY GILLOW OF LANCASTER

INDEX OF ILLUSTRATIONS

Chapter I

Chapter II

THE GOTHIC

Chapter III

THE HALF-TIMBER HOUSE

Chapter IV

THE TIMBER ROOF OF THE MEDIÆVAL CARPENTER

Chapter V

PANELLING AND INTERIOR WOOD-WORK: THE SMALL PANEL

Chapter VI

PANELLING AND INTERIOR WOOD-WORK: THE LARGE PANEL

Chapter VII

OAK FURNITURE

INDEX OF ILLUSTRATIONS

Chapter VIII

WALNUT FURNITURE OF THE SEVENTEENTH CENTURY

Chapter IX

MARQUETERIE FURNITURE

Chapter X

ENGLISH NEEDLEWORK

Chapter XI

QUEEN ANNE WALNUT FURNITURE

Chapter XII

ENGLISH WALL MIRRORS

Chapter XIII

LACQUER-WORK IN ENGLAND

Chapter XIV

EARLY MAHOGANY FURNITURE

INDEX OF ILLUSTRATIONS

Chapter XV

THOMAS CHIPPENDALE AND THE "DIRECTOR"

Chapter XVI

THE CHIPPENDALE STYLE

Chapter XVII

ROBERT AND JAMES ADAM

Chapter XVIII

THE STYLE OF THE HEPPLEWHITE SCHOOL

Chapter XIX

THE STYLE OF THE SHERATON SCHOOL

BIBLIOGRAPHY OF ANCIENT BOOKS

ADAM, R.
Ruins at Spalato, 1764

ADAM, R. AND J.
Works in Architecture, 1773–1812

ALDRICH, H.
Elements of Civil Architecture, 1789

BRENTHAM, J. AND B. WILLIS
History of Gothic and Saxon Architecture in England

BRETTINGHAM, M.
Holkham Hall (1st Edition), 1761

BRUNETTI, G.
Ornaments (1st Edition), 1731. Ornaments (2nd Edition), 1736

CAMPBELL, C.
Vitruvius Britannicus (Vol. 1), 1715. Vitruvius Britannicus (Vol. 2), 1717. Vitruvius Britannicus (Vol. 3), 1725

CARTER, J.
Ancient Architecture in England, 1795

CHAMBERS, E.
Translation of Le Clerc's Treatise on Architecture, 1724

CHAMBERS, SIR W.
Designs of Chinese Buildings, 1757. Buildings at Kew, 1763. Civil Architecture (1st Edition), 1765. (2nd Edition), 1768. (3rd Edition), 1790

CHIPPENDALE, THOMAS
The Gentleman and Cabinet Maker's Director (1st Edition), 1754. (2nd Edition), 1759. (3rd Edition), 1762

CHIPPENDALE, THOMAS JR.
Ornaments, 1779

CIPRIANI, J. B.
Ornaments, 1786

COLUMBANI, PLACIDO
Ornaments, 1775. Capitals, etc., 1776

COPELAND, H.
New Book of Ornaments, 1746

CRUNDEN, J.
The Cabinet Maker's Darling, 1765. Ornamental Architecture, 1770

DARLY, M.
Sixty Vases, 1767. Ornamental Architecture, 1770

EDWARDS & DARLY
Chinese Designs, 1754

FISCHER, J. B.
A Plan of Civil and Historical Architecture, 1730

GIBBS, J.
Architecture (1st Edition), 1728. (2nd Edition), 1739. Shields and Tablets, 1731. Rules for Drawing the Five Orders, 1732. Radcliffe Library at Oxford, 1747

GWYNNE, J.
Essay on Harmony in Building, 1734

HALFPENNY, W.
Practical Architecture, 1724. (2nd Edition), 1736. Magnum in Parvo, or The Marrow of Architecture, 1728. Art of Sound Building, 1725. Compleat System of Architecture, 1749. New Designs for Chinese Temples, 1750. Useful Architecture, 1755

HALFPENNY, W. AND J.
The Modern Builder's Assistant, 1757

HAWKSMOOR, N.
Account of London Bridge, 1736

HEPPLEWHITE, A. & CO.
The Cabinet Maker and Upholsterer's Guide (1st Edition), 1788. (2nd Edition), 1789. (3rd Edition), 1794

HOPPUS, E.
Palladio's Architecture, 1735. The Gentlemen's and Builders' Repository, 1737

INCE & MAYHEW
A System of Household Furniture, 1763

JOHNSON, T.
Designs for Picture Frames, 1758. New Designs, 1761

JONES, W.
The Gentleman and Builder's Companion, 1739

K. C.
Art's Masterpiece, or a Companion for the Ingenious of Either Sex, 1697

KENT, W.
Designs of Inigo Jones, 1727

LANGLEY, B.
Practical Geometry, etc., 1726. New Principles of Gardening, 1728. A Sure Guide to Builders, 1729. The Young Builder's Rudiments, 1734. Ancient Masonry, 1736. Designs for a Bridge at Westminster, 1736. The Builder's Compleat Assistant, 1738. A Treasury of Designs, 1740. The Builder's Bench-Mate, 1746. The Builder's Director, 1767

LANGLEY, B. AND T.
Ancient Architecture, 1742. The Builder's Treasury of Designs, 1745. Gothic Architecture Improved, 1747

LEONI, G.
Architecture of Palladio (1st Edition), 1715. (2nd Edition), 1721. Architecture of Alberti (1st Edition), 1726. (2nd Edition) 1755. Architecture of Palladio (3rd Edition), 1742

LEWIS, J.
Designs in Architecture, 1780

LOCK, M.
Six tables, 1746. Book of Tables, etc., 1768. Six Sconces, 1768. Pier Frames, etc., 1769. The New Book of Foliage, 1769

LOCK AND COPELAND
Ornaments, 1752. Ornaments, 1768

MANWARING, R.
The Carpenter's Compleat Guide, 1765. The Cabinet and Chairmaker's Best Friend, 1765. The Chair-maker's Guide, 1766

MIDDLETON, C.
Cottages, 1795

MILTON, COLUMBANI, CRUNDEN AND OVERTON
The Chimneypiece Maker's Assistant, 1766

MORRIS, R.
A Defence of Ancient Architecture, 1728
Architecture Improved

NEWTON, W.
Civil Architecture of Vitruvius, 1791

NICHOLS, J.
Antiquities of Lambeth Palace, 1782

NICHOLSON, P.
Principles of Architecture, 1795–98

OAKLEY, E.
The Magazine of Architecture, etc., 1731

OVERTON, T. C.
Designs for Temples, 1766

PAINE, J.
Plans of Noblemen's and Gentlemen's Houses, 1767–70. (2nd Edition), 1783

PAINE, W.
The Builder's Companion (2nd Edition), 1765. (3rd Edition), 1769. The Practical Builder, 1774. The Practical Builder, 1793. The Carpenter's Repository, 1778

PAINE, W. AND J.
The British Palladio, 1786

PASTORINI, B.
Designs for Girandoles, 1775

PERGOLESI, M. A.
Designs, 1777
Perrault's Architecture of Vitruvius, 1692

RICHARDS, G.
Palladio's First Book of Architecture, 1721

RICHARDSON, G.
Ceilings, 1776. Chimney Pieces, 1781. The Five Orders of Architecture, 1787. New Designs in Architecture, 1792. Designs for Tripods, etc., 1793. Ceilings (2nd Edition), 1793. Designs for Country Seats and Villas, 1795

SALMON, W.
Palladio Londoniensis, 1743. Polygraphica, or the Arts of Drawing (4th Edition), 1701

SHEARER, HEPPLEWHITE AND OTHERS
Cabinet Maker's (London) Book of Prices (2nd Edition), 1793

SHEARER, T.
Cabinet Maker's (London) Book of Prices, 1788. Designs for Household Furniture, 1788

SHERATON, T.
The Cabinet Maker and Upholsterer's Drawing Book (1st Edition), 1791. (2nd Edition), 1793

SOANE, SIR J.
Designs in Architecture, 1778. Plans and Elevations of Buildings, 1788. Sketches in Architecture, 1793

SOCIETY OF UPHOLSTERERS
Household Furniture in Genteel Taste, 1760

STALKER, J. AND PARKER
A Treatise on Japanning, etc., 1688

SWAN, A.
Staircases (1st Edition), 1745. (2nd Edition), 1750. Designs in Architecture, 1757. British Architecture (3rd Edition), 1758. Designs in Carpentry, 1759

TATHAM, E. H.
Examples of Ancient Architecture, 1794

THOMAS, W.
Designs in Architecture, 1783

TIJOU, J.
Designs for Ironwork, 1693

WALLIS, N.
Book of Ornaments, 1771. Compleat Joiner, 1772

WARE, J.
Rookby Hall, Yorks, 1735. Designs for the Mansion Home, 1737. Palladio's Architecture, 1738. Designs of Inigo Jones, 1743. Compleat Body of Architecture, 1756. Kent and Ripley's Designs for Houghton Hall, 1760

WOOD, J.
Origin of Building, 1741

WOOD, R.
Ruins of Palmyra, 1753

WOOLFE & GANDON
Vitruvius Britannicus (Vol. 5), 1771

WRIGHT, W.
Grotesque Architecture, 1768

BIBLIOGRAPHY OF MODERN BOOKS

ADDISON, JULIA DE WOLF
Arts and Crafts in the Middle Ages, 1908

BELL, J. M.
Furniture Designs of Thomas Chippendale. Furniture Designs of Thomas Sheraton. Furniture Designs of George Hepplewhite. (Reprints), 1910

BENN, H. P. AND BALDOCK, W. C.
Characteristics of Old Furniture, 1600–1800

BENN, R. DAVIS
Style in Furniture, 1904

BINSTEAD, H. E.
Furniture Styles, 1904

BLAKE, J. P. AND REVEIRS-HOPKINS, A. E.
Little Books About Old Furniture, 1911

BLOMFIELD, R. T.
A History of Renaissance Architecture in England (2 Vols.), 1897

BOLTON, ARTHUR T.
The Architecture of Robert and James Adam (1758–1794) (2 Vols.), 1922

BRACKETT, OLIVER
Thomas Chippendale, 1927

BRITTEN, F. J.
The Wetherfield Collection of Clocks, 1907. Old Clocks and Watches and Their Makers—3rd Edition, 1911. 4th Edition, 1919

BURGESS, F. W.
Antique Furniture, 1915

CESCINSKY, HERBERT
English Furniture of the Eighteenth Century (3 Vols.), 1910. The Old World House (2 Vols.), 1924. Chinese Furniture, 1922. English Furniture, From Gothic to Sheraton, 1929

CESCINSKY, HERBERT AND GRIBBLE, E. R.
Early English Furniture and Woodwork (2 Vols.), 1922

CESCINSKY, HERBERT AND HUNTER, GEORGE LELAND
English and American Furniture, 1929

CESCINSKY, HERBERT AND WEBSTER, M. R.
English Domestic Clocks, 1912. 2nd Edition, 1914. 3rd Edition, 1928

CHANCELLOR, E. BERESFORD
The Eighteenth Century in London, 1920. The Private Palaces of London, 1908

CLARK, HARTLEY
Bokhara, Turkoman and Afghan Rugs, 1922

CLAYTON, J.
Ancient Timber Edifices of England, 1846

CLOUSTON, R. S.
English Furniture and Furniture Makers of the Eighteenth Century, 1906

CROSELEY, F. H.
English Church Monuments, 1921

DAVIE, W. G. AND DAWBER, E. G.
Old Cottages and Farmhouses in the Cotswold District, 1905

DOLLMAN, F. T.
An Analysis of Ancient Domestic Architecture in Great Britain (2 Vols.), 1864

EBERLEIN, H. D. AND McCLURE, A.
The Practical Book of Period Furniture, 1914

EBERLEIN, H. D., McCLURE, A. AND HOLLOWAY, E. S.
The Practical Book of Interior Decoration, 1919

ELLWOOD, G. M.
English Furniture and Decoration, 1680–1800
(No text to this book)

FENN, F. AND WYLIE, B.
Old English Furniture

FOLEY, E.
The Book of Decorative Furniture, 1910

GOTCH, J. A.
Architecture of the Renaissance in England (2 Vols.), 1891–94. Early Renaissance Architecture in England, 1901

GREGORY, E. W.
The Furniture Collector

HABERSHON, M.
Ancient Half-timber Edifices of England, 1836

HACKETT, W. H.
Decorative Furniture, 1902

HAKEWILL, F.
An Attempt to Determine the Exact Character of Elizabethan Architecture, 1835

HALL, S. C.
Baronial Halls and Ancient Edifices of England (2 Vols.), 1850

HALSEY, R. T. H. AND TOWER, ELIZABETH
The Homes of Our Ancestors (New York), 1925

HEATON, J. ALDAM
Furniture and Decoration, 1892

HELM, W. H.
Homes of the Past, 1921

HOLLOWAY, E. S.
The Practical Book of Furnishing the Small House and Apartment, 1922

HOWARD, F. L. AND CROSSLEY, F. H.
English Church Woodwork, 1917. 2nd Edition, 1919
(See also Croseley, F. H.)

HUNT, T. F.
Exemplars of Tudor Architecture, 1836

HUNTER, GEORGE LELAND (See also Cescinsky, Herbert)
Tapestries, Their Origin, History and Renaissance, 1912. Decorative Textiles, 1918. Decorative Furniture, 1923. The Practical Book of Tapestries, 1925. English and American Furniture, 1929

HURRELL, J. W.
Measured Drawings of Old English Oak Furniture, 1902

JACQUEMART, SEBERT
A History of Furniture, 1908

JOURDAIN, M.
English Decoration and Furniture of the Early Renaissance, 1924. English Decoration and Furniture of the Late Eighteenth Century, 1922

JUSSERAND, J. J.
English Wayfaring Life in the Middle Ages, 1890

KENDRICK, A. F. AND TATTERSHALL, C. E. C.
Handwoven Carpets (2 Vols.), 1922

KIMBALL, FISKE
Domestic Architecture of the American Colonies and of the Early Republic, 1922

LACROIX, PAUL
Manners, Customs and Dress during the Middle Ages, 1874. Military and Religious Life in the Middle Ages, 1874

LAKING, GUY FRANCIS
The Furniture in Windsor Castle, 1905

LAMB, S. B.
Studies of Ancient Domestic Architecture, 1846

LATHAM, C.
In English Homes (See Tipping, H. Avray)

LAW, E.
History of Hampton Court Palace (3 Vols.), 1888–1891

LENYGON, FRANCIS
Decoration in England from 1660–1770, 1914. Furniture in England from 1660–1760, 1914

LETHABY, W. R.
Leadwork, Old and Ornamental, 1893

LEWER, H. W. AND WALL, J. C.
The Church Chests of Essex, 1913

LITCHFIELD, F.
How to Collect Old Furniture, 1904. Illustrated History of Furniture, 1907

LLOYD, NATHANIEL
A History of English Brickwork, 1925

LOCKWOOD, LUKE VINCENT
Colonial Furniture in America, 1902

MACQUOID, PERCY
A History of English Furniture (4 Vols.), 1904–08

MACQUOID, PERCY AND EDWARDS, RALPH
The Dictionary of English Furniture (3 Vols.), 1926–27

MALLETT, W. E.
Introduction to Old English Furniture, 1906

MASKELL, ALFRED
Wood Sculpture, 1911

McCLELLAND, NANCY
The Practical Book of Decorative Wall Treatments, 1926

MOORE, N. H.
Old Furniture Book, 1903

MORSE, FRANCIS CARY
Furniture of the Olden Time, 1902

MULLINER, H. H.
The Decorative Arts in England (1660–1780), 1924

NASH, J.
Mansions of England in the Olden Time (4 Vols.), 1839–49. Another Edition (4 Vols.), 1869

NUTTING, WALLACE
Furniture of the Pilgrim Century, 1921

OLIVER, BASIL
Old Houses and Village Buildings in East Anglia, 1912

PAPWORTH, W.
The Renaissance and Italian Styles of Architecture in Great Britain (1450–1700), 1883

PARKINSON, J. AND OULD, E. A.
Old Cottages and Farmhouses in Shropshire, Herefordshire and Cheshire, 1904

POLLEN, JOHN HUNGERFORD
Ancient and Modern Furniture and Woodwork, 1908

PUGIN, A.
Specimens of Gothic Architecture in England (2 Vols.), 1821

PUGIN, A. AND E. WELBY
Examples of Gothic Architecture in England (3 Vols.), 1831

RICHARDSON, C. J.
Specimens of the Architecture of the Reigns of Elizabeth and James I, 1840. Studies from Old English Mansions (4 Vols.), 1841–48

ROBINSON, VINCENT J.
Ancient Furniture and Other Works of Art, 1902

ROE, FRED
Old Oak Furniture, 1905

ROGERS, JOHN C.
English Furniture, 1923

SANDERS, WILLIAM BLISS
Half-timbered Houses and Carved Oak Work of the Sixteenth and Seventeenth Centuries, 1894

SHACKLETON, R. AND E. H.
The Quest of the Colonial Furniture in the United States, 1907

SHAW, H.
Details of Elizabethan Architecture, 1834

SHUFFREY, L. A.
The English Fireplace, 1912

SIMON, CONSTANCE
English Furniture Designers of the Eighteenth Century, 1905

SINGLETON, ESTHER
The Furniture of Our Forefathers, 1901. French and English Furniture, 1904. Dutch and Flemish Furniture, 1907. Furniture, 1913

SMALL, J. W.
Ancient and Modern Furniture, 1903

SPARROW, W. SHAW
The English House, 1908

STRATTON, ARTHUR
The English Interior, 1920

SWARBRICK, JOHN
Robert Adam and His Brothers, 1915

SYMONDS, R. W.
The Present State of Old English Furniture, 1921. Old English Walnut and Lacquer Furniture, 1923

TANNER, H.
English Interior Woodwork of the Sixteenth, Seventeenth and Eighteenth Centuries, 1902

THOMSON, W. E.
A History of English Tapestry, 1906

TIMMS, W. H. AND WEBB, G.
The Thirty-five Styles of Furniture, 1904

TIPPING, H. AVRAY
English Homes "Country Life" Series. Various dates. English Furniture of the Cabriole Period, 1921

TURNER, I. H. AND PARKER, J. H.
Some Account of Domestic Architecture in England during the Middle Ages (3 Vols.), 1859–77

TWOPENY, W.
English Metal Work, 1904

WARING, J. B.
Furniture and Decoration

WELLS, PERCY A. AND HOOPER, JOHN
Modern Cabinetwork, Furniture and Fitments, 1909

WHEELER, G. OWEN
Old English Furniture, 1909

WILLIS, J. AND CLARK, J. W.
The Architectural History of the University of Cambridge (4 Vols.), 1886